Growing Up at the Margins

Growing Up at the Margins:
Young Adults in the North East

Frank Coffield, Carol Borrill and Sarah Marshall

Open University Press

Milton Keynes · Philadelphia

Open University Press
Open University Educational Enterprises Limited
12 Cofferidge Close
Stony Stratford
Milton Keynes MK11 1BY, England
and
242 Cherry Street
Philadelphia, PA 19106, USA

First Published 1986

British Library Cataloguing in Publication Data
Coffield, Frank
    Growing up at the margins: young adults
in the North East.
    1. Youth   England, Northern   2. England,
Northern   Social Conditions
I. Title II. Borrill, Carol III. Marshall,
Sarah
305.2'3'09428   HQ799.G7

    ISBN   0-335-15134-5
    ISBN   0-335-15114-0 Pbk

Library of Congress Cataloging in Publication Data
Main entry under title:
Coffield, Frank
    Growing up at the margins.

    Bibliography: p.
    Includes index.
    1. Young adults—England—Social conditions—Case
studies. 2. Young adults—England—Economic conditions—
Case studies. 3. Labor and laboring classes—England—
Case studies. I. Borrill, Carol. II. Marshall, Sarah.
III. Title.
HQ799.8.G72E5325 1985   305.2'35'0942   85-29740
ISBN   0-335-15134-5
ISBN   0-335-15114-0 (pbk.)

Text design by Nicola Sheldon
Typeset by Gilbert Composing Services
Printed in Great Britain by St. Edmundsbury Press,
Bury St Edmunds, Suffolk

This book is dedicated to the children who were born while it was being researched and written: Rachael, Emma, Laura, Toni Anne and Kate.

Contents

Acknowledgements

We wish to acknowledge the financial help we received from the ESRC and Durham University. Throughout the study we consulted many people, professionals, colleagues and personal friends: we wish to thank them all for the various forms of assistance they gave us. We also owe a large debt of gratitude to our secretary, Margaret Newton, whose loyalty, cheerfulness and skills continued to be put at our disposal long after the project had officially ended. We also want to put on record our thanks to the young people of this study who put up with our questions, our 'daft lists', and our intrusions into their personal lives for two-and-a-half years and who were still prepared to meet us at the end of it.

Introduction

Since the last war, the young have never had it so bad. In the view of the young adults we met, the twin evils of mass unemployment and the nuclear arms race have given them the bleakest prospects experienced by any young generation since their grandparents went to war in 1939.

The young women and men we came to know through our research project in the north east of England were bright, friendly, full of life and fun, and yet poor, hemmed in by their poverty and deeply worried about the future. Their flat pessimism extended to all futures, personal, national and global, but they rarely let it affect their lives from day to day. A few years out of school, the young adults we knew were under no illusions about their prospects, they just got on with life. They coped with their anxieties, just as most people do, by pushing them out of their minds and living in and for the present. Why and how did we come to know them and learn their views?

Between January 1982 and August 1984 we carried out two-and-a-half years' fieldwork in a study of 'around fifty' working-class young women and men in the north east of England. They were aged between sixteen and twenty-eight when we first met them.

The project was jointly funded by the SSRC (now the ESRC) and Durham University and was part of the SSRC's research initiative into 'Young People in Society'. The main aims of the initiative were to study older adolescents and young adults; to encourage research that tried to relate individuals to their social surroundings, to concentrate on young people growing up in society rather than to focus on problems such as delinquency; and to encourage approaches based on talking to young people in their homes, in pubs and night clubs and in and out of jobs.

In aims and approach, our project sought to embrace all these points. Our sample covered a wider than usual age range, reflecting the lack of chronological age barriers outside institutional settings such as school or administrative categories such as 'sixteen to nineteen-year-olds'. We also included women and men in equal numbers because too frequently in the past the focus has been on one or other sex. The early concentration on studying boys and young men from Thrasher (1927) and Whyte (1955) to Parker (1974) and Willis (1977) has been partially corrected by more recent studies of young women by McRobbie and Garber (1975), Davies (1979), Griffin (1985) and Breakwell (1984). The book considers *both* young women and men and how they interact, which is after all one of the main activities of the age group.

Our methods were also very different from the standard approach of

1

the mass media and of professional conferences on adolescence, both of which tend to sensationalize the scabrous deeds of a few rampant or exotic adolescents. Too often, discussions of young people are confined to a catalogue of 'teenage problems' such as glue sniffing, schoolgirl pregnancies, vandalism, aggro and delinquency. In contrast, our fieldwork constantly underlined the essential normality and conformity of most young adults. Our aim, then, is to present a rounded account of their lives which puts issues such as crime or drunkenness into perspective.

We also accept that discussing such issues as unemployment and social security rates with sixteen to twenty-eight-year-olds involves us in taking a political stand. We attempted to reflect this political stance in our research by combining theory and method, and by inviting the young adults to join us in an examination of the main issue in their lives. For example, we encouraged them wherever possible to decide on the main questions and areas to be discussed rather than always supplying them ourselves. We negotiated our accounts of their lives with the young people and for the most part we met with confirmation and approval. We are inclined, however, to challenge the notion of Rom Harré (1980) that relatively inarticulate, unreflective and inexperienced young people can be 'the prime sources of *theories* about their actions and thoughts' (our emphasis). It would be disingenuous of us not to admit that the selection from the wealth of data we collected, the organization of the material, and the final conclusions are all our work, although heavily influenced by discussions with young adults.

In trying always to recognize the distribution of power between ourselves and our sample, we constantly restated our promise of confidentiality. Asking them to choose their own pseudonyms for this book resulted in further insights into some of their characters. Kirsty and Clara chose their names because they preferred them to their own, Asia named herself after a little three-year-old girl down her road and Shuk decided on hers because she liked her friend Shuk at work. Joe (Tetley) and Scotch were influenced in their choice by their favourite beer, and Jimi named himself after Jimi Hendrix, while Max and Ricky were indicating their favourite film stars from action-packed 'macho' movies. Troy later denied that he had chosen his name: 'I must have been drinking at the time'. He had been, but he was pleased to learn that he had changed from his first choice of Sinbad!

We also decided to omit a large amount of the richest (traceable) data, on the principle that those who are researched own the facts of their own lives and have the right to decide what should and should not be published. The paramount concern in our type of research is to protect those who have participated from unwelcome attention. Many of the young women and men said they did not mind whether they were identifiable or not, and some even wanted their photographs to be included. For us, the ethics of our relationship demanded that anonymity rule the day, even at the cost of some of the best illustrative material.

We have tried to produce a text in clear, simple English, devoid of the jargon of the social sciences which is becoming impenetrable even to students of the subject. We want to speak directly to as many young adults as possible as well as to students of the social sciences and to those professionals in the civil service, politics, education and the social services who take daily decisions affecting young people. This book has not been written for the academic specialist.

Three points of style in particular illustrate three major themes in the book: age, gender and region. First, the notion of age: young people in British society are neither fish nor fowl nor good red herring. There is not even an appropriate term to describe this section of the population. 'Kids' is patronising, 'teenagers' is similarly dismissive, 'adolescents' is unattractive and never used by the people so described, according to Simmons and Wade (1984), 'children' is insulting (although used by many professionals), 'youth' rhymes with 'uncouth', and even 'young adults' appears grudging in its recognition of status. 'Young people' is less objectionable, but bland. In the absence of any other terms, we have decided to use the latter two, and just as often we refer simply to either 'the women and the men', in an attempt to accord sixteen to twenty-year-olds some status or to the 'lasses and lads', which was the phrase employed by the young people themselves. The lack of an acceptable phrase typifies the anomalous position of young people in western societies.

Second, throughout the text we have regularly put women first, both in terms of style (the women and the men, Kirsty and Phil) and in order of our considerations of the two sexes. This came from Carol and Sarah's awareness that, in team discussions, all three of us unthinkingly discussed the males in our sample first, and only afterwards would we turn to consider the females. We therefore made the conscious decision to consider the women first and we believe this has made them more visible both in our thinking and in these pages (see Marshal and Borrill, 1984).

Our third stylistic and political point concerns the representation of the Geordie dialect. Our first preference was to include as much dialect as possible to provide splashes of local colour, but we have been persuaded that this approach might be seen by North Easterners as patronising. They disagree among themselves about who is entitled to be called a Geordie and whether it is desirable to speak Geordie. In the event, we have compromised, by including some dialect words, which are listed in a glossary, but generally keeping phonetic spelling to a minimum. Our reasons are the same as those given by Jack Common (1954, p.149), whose autobiography about growing up in the North East faced the same problem:

> Most of the characters are of course people who speak in dialect . . . Readers may wonder why they are not treated to the traditional outbreaks of funny spelling and if in their absence they are expected to regard all dialogue as being conducted in Standard English. They are not. Funny spelling is avoided . . . just because it won't work in this case . . . Try to spell the north eastern dialect and the result is something nobody can understand for more than a line or two . . . The short way out is to print all plain.

We worked with young adults from three different areas in the North East to which we have the pseudonyms Shipton, Milton and Hillsborough. Shipton and Hillsborough were urban town and city respectively and Milton was a large rural area incorporating a number of small towns and villages.

We met these groups after a series of initial visits to various parts of the North East and interviews with officials from agencies including Education departments, the Careers Service, the police and the Manpower Services Commission (MSC) to give us some notion of the official version of local provision for young people.

In Shipton, we met the group in January 1982 through the local Technical College. They were all participating in the MSC's Youth Opportunities Programme (YOP). We attended a 'Life and Social Skills' course and a residential weekend away with twenty-four YOP 'trainees' of both sexes.

The second group we contacted at the same time though the Milton Training Workshop where we carried out interviews and group discussions with six young women and six young men during the first six month period.

Over these early months, we concentrated on building up good relationships with our sample. Once the young people (at this stage eighteen women and eighteen men) had finished their government schemes, we kept in touch with them at informal monthly meetings in pubs, cafes or in their homes, seeing them in small groups or on a one-to-one basis. We then concentrated on getting to know our sample well and building up an easy atmosphere of mutual trust, disclosure and respect.

In September 1982, work began in the third area, Hillsborough, where contact was made with a 'natural group' of eight men aged sixteen to twenty-eight. They all lived on the same estate, Marlow Dene, and were all unemployed. With the help of a local youth project, we had regular weekly meetings with the lads and a series of evening meetings with a small group of women from a nearby estate. After ten months, contact was also established with the wives and girlfriends of the men.

As fieldwork started later with the Hillsborough group, contact was deliberately more intensive: we spent whole days with the lads plus several residential periods organized through the youth project. As it was an informal group, however, the circumstances of their everyday lives (for example, commitments to partners and family ties) affected the attendance of individual members. This drifting in and out highlighted the constantly changing patterns of young adults' lives.

Intensive fieldwork in all three areas ended in August 1983. Over the following year, however, we maintained regular contact by letter, telephone and with occasional meetings in order to keep up with any changes in their lives. We also held special feedback sessions to give the women and men the opportunity to comment on our ideas and emerging conclusions. We met them for a final time in August 1984.

Although unstructured interviewing and observation of individuals, couples and groups were our principle methods of gaining information, we also devised some basic questionnaires and asked young people to complete diaries for us. We deliberately employed a mixture of methods in order to check and recheck the validity of our data.

When discussing the size of our sample, we have always referred to 'around fifty' young women and men. Perhaps an explanation of the word 'around' would help as much as anything to convey the qualitative nature of our work. Unlike most research projects, we are unable to give a simple answer to the question: what is the size of your sample? Some young people, for instance, faithfully turned up to meet us for over a year and then, for a variety of reasons such as searching for work in London, or going steady with their lass or lad or moving home, they stopped seeing us. Others slowly became members of our project because they were the partners or close friends of our original contacts. Again, our sample size varies depending on whether we stress the depth or the regularity of contact established with us. For instance, we met Clara infrequently, but gained as much information about her life and the life of her street in ten minutes as we did from, say, Winnie after hours of monthly meetings. The type of information we received also varied: we learnt more, for instance, about relationships with partners from the women than from the men. The sample number changed, therefore, from week to week throughout the life of the project. In all, we met far more than fifty young people but we are claiming to have established good relationships for two-and-a-half years with around fifty. What matters, however, in a study such as ours is not the seductive certainty produced by percentages or statistical tables but the quality of the understanding reached and of the explanations offered. Surveys of large numbers of young people by means of questionnaires have their place and importance, but the very technique prevents much being discovered about the nature of young adults' personal relations or how they develop tactics or strategies to cope with unemployment, for instance.

The size of our sample was not the only variable that changed constantly over time. Some moved away from the parental home to set up on their own. Only fourteen women and men were kept on after their government training schemes ended and were in full-time employment for the period of the study. All the others moved on and off schemes and in and out of jobs, particularly when they were still eligible for youth training placements in the early stages of our fieldwork. We were in fact monitoring a moving picture with constant scene changes rather than a still; and those behind the camera changed their angle and their view as much those in front of it.

The three areas

We deliberately worked in three different geographical areas to prevent us putting all our eggs into one (perhaps atypical) basket. While the anonymity of our sample remains important, so does a basic knowledge of the social and economic backgrounds of the areas in which the women and men lived. We therefore present here brief accounts of Shipton, Milton and Hillsborough, from which we have omitted details which would make them instantly recognizable. Their place in the culture and economic prospects of the North East will be discussed in the final chapter.

Shipton

Southern historians and travellers have dealt harshly with Shipton. In the middle of the nineteenth century it was described as 'a centre of work, noise, smoke and dirt; iron-works, brass-works, chain cable-works, glass-works, bottle-works and chemical-works lie on all sides . . . The town has little interest except for its manufactures'. At the turn of the century, a travel guide dismissed it in one line, 'Hotels hardly to be recommended. Sleep elsewhere'. By the 1930s, few if any improvements were visible to the commentator who wrote: '(Shipton) is, I am afraid, as unattractive a place these days as you could find. Wholly industrial now, all charm has left it . . . . The houses are mean and the whole appearance of the place unpleasing and squalid'. The verdict on Shipton in the 1960s was very much in the same vein, 'No one could really want to see the town except on business'.

The main shopping centre in 1984 consisted of a few high-rise chain stores, the usual range of banks, chemists, dairies, shoe shops and pubs, amusement centres packed with young people playing 'Space Invaders', bingo and billiard halls, video centres and second-hand furniture shops with large orange notices in their windows declaring 'DHSS estimates given free'. In a town with a population of a quarter of a million, the noise and bustle of shoppers and business people does not last for the length of the main street, but soon peters out amid empty premises, abandoned yards and deserted cafes. The local libraries are now full of men of all ages listlessly reading newspapers in the hope of passing the time; some younger men can be seen joining the women shopping, pushing prams or waiting to collect their children from nursery or primary school. In the words of the Goftons (1984):

> The Giro Cities of the North East have developed a culture of worklessness . . . the commercial geography of these towns has been transformed. The shops which have been there for years have been swept away, rationalized into new sites in the new shopping malls. They have been replaced by what are called locally 'cheap shops' . . . Here in the North East, the 1930s have never really gone away.

Since the mid-1970s, a stream of official reports on Shipton have made public a grim catalogue of deficiencies in health, education, housing and employment. Local histories, however, reveal that the problems of poverty, unemployment, overcrowding, ill-health and poor education have not suddenly emerged in the last ten years nor are they a throwback from the 1930s, but they have been endemic in Shipton since it became an early boom town in Victorian times. To take one example from the world of education, provision for technical and commercial education has long been seriously inadequate, especially for an industrial town such as Shipton. All manner of industries thrived and private fortunes were accumulated for over a hundred years before a Technical Institute was established after the Second World War. It should come as no surprise, therefore, that the proportion of professional people is and always has been low: in 1865, for example, out of a total population of 39,000 there were 6 lawyers, 12 doctors, 27 teachers, 9 chemists, 1 land surveyor and 158 publicans.

Milton

Milton is an area roughly triangular in shape which covers thirty square miles and embraces the townships of Thealby and Runswick and a handful of smaller villages, including Monkton and Hambridge. Essentially a rural community until the mid-nineteenth century, the population of Milton trebled and then trebled again during the Victorian age with the development of the towns and villages into industrial settlements based on coal mining. Monkton, for example, had less than 100 inhabitants in the 1840s, but within forty years, its population had increased to nearly 3000. Migrant labour flocked to the area from Ireland, other counties of England, and some from the continent. New shafts were being sunk regularly and in 1900, the largest pit employed as many as 10,000 people.

At the turn of the century, Milton was a thriving area with its busy population, its clanking railways full of coal, its market days, chapels, pubs and clubs. On Saturdays in Runswick, the shops stayed open until midnight; and football matches, quoits, 'fives' and a theatre provided entertainment. Throughout the nineteenth century, the crime rate in the area was high. One commentator noted:

> There is no doubt that alcohol played a major role in the troubles that plagued Milton. Engine drivers and firemen seemed to spend every penny they possessed on ale, then, after a 'belly full', plan a full-scale battle with the police or anyone else who tread their path.

The hard, dangerous and uncertain work of the miners underlay their physical and mental toughness, and according to Williamson (1982, p. 36), it was the proximity of death which explained 'both fatalism and hedonism which have been so much a part of working-class life, particularly in mining districts'. Their solidarity was a consequence of a shared history of living and working in one place, of the need for cooperation among colliers underground, and of often bitter struggles with the coal owners. Strikes over matters of wages, hours and working conditions occurred regularly throughout the century, but the trade unions were not formed until the 1860s when the Durham and Northumberland Miners' Unions came into being. The history of coal mining in the area cannot be discussed 'with miners without their recalling, conflict, exploitation and hardship: their historical self-image is that of an exploited class' (Williamson and Quayle, 1983, p. 18).

Socially and geographically isolated, these insular communities were forced back on their own resources. The Co-operative movement grew out of this need. The Store, as it was known, was run by the miners' families for themselves: the more they spent, the bigger the 'divvy' they received twice a year. Credit helped families to survive between one payday and the next; and during strikes it was the Store that kept many from starvation. When work resumed, debts were paid out of accumulated dividends and once again goods were paid for with cash.

Employment was hard but, when it came, unemployment was harsher. Exhausted pits were being closed from the 1870s and mass redundancies through closure gradually increased, accelerating into a total decline after the First World War, when between 300 and 2000 men were being laid off at a time. As a coal-exporting district, Milton was particularly susceptible to fluctuations in the trade cycle. The slump of the 1930s saw 60 per cent male unemployment in Hambridge. The whole of the Milton area took on an air of dereliction as the pits closed down and left deserted slag heaps in their place. Encouraged by Family and Juvenile Transference Schemes introduced by government in the mid 1930s (see Rees and Rees, 1982), some of the young migrated south; the men were offered places on training schemes and the women the opportunity to go into domestic service. The majority who remained behind, young and old, soon suffered long-term unemployment. The population of the area reached a peak in the early 1920s and has declined every decade since; by 1981 more than one-third of the total population in 1921 had drifted away in search of work.

Although Runswick had two new factories as early as 1938, it was not until after the Second World War that Industrial Training Estates were established generally in the Milton area. Agricultural and electrical engineering works and clothing factories soon provided jobs for both women and men. The 1950s saw increased diversification of trade and industry with textile and food manufacturers, mechanical engineering and firms that exploited the natural mineral wealth of the area in tin, silica and lime. Industrial diversification has doubled the proportion of jobs taken by women in the last twenty years. Coal mining by now was drastically reduced and in Thealby the last pit closed in the late 1960s. The run down in coal mining has been relentless: almost 5000 jobs were available locally in the industry in 1951, 3500 in 1961, 150 in 1971 and none in 1981. Alternative employment, however, has never fully taken up the labour force left behind in the wake of pit closures and Milton has continued to suffer disproportionately high unemployment rates to this day.

As people have continued to drift away in search of work, the village communities have contracted still further, leaving houses empty and shops closed and boarded up. The pit closures left behind acres of derelict land, waste heaps and abandoned railway lines: energetic local councils have reclaimed and landscaped the worst eyesores, but the only new buildings in the area appear to be a string of local authority sport centres and leisure complexes which are no doubt intended to produce the fittest unemployed in the country. Research quoted by Townsend (1985) shows that such centres are mainly used by middle-class residents.

Hillsborough

In the mid-eighteenth century, a visitor to Hillsborough commented, 'I was struck by the bustle and prosperity of the town'. Over the next hundred years, it continued to develop as a port and centre of industry based on fishing, shipbuilding, the mining of coal, copper and salt and the manufacturing of cloth, rope, leather and pottery. In light engineering, it contributed to the most advanced technology of its time and attracted skilled workers from outside the north east by paying high wages. Most of the new housing built for workers was of a relatively high standard thanks to the good quality of locally produced bricks and mortar, although fewer than one in ten had running water. The business class built themselves grandiose houses on certain streets, often protected by their own walled grounds.

Prosperity in Hillsborough reached a height in the mid-nineteenth century, which it has not seen since. The fortunes of the town reflect the region's history and its dependence on a few heavy industries with their boom periods and corresponding troughs. In 1891, an official report noted the deterioration in the city since the 1850s: 'Even if employment were regular, the wages are so low that existence must be a struggle at the best of times' and it expressed concern at the poor living conditions of unskilled workers and their families who made up the largest proportion of Hillsborough's population. At the turn of the century there was official recognition of people's attachment to housing that was often run-down and overcrowded. One reason to stay in the same neighbourhood was because of the credit built up with 'the little shopkeepers of the district'. Another was linked to employment: the dock labourers are a class that must be on the spot because they have always to wait for calls that may arise at any moment.' In these ways, people were hooked into a local network of mutual support, credit and job opportunities.

By the beginning of the twentieth centure, Hillsborough had stopped growing and, after years of slow decline, by the 1930s production was lower that it had been for over two hundred years. Unemployment was endemic. At this time, there was a policy of rehousing on a large scale: 77 per cent of all rehoused families were in receipt of some form of public assistance. The local authority, which by now had superseded the local industrialists as providers of housing and civic amenities, found that its programme of slum clearance met with some opposition. Families so long established in certain areas and whose fortunes were so intrinsically linked with the local yard or pit were no more inclined to move than was their grandparents' generation. Over the last two hundred years the indigenous population of Hillsborough has become attached to the town and remains fiercely loyal to particular neighbourhoods.

There was an upsurge in productivity during the war and along with most parts of the country, the town enjoyed a brief return to prosperity until the late 1960s. The decline which began then spans the lifetime of the young people in this study and continues to this day. Hillsborough in the 1980s provides better housing, but less employment that ever before for its population of several hundred thousand.

In the areas where we knew most young people, housing was predominantly council owned and exclusive use of basic amenities (water, bath and inside toilet) was high, but so too was the incidence of overcrowding as there were many large local families. The age distribution was out of balance, with more elderly on the one hand and an above average number of children of school age on the other. There was also a disproportionate number of single-parent families. Car ownership was two-thirds the average for the borough as a whole and travel to work was mostly by bus or on foot.

Over the period we visited these estates the rates of unemployment were consistently above the already high average for Hillsborough of 16.7 per cent. The unemployment rates for the estate we came to know best and its two adjoining estates were 31.2 per cent, 43.2 per cent and 32.6 per cent in the summer of 1984. The rate for male unemployment reached more than 50 per cent in one estate, showing dramatically the changes in the structure of the local job market.

The North East

Not even the proudest Geordie would claim that the north east was a prosperous or trouble-free region, but there is something of the very essence of the three areas missing from the above accounts. The usual picture of the North East presented by official statistics and by the media is all too depressingly familiar; to those who come for a full weekend and stay in first-class hotels in order to write a lurid article or to make a socially relevant, three-minute television report, the north is distant, drab and perhaps in irreversible decline. If that is an accurate picture, then how is the intense loyalty of local inhabitants to the area to be explained? How are we to account for the attachment of newcomers, so many of whom decide to settle in the north? What the camera cannot see and the estate agent's blurb is silent about is the vibrant culture of the north east: the pride the older generation had in their work and craftsmanship; the rich networks of mutual support which have been built up over generations by families, neighbours and friends, self-sufficient and resourceful communities, which have not lost hope for themselves and their children and which give security and warmth to those members who are unemployed, and thousands of talented young people who want nothing more and nothing less than a place in society. There is, of course, the danger of middle-class outsiders romanticizing what local people see as the harsh realities of their lives. We have tried to remain alert to that danger and discussions in subsequent chapters of the collapse of the traditional apprenticeship system, of the strains put on family life by unemployment, and of fragmentations among working-class communities should help to make the picture more complete. On the other hand, if the following pages do not convey something of the collective excitement, pleasure, and sheer fun that young people enjoy in the north east, then we will have failed those who helped us so generously.

Such vitality, however, does not take place in a vacuum. We sought at all times in our work to link the personal experiences of our sample to national economic changes and to the continuing slide in the fortunes of the economy of the North East. From a dominant position at the very heart of the industrial revolution in nineteenth-century Britain, the north's economy has been transformed into a series of branch plants; and regional policies have so far failed to halt the persistent decline. The decisions of the largest employers in the area—the nationalized industries of coal and steel—to close plant after plant have resulted in the highest unemployment figures in mainland Britain.Behind, then, the portrayal of individual lives in the following pages march economic and political forces which will be more fully analysed in the final chapter; the modest hopes and job aspirations of young adults, for example, were soon reduced by the realities of local labour markets to a 'choice' between (in their words) 'a shit job, the dole or a govvy' (scheme).

The organization of the book

The young women and men are central to the chapters which follow: their lives and their views are always described first, our own commentary and observations coming second to allow readers to form their own impressions before presenting our own interpretation. We have organized the material into four sections with two chapters in each. Read in sequence, they present a multi-dimensional picture, built up in layers, of life as experienced by around fifty young adults in the North East in the 1980s. Can one, however, generalize safely from a sample of around fifty to the total population of young adults in the North East, never mind in the rest of Great Britain? We have examined a number of local studies in Gateshead (King, 1984), Newcastle (Blackie, 1983), and in County Durham (Kirton, 1983); we have discussed our conclusions with local professionals and have read various higher degree theses on aspects of the same theme; taken together these different types of evidence suggest that our findings fit into a pattern typical of young, working-class adults in the north east. Our own previous experiences and the published work of Parker (1974),

Rees and Atkinson (1982), Jenkins (1983), Roberts (1984) and others would further suggest that our sample can be safely compared with other working-class young people in similarly depressed areas of the North West, Northern Ireland, and the industrial areas of Scotland and Wales, although there are significant regional differences particular to the north east. If we had studied another fifty women and men in three different areas of the north, then the details of individuals lives would obviously have changed, but the main parameters within which those lives were being lived (such as government schemes, job opportunities or local responses to unemployment) would have remained much the same.

The first two chapters present short portraits of young women and men. The intention is to give an overall sketch of their lives before certain aspects are focused on more closely in the following sections. The portraits describe them with their friends and families, going to rock concerts, on holiday, courting, splitting up with partners, getting engaged and married, learning to live with unemployment, with each other, discovering good things about jobs and bad, fighting with the lasses or getting 'done over' by lads from a rival town, borrowing money as well as saving it, growing up and settling down with children of their own. Implicitly, these two chapters describe the strength of local ties, the social networks, the poverty and lack of opportunities confronting women and men alike and their ways of surviving.

Chapters 3 and 4 follow the young adults out into the world of jobs, government schemes and unemployment. Their experiences reflect the crisis in the labour market which came to a head during the period of this study. The accounts of individual employment histories add, we hope, detail and colour to the empty canvas of youth employment statistics. There is no homogenous group such as 'the unemployed'; those who were at times unemployed were the same people as those who at other times were in employment. We also describe the survival tactics used by the young people to show how these tactics grow out of day-to-day family and community life.

Chapters 5 and 6 deal more specifically with their backgrounds and their relationships with families, neighbours and especially friends. They take us round the neighbourhoods and homes in Shipton, Milton and Hillsborough from which the young adults came. As their emotional dependence on family decreased, friendships with contemporaries became more important. We look at a wide range of experiences from hectic social lives to loneliness and isolation, from young couples who married and produced their first children to those who never had a partner.

In the fourth and final section, we look at wider perspectives. In

Chapter 7, we consider how far young people were prepared to explore the world, both physically and intellectually. We discuss their reflections on their transition to adulthood, their treatment by older adults and the media, and their views on politics, race and other social issues; we also try to estimate the extent of our own influence upon them.

In the final chapter, their futures are assessed in relation to the economic prospects for the North and that assessment reinforces the overriding importance of regional differences. There is no uniform process of growing up in Great Britain which can be applied to the millions of young people in the sixteen to twenty-four-year-old age group. The middle-class girl from the south east of England who attended a private school on her way to Durham University and a professional career has little beyond her nationality in common with a working-class lad who left a Newcastle comprehensive at the earliest possible moment for the Youth Training Scheme and then the dole. We also attempt in the final chapter to combine psychological theories of adolescence with sociological explanations of youth; normally such competing schools of thought either ignore or deride each other's contribution. We have tried to integrate the insights from both disciplines: individual factors such as physical attractiveness or a warm personality are obviously important to eighteen-year-olds and all those around them, but equally there are structural factors, such as inequalities in the provision of health or education services, which are not explicable in terms of individuals. By simultaneously looking up at society from the perspective of one young woman or one young man and looking down from the level of government policy and its effect upon them we hope to avoid the dangers of concentrating on only *one* level of explanation.

Thus, we begin our account by looking rather narrowly at individuals and end by assessing more widely their place in society. What unites the chapters is a common theme: our belief that the women and men have been created by their society and its history just as that society and its history are likely in turn to be fashioned by them and their contemporaries. In other words, we shall argue that personal identity and social structure are best understood not as two separate or opposing strands, but as one interwoven thread in the single process of growing up. We tried to capture some of the above themes in the title of the book *Growing Up at the Margins* which underlines the fact that all young adults have been pushed to the very periphery of British society and that some are further disadvantaged by living in areas like the North East which have become neglected, economic outposts.

Section I
Young Adults' Lives

1 Portraits

Stephanie

Stephanie was above average height, with a trim figure and light brown hair which she cut short around her face to emphasize her large eyes. She worse steel rimmed glasses and put on make-up if she was going out. She took great care over her appearance and always liked to look at clothes when we met her shopping on market days in Runswick, the local town. Over one summer, she lost a stone in weight by choosing to eat boiled potatoes instead of chips. Perhaps Stephanie was extra careful about how she looked because she was self-conscious about her legs which had required periodic surgery due to a congenital complaint.

It was difficult to get to know Stephanie as she was not naturally talkative or outgoing. Her shy, uncommunicative manner set her apart at the Milton Training Workshop. Over time, however, in long one-to-one meetings, we became friends with Stephanie. We knew her through seventeen months of lonely unemployment and ups and downs at home, and followed her change in fortune as she did nine months on a government scheme and became engaged. Eventually, we attended her wedding and visited her in her married home.

Although Stephanie was a woman of few words, we came to know her as a forceful character. After meeting her family it seemed that she got her strong will from her mother, her quietness from her father.

Ivy and Will Harrison were in their mid-forties. Stephanie, seventeen when we first met at the beginning of 1982, was the eldest of their three children. Jenny was fifteen at this time and Billy seven years old. The family had recently moved to a council estate in Green Fell just outside Runswick. Previously, they had lived for a year in another village nearby and before that, around Consett, where Stephanie had gone to school. She said that five years was the longest they had ever lived in one place. Her mother always found something wrong, like the

15

neighbours, or dogs, or the local children, and would move house.

After six months in Green Fell, we asked Stephanie her opinion of the area. 'Wey, I don't like it ... there's nowt, just a few shops ... you always have to get the bus into town and there's nowhere to go. And the neighbours are always talking among themselves.' But in one respect, she said, it was better than their old place. There the local kids used to throw stones or snowballs at their windows. This had not happened in the new house.

The Harrisons seemed an insular family. Ivy and Will's only involvement outside the home was with their local chapel. Will had been employed all his life in the steelworks, but he had accepted redundancy because of his heart condition. Stephanie said he used to bring home between £80 and £100 week, but in November 1982, 'He had £41.50 for the four of us'. There was still some redundancy money at this time and the Harrisons were able to replace their old carpet and buy a new sideboard of which Ivy was very proud. Unlike the one 'they' had next door, hers had lights which lit up the ornaments on display. Will became eligible for unemployment benefit in January, 1983 and the family received a rent rebate. We asked Stephanie how her father filled his unemployed days: 'He hardly ever goes out'. She explained that he helped in the house, walked the dogs and went to chapel, but he did not drink and had lost touch with his old workmates through the steelworks closure, plus their moving to another area.

Ivy loved the television which was always on in the front room. She was extremely talkative whenever we met her: Stephanie said, 'She gets lonely, she has no one really to talk to.' Ivy's conversation including opinions about leading politicians, seemed mostly inspired by what she had heard on the TV. She was kept busy washing, ironing and knitting and early in 1982, she had the added responsibility of caring for her mother, Mrs Bootle.

We had first heard of Mrs Bootle when Stephanie mentioned she was organizing her own eightieth birthday party. She still lived in Consett where Stephanie visited her regularly to help with the shopping. Mrs Bootle had lived in the same mid-terrace Victorian house for seventy-eight years. The house had never been modernized and not redecorated since the 1930s. On one visit, Mrs Bootle gave Stephanie her shopping requirements: 'a pound of stewing meat for beef tea and a cough bottle' for her cold. A few days later the house was burgled and Ivy and Will insisted that she came to stay with them. As the Harrisons' house had only three bedrooms, the arrival of Ivy's mother meant Stephanie had to sleep on the couch in the living room. After seven weeks of this arrangement, Stephanie developed a bad back and insisted that she had her bedroom once more. Grandmother moved in with Jenny, and Billy had to sleep in with his parents. Not surprisingly, tensions rose in the crowded household. Jenny, who was on medication for epilepsy and seeing her doctor once a month, seemed to cut herself off from the rest of the family. Her mother said, 'she doesn't live with us, when she gets in, she's straight up to her room.' She was proud of Jenny, though, as she went to an English Literature evening class. Stephanie described her sister as 'always writing stories'.

The closest relationship in the family seemed to be between Stephanie and Billy. She took him to the swimming baths with his friend because their parents would not let the lads go alone and at Christmas she 'spent a fortune on the bairn'. Stephanie liked the company of young children, but then she did not consider she had any friends of her own age. She had lost contact with her best school friend not long after moving to Green Fell.

Of her school, Stephanie commented, 'I was always in the bottom class'. She had never taken any examinations because of the time she had had to spend in hospital. Of herself, she said: 'I'm not very brainy, in fact I'm thick'. Other observations Stephanie made belied this analysis. In describing her relationship with her parents, she once made the fine distinction between her father talking *with* her and her mother talking *at* her. On another occasion, she remarked that she thought schools ought to teach more up-to-date subjects like politics, 'so you know what everything's about when you leave'. When discussing orders for steel now going to yards in the south, Stephanie's sense of justice came out: 'I don't think that's right that, they've got more jobs down there'.

Stephanie had a raw deal in the labour market. After leaving school at Easter in 1981, she was in hospital and had six weeks' unemployment before starting at the Milton Training Workshop. From there she went on a Work Experience on Employers' Premises (WEEP) scheme at a local factory, Toulons, but she was dogged with ill health, first with an allergy to one of the plastics she dealt with on the production line and later with glandular fever. She did six weeks in total on the scheme but lost her place after three weeks continuous absence, because of MSC regulations.

Previously, the Careers Office had put her on to evening classes at the local technical college. She had attended for nearly a year, but when she failed both the typing and English exams, she declined to retake them because it meant sitting through a second year of the same classes. Her image of herself had become set: 'I don't seem to be too good at studying'.

Stephanie signed on as unemployed again in May 1982. She was seventeen and a half and over a year's unemployment was to follow. Never having paid National Insurance, she was not eligible for Unemployment Benefit. Her weekly social security payments were

£16.85 at first, rising to £22.85 when she was eighteen and subsequently to £23.65 with the standard annual increase. After April 1984, however, this dropped to £20.55 when the government retracted £3.10 housing allowance. She paid her parents £8 a week for her board, which along with her grandmother's contribution to the household, meant that her father's benefit was reduced accordingly.

After four months of unemployment, Stephanie was very bored. She played with the kids in the street, watched television or went into Runswick. With her dad's help, she redecorated her bedroom. They then moved on to the living room, but soon that was done too. Occasionally, she went swimming, as much for the company as for the exercise: although it was half rate for the unemployed before 4 pm she preferred to pay the full 30p. admission to go at the more sociable time when the baths were busier. Stephanie took up learning to drive and she started to make her own clothes on a second hand sewing machine which her father lent her the money to buy. He also paid for her driving lessons, but at £6 an hour, it was hard to find the money on a regular basis. Stephanie had lessons intermittently, but when her provisional licence expired, she never had a spare £10 to renew it.

She looked in the paper every day and sometimes phoned about jobs, but they always asked for two or three years' experience. In the Milton area, there was a pool of experienced unemployed workers which firms could choose from. Once when she had been to sign on, she said she had 'been told to look' for jobs. In fact, that week she had followed up an advertisement in the Herald for a clerical post, but when she went for interview, she had failed the typing test because of her speeds. Another time, in response to a letter from the Careers Office, Stephanie went for interview at a local factory for what she believed to be a job on the production line. It was only after she spent half a day waiting to be interviewed that she learnt the opening was in fact just another WEEP scheme. It would in effect have meant her working a forty hour week for an extra £1.35 pence; that is, the difference between her social security payment and the scheme allowance.

Stephanie suffered her unemployment alone, although she got on well with father and sometimes they would talk about topical issues together. One day, Will related the story of a local employer of a workforce of twelve men. Gradually, he had got rid of them all, saying he could no longer afford to keep them, but he had then accepted young people on WEEP schemes. It was Ivy who commented: 'He was thinking of the jam on his bread'.

The two brightest spots in Stephanie's first year of unemployment came at Christmas and Easter. What social life she did enjoy was mainly with her cousin, Paula, who invited her over to Darlington at weekends. In January, Stephanie was a lot chirpier than usual: over

Christmas, when out with Paula and her boyfriend, Alan, she had met Alan's friend, Dave, and over the New Year the four of them had been out together four nights in a row. Stephanie's comment, 'It makes a change from staying in all the time', seemed an understatement of what she was really feeling during this happy spell. Her courting did not last long though. The distance of twenty miles between Green Fell and Darlington meant that she only saw Dave at weekends and, in March, he suggested that they just be ordinary friends. Stephanie's life reverted to its main base – her family.

At Easter, Stephanie had a holiday in Penrith with her aunt and uncle. She went to help with her grandmother who after three months was still living with the family. The holiday provided some short relief for the Harrison household. After the trip, Stephanie happily showed photographs of days visiting the Lakes and announced: 'I got drunk'. She had been out with her aunt and uncle one evening, playing darts in a pub, and had managed five lagers and black and five whisky and oranges! The occasion was memorable for Stephanie as she had never done anything like it before, never having belonged to a group of friends the same age with whom she might have celebrated.

Stephanie's principal pastime over her months of unemployment was going to the shops. After paying her board, a good share of her money went on bus fares into town which cost 40 pence one way. The General Election in the first week in June, 1983, was less important to her than the long awaited opening of a large new discount supermarket in Runswick. Through force of circumstance, Stephanie had a strong sense of value for money. She knew the prices of different commodities in the stores all over the town. Shopping, in a sense, was her hobby. On her very limited budget, in her own way, she was a consumer par excellence, looking in the shops almost daily to see what she fancied or what she could pick up at a reasonable price. Most of the things she bought were given as presents, a potted plant for her mother, a jumper for her brother.

In June 1983, it appeared Stephanie's luck had at last changed when her mother told us on the phone that she had found a job, but then came the news: 'It was one of those twopenny-ha'penny jobs... They weren't telling the truth, they just wanted cheap labour, they weren't paying the full rate'. Stephanie told us about it a few days later. A cousin had told her there were trainee jobs advertized at a clothing factory in Consett. Stephanie went for a practical test on the Tuesday and was 'started on' the following Monday, when she was given minimal instruction on a type of machine she had never used before. She tried her best each day, but on Friday, at 4.15 pm, she was told not to bother coming in the following week. In her own word, she was 'stunned' at being given just a half an hour's notice. The supervisor simply said that she was not good enough at the job. Stephanie went back to collect her wage for the week: £55 for 40 hours 45 minutes. Deductions came to £6.10 tax and £5.11 insurance. The bitter experience left Stephanie reeling in disbelief for weeks to come. After a full year's unemployment, she thought she had broke the mould, only to find herself thrown back into it with a vengeance after just one week.

Only two events of note happened in the following months. In September 1983, Stephanie and her neighbour whom she counted as 'my one friend' started to attend local keep fit sessions together at £1 a time on a Monday evening. Stephanie was also looking forward to the wedding of one of her cousins. For months beforehand, she saved up for a present and anticipated the day with excitement, but when she came to described it afterwards, she simply said it was 'all right'.

Then, suddenly, life for Stephanie changed completely. In the Jobcentre, she saw a vacancy for a canteen assistant and, on enquiring, learnt that the interviews were to be the following week. She went and, the next day, heard by letter that she was to start that Monday. It was in fact an MSC funded Community Programme (CP) post of twelve months duration. Stephanie knew this, but she still called it a job. It was to pay £54 for a 35 hour week. After five days' employment in seventeen months and existing on £22.85 a week, at this time it seemed to Stephanie to be as good as a job.

The next we heard was one month later: Stephanie was getting engaged–to Rob, also a CP worker, whom she had met on the project. He was a local lad who had been unemployed for over a year, after three years in the Army. At Stephanie's invitation, he moved in to live with the Harrisons, sleeping on a bunk bed in the back of the living room. After a few weeks, family relations were strained to new heights with the overcrowding and having to make the wedding arrangements. Rob moved back to live with his married brother and then, at Easter 1984, he took rented accommodation. Stephanie joined him there for a month but two weeks before the wedding, she moved back with her family, to be properly married from home.

In the early summer of 1984, nearly two and a half years after we first met Stephanie, we attended her wedding. She was nineteen and a half; Rob was twenty-three. Stephanie had bought her white lace dress months before. (Even before she met Rob, she had been window shopping for wedding dresses.) Her sister Jenny headed the three bridesmaids and the service was held in Stephanie's parents' favourite chapel. The congregation numbered about sixty, with more guests on Rob's side as he was one of fifteen children, all of whom were married and lived locally. Afterwards everyone enjoyed themselves at the buffet and disco reception in a nearby club.

Stephanie and Rob could not afford to go away afterwards. Two weeks previously, Rob had finished his scheme prematurely and within the following two weeks, Stephanie gave up her post, four months short of the expected date. They explained that it was to do with MSC cutbacks on CP schemes in that area and none of those who had been taken on the previous autumn would be completing their full twelve months. Once Rob was unemployed, they said, financially it was not worth Stephanie continuing.

Rob had had his name on the housing list for two years and shortly after they were married, was offered a house on his home estate in Runswick. In July 1984, the couple moved in. Rob said they were lucky to have a house in such good order 'with the estate being a bad one'. They furnished it completely with the help of relatives, only having the carpets to buy.

On our last visit to Stephanie, she was sitting in her smart new home watching afternoon television with Rob. She said they watched a lot 'because there's nothing much else to do'. Rob was signing on unemployed and claiming for Stephanie who was no longer registered independently. When we asked, neither of them could see any new prospects for themselves in the near future.

Max

During the life of our project, Max changed physically and emotionally from a plump, boyish faced, shy and rather immature lad who had little self-confidence into a tall, lean and fit young man with a relaxed and accepting attitude towards the world. He was invariably friendly and gentle mannered. We first met him at the Training Workshop in Milton when he was just over sixteen-and-a-half years old, at which time he weighed thirteen stone and was five foot two. On his nineteenth birthday, he was ten-and-a-half stone and six foot one.

Max was born in Germany where his father, a Welshman, was serving with the British Army. When he was ten, the family returned to the south of England and then to County Durham where his mother's family came from. Since leaving the Army, his father had been able to find only seasonal work with Shales, a firm of landscape gardeners who laid him off every winter. To help bring up Max and his three older sisters, all four of whom had been born within the space of four years, his mother worked full time at a local factory 'at the top of the road' as a machinist.

Max had never been on holiday in his life, although he had once visited his father's mother in North Wales for a few days. The family had no car, his mother having bumped into another car while learning to drive without insurance or motor taxation: the fines put the family off the road for good. They lived in Redshaw in a three-bedroomed council house, the front door of which was badly scratched by their dog; Max had shared a bedroom with the sister nearest in age to him until he was sixteen. The two eldest girls then left home, one to get married and the other to live with her boyfriend. The youngest sister gave birth to a son and continued to live with her parents for a further year until provided with her own council house. Max's first reaction was that he could now play his records as loudly as he liked, but, as time progressed, we noted that he made frequent visits to see his sister and the 'canny bairn'.

Max went to the local comprehensive school where his strongest memories were of being bullied by the boys and bored by the teachers. During his first year at the school, Max witnessed a fight caused by the rivalry between two neighbouring villages; it involved hundreds of pupils whom, it was reported, had stolen knives from the dining-hall and then smuggled them out of school for a battle in a local field. Four years later, there were riots on two consecutive days which resulted in £20,000 worth of damage being done to large, plate glass windows and a gymnasium flooded by fire hydrants. The violence, caused by senior girls and boys, was only brought to a halt by the intervention of the police. When Max was presented in his fifth year with the same work sheets in English as in the previous year, he resorted to 'playing the nick . . . a lot'. He left school in the summer of 1981 with one CSE grade 4 in Design Technology. He thought he would have achieved a higher grade if only some of his continuous assessments had not been mislaid by the staff.

Max sported a skinhead haircut in his last year at school but gave it up when he started looking for a job. After three weeks of unemployment, his dad fixed him up with sixteen weeks of summer work at Shales. Max had problems in adjusting to the adult atmosphere at work: at first he noted how 'the grown men' were calling each other (and him) by their first names and he was unsure about how he should reply, but by the end of four months, and by dint of hard graft, he slowly developed the courage to address them by their Christian names. He then returned to the dole queue for three months before starting at the Training Workshop.

At the Workshop he preferred to be on his own or with only one or two lads rather than in a larger group where his work tended to be criticized, 'If a job comes wrong, it's my part that usually goes wrong. I get the measurements wrong'. He was assigned to the joinery department, although he had always expressed an interest in farming and had in fact helped out in a voluntary capacity on a farm for a year while at school. Max decided 'to finish myself at the Workshop' after a quarrel with the manager, Mr Long, who had told him to clear a path of stones with his hands. Max had insisted on using a shovel and was sent home for the day; at a meeting the following morning, Max refused to admit he was at fault and left after the only quarrel he had had with a member of staff in seven months.

While at the Workshop he received £23.50 (later increased to £25) from which £3 was deducted for transport to and from home in a minibus. In the summer of 1982, he was giving his parents £10 for bed and board, which left him with £10.50. He was worried about having his allowance 'docked' by the Manager, and he saw his friends losing money for being late, for failing to 'phone in if ill, for 'gannin' down the shops for a bag of crisps or cream cakes for the supervisors', but Max himself was never fined. After he left the Workshop, his income was reduced to £33 social security every fortnight which left him with £6.50 a week. He gave up going to see action-packed movies at the cinema in Runswick (he chose the pseudonym Max from the hero of the *Mad Max* films), because it cost £2.20 a time; he also stopped skating because of the price of admission and the bus fares. He received his social security girocheque on Thursdays and regularly ran out of money before the following Sunday. He applied to have his cheque sent to him every week as he could not manage his money over a two week period.

After a second spell of three months' unemployment, Max started a three weeks course recommended to him by the Careers Office which led to a six months WEEP scheme with a carpet firm. He took to this job, learning about the different makes and qualities of carpet and how to lay them, describing it to his contemporaries as 'brilliant'. The owner of the shop treated him well and took him out for a free Christmas dinner and drink, but at the end of the scheme he was unable to keep him on because business was so poor. He did, however, describe Max to Carol as 'a very hard worker' whom he would have liked to have kept on.

Max became unemployed again, this time for five weeks before his father found him another summer job at Shales which last twelve weeks until August, 1983. Because the hourly rate of 78p was so low, Max began working long hours of overtime and had to travel as far as Barrow-in-Furness with the firm. This meant leaving at 6 am and travelling three hours there and back in a mini van with nine other workers. Every so often they arrived home much later than intended because the mini van had broken down: 'he's so mean, he won't pay for proper tyres, just remoulds . . . everything (in the firm)'s cheap and nasty', explained Max. One week he brought home £49.57 for 55 hours of work and the next week £66 for 82 hours. As he anticipated further periods of unemployment, he saved £78 from his job with which he later bought a CB radio. Saving meant, however, that he stayed at home much more than he wanted to.

Eleven months of unemployment followed during which Max and

his father spent all day and every day of the winter together at home, getting on each other's nerves. His relationships with both his parents were good on the whole, the only arguments being about his untidy bedroom: 'I know it's in a state, but I know where everything is'. His father explored the possibility of setting Max up on his own as a gardener now that he had learned the rudiments of the job at Shales, but the price of the tools and machines needed to tackle large jobs proved prohibitive. Anyway, all the neighbours did their own gardening.

For over a year we developed a consistent picture of Max as a rather quiet and perhaps lonely boy who kept his problems to himself, who had one good male friend with whom he 'went down Runswick and walked about', buying posters and records of his favourite singer, Toyah. In good weather he travelled alone on his push-bike around the countryside, preferring, he said, to cycle uphill because of the exercise it gave him. Most of the time he was unemployed, however, he spent at home playing records or watching war films on video. When asked what he was doing to pass the time, Max gave the typical reply: 'nowt'. We encouraged him on one occasion to describe what he had done the previous evening. He and his best mate had sat on a wall outside the local 'chippy'. They had no money – not even for 'scrapings' – and so they just sat there and talked. Then his mate said, 'Let's go for a walk.' They walked round the block, came back to sit on the same wall and talked until 10 pm and then went home.

Three incidents broke the repetitive pattern of his life at this time. He volunteered all the details about the first event because it had a major impact on him, while we discovered the second by chance. One evening Max told us as soon as we met that he had 'been in trouble with the police' and had been caught red-handed, stealing an old car from the centre of Runswick on a Saturday night. When he appeared in court he was fined £100 plus £10 costs, which he subsequently paid off at £5 per week, was banned for driving for six months, and had eight points set against his non-existent driving licence. The friend who broke into the car and was driving it when they were stopped by the police was fined £165 and was penalized ten points. Max added that appearing in court had given him a fright and he resolved never to get into trouble again. Neither of them had any previous convictions nor any prior involvement with the police. There had been a fourteen-year-old schoolboy with them who sat in the back of the car; 'he was sent away 'cos he'd been in so much trouble before'. Even six months later, the only explanation Max could offer for the incident was, 'I dunno . . . there's nothing to do, no money, nowhere to go . . . it filled in the time'. It had also created some excitement.

Later that summer, Frank noticed Max rubbing his chest one evening and thought nothing of it until he repeated it so often that he asked about it. Max explained that he had been spotted one Saturday evening in Runswick by a lad he had never got on with at the Training Workshop and who knew that he came from Redshaw. Partly because of their personal unfriendliness and partly because of the rivalry between neighbouring villages, Max had been chased, trapped on a bridge, kicked on the legs and chest and was only prevented from being badly beaten by the arrival of his mate and some other friends. Six days later his ribs and chest still hurt enough to make it difficult for him to lift objects and yet Max treated the incident as a matter of routine, not worthy of mention.

Thirdly, we began to notice a distinct difference in Max when, a month short of his eighteenth birthday, he casually dropped into the conversation that he was going out with a girlfriend. Previously, he had been embarrassed when asked about relationships with the opposite sex. At the Workshop he had been rather brutally dismissed by the lasses for showing little interest. Now he began to spend most of this time with his girlfriend after she finished school, mainly at her house or walking round the town or occasionally they would go into a local pub. She was a cousin of his best friend and they first met when he was unemployed. During this time their relationship flourished but, when he became employed again, he gradually saw less of her and eventually they stopped seeing each other. They had been together for four months.

Max did not vote in the General Election of June, 1983, he did not know the name of his local MP or of any of the local councillors, and he tore up the election addresses as they came through the door. He had never belonged to a Trade Union and was not prepared to join one. Why not? 'You've to go on strike and if you go on strike, you don't get paid'. He later added that unions were banned at Shales: 'if y' ask for a rise, he finds a reason to finish you'. He did not believe that politics had any effect on his life and professed on a number of occasions to know nothing about the subject; and yet he was engrossed by the Falklands war, knew all the details of ships, aircraft, missiles and of men killed and injured. Nor did he refrain from political judgement; he felt, for instance, that the British government had not acted swiftly enough to prevent an invasion and that the islands would sooner than later be handed to Argentina because of their proximity to the mainland and the huge costs of defending them.

When we discussed with Max subjects that interested him, his diffidence fell away and he became excited and talkative. It took us months, for instance, to discover the deep knowledge and interest which he himself had developed in the American Civil War, where he identified with the southern states. He also pointed out to us mistakes in war films where modern German tanks were used instead of ones from the Second World War.

Max tried all he knew to avoid long-term unemployment. He applied to join the Territorial Army and the Royal Corps of Transport, but was turned down because he had no driving licence. The only jobs he fancied among those advertized in the local Jobcentre called for the same qualification. He had not heard about TOPs courses until Carol explained what they were. By the time he was nineteen, his life had become like that of his father's. The most he looked forward to was being taken on again by Shales for the summer to work for 78p an hour In the meantime, he walked the dog, visited his sister and her baby, and met his mother's sister and children three days a week for a cup of tea.

When the summer of 1984 arrived, Max phoned the owner of Shales and asked to be taken on but 'was given the brush off'. His father made enquiries on his behalf only to be told that, in the opinion of the boss, Max had not worked hard enough the summer before. His father argued that Max had worked seven days a week throughout that summer. Still no job. Instead Shales offered places to the Youth Training Scheme and the MSC paid the wages of the sixteen-year-olds who carried out the work formerly done by Max and other eighteen and nineteen-year-olds.

When we last met Max in August 1984, he was about to start on a one-year Community Programme as a labourer for the local council. Because of government cuts, the job was only twenty-eight hours per week for which he was to be paid £51, an hourly rate of £1.82 which compared favourably with 78p per hour at Shales. Max was delighted to have something to do at last: 'I'd rather work than be on the dole'. When asked what he thought about his future, he replied: 'Not a lot ... take it as it comes.' The other young men who were present agreed. We calculated that in the 40 months since he left school, Max had experienced five separate periods (amounting to 19 months) of unemployment without becoming one of the long-term unemployed, had spent 14 months on three different government schemes, was about to start a fourth, and had worked for 7 months over two summers on the same 'shit job'. His fatalistic attitude to the future appeared both sensible and appropriate.

Reg and Carol Ann

During a weekend in February, 1982, which we spent in the country with a group of young people from Shipton, Carol Ann met Reg for the first time. Within six months Reg proposed to her on the Tyne bridge and was accepted; they became officially engaged on the first anniversary of their first meeting; fifteen months later, they were married in church. We therefore saw their relationship develop from the very beginning, as Reg and Carol Ann went through all the main stages of courtship within the space of our project.

A year after their first meeting Carol Ann reminisced with us one evening about their earliest days together. Reg had helped Carol Ann out of a stream during a walk through a forest on the Saturday of the weekend in the country. She had taken no notice of him then, but they met again at the disco on the Saturday night when they drank, danced and talked together. On the return journey the following day in the coach, they did not sit together and Reg, sitting among the lads, left it to the last minute to ask Carol Ann to meet him again. The next night, Monday, they went to the pictures in Shipton. Two or three days passed, Reg did not phone and so Carol Ann thought it was over. Then he did phone and they went out together on Friday evening, the big night out in the North East. Within two weeks they started to see each other every night and ever since they had spent as much time as possible together.

Neither Reg nor Carol Ann had been involved in a steady relationship before they met. Both had gone out with the other partners but a month had been the longest period any relationship had lasted. These earlier liaisons had, as Carol Ann put it, 'just sort of fizzled out' through a mutual lack of interest. It therefore came as a pleasant shock to them both to find someone with whom they got on so well and for whom they had such genuine feelings.

At this early stage, Reg had very firm views about couples living together before they were married and swore that he would never be party to such an arrangement. (Carol Ann moved in with Reg within ten months of their first meeting.) A year later, when they became engaged at the age of eighteen, Reg was adamant that he would not get married until he was twenty-one. (They were both nineteen on their wedding day.) Reg had watched his two elder brothers getting married, one at the age of sixteen and the other at eighteen, and had thought that they were too young to be tied down. He insisted to us that he would not follow suit.

Both Carol Ann and Reg were close to their respective families, although their relationships and circumstances were somewhat different. Carol Ann lived in a comfortable, well-furnished modern home, owned by her parents, on a well-cared-for and well-respected council estate. She was the youngest of three girls, the eldest of whom was twenty-six and living at home. The second daughter married shortly after we met Carol Ann who, at the age of seventeen, was then given a bedroom of her own for the first time; she reported being unable to sleep because she was unused to it.

Her father had been a military policeman in the Royal Air Force and was currently employed as a technician in a local hospital. Carol Ann's mother was not in paid employment. Both her parents had firm

religious views. The family, according to an early statement from
Carol Ann, got on well together apart from minor tiffs among the
sisters and complaints from their father about the size of the electricity
bills caused, in his view, by hair dryers and curling tongs being in
constant use.

Right from the beginning Mr and Mrs Connelly objected to Carol
Ann going out every night with Reg; her relationship with her parents,
and especially with her father, deteriorated as she became steadily
more involved. As the rows became more frequent and more serious,
Carol Ann talked to us about her father's possessiveness with all his
daughters and particularly with her, the youngest. She felt that both her
parents were strict but her father was much more so, 'He doesn't let me
do anything . . . anything that's good fun is banned in my family'.
Before Reg arrived on the scene, she had been prevented by her parents
from going to London with Fenwick, her closest friend, to find work as
nannies. She felt sure they would oppose her engagement: in fact, none
of her family attended her engagement party. She found an
unfurnished flat close to where Reg lived for £10 a week but her parents
would have none of it. After they had been going out together for eight
months, Reg visited the Connelly home but the couple were left sitting
alone in the front room as the rest of the family withdrew into the
kitchen. Her parents stopped speaking to her and she began staying
overnight at Reg's house. Eighteen months after their first date, Reg
had still not met her father. Matters came to a head when Reg went to
collect her one evening and found that Carol Ann's face and arms were
bruised. Her father had locked her in her room and when finally she got
out, Reg had said, 'Right, that's the end of it. You come down with me'.
She packed her clothes and left.

It was just before Christmas, 1982 when Carol Ann moved in with
Reg to a small, self-contained flat in his parents' house. Within three
weeks her parents visited her and their relationship temporarily
improved with her mother meeting her from time to time at her
workplace. Carol Ann began making trips back to her own home but
always at times when her father was out. The rift with her parents
then became a bone of contention between Reg and Carol Ann, partly
because the contrast with Reg's easy going and tolerant parents was so
striking. At a funeral for Fenwick's (her best friend) grandmother,
Carol Ann made up the quarrel with her parents and began visiting
and phoning them regularly: Reg and Carol Ann had at this point been
going out for sixteen months and had been engaged for four.
Understandably perhaps, her parents found her relationship with Reg
more acceptable the longer it lasted. They now began to view and to
treat them, in Carol Ann's words, 'as though we were already married'.
On the day she married, her sisters acted as bridesmaids and her

father, as the saying goes, gave her away, even though she had left home some eighteen months previously.

Reg talked of close, warm relationships within his large family, spontaneously telling us one evening that his best friend had just become fifty. He was referring to his mother, who had a full-time job as a superintendent of the dinner ladies at a large local school, 'She's great . . . I'll never want to leave her'. One of our questionnaires on family life asked our sample when they thought they would move away from their parents. Reg replied:

> 'I'll never move away from them . . . I'd miss them. That's one of the reasons why I'd never go in the army or owt like that . . . Wey, in the morning me dad'll do us me breakfast.'

His parents lived in the centre of Shipton, in a large, ramshackle old house which they had bought when Reg was one-and-a-half years old. His mother's family had lived in the same area since before the First World War and both her brothers and married sons had congregated round her with homes in the same street or in the immediate vicinity. Hence the front door of Reg's home was always open for members of the family to come and go as they pleased. Some new council housing had recently been built in the area and Reg commented to us, 'the people there try to be posh but they're as common as me'. Four members of Reg's family were employed by the same local newsagents, some serving behind the counter, others driving vans. When Reg latterly found a job less than two minutes walk from his home, he was able to visit his two elder and married brothers and their children three or four times a day on his way to or from work. Reg felt closer to one of his brothers:

> 'Well, I pop in at dinner time, pop in at night time before I go home and later on I pop in an' see him. Saturday, we usually pop in after we've been over the toon to see him.'

According to Reg, his maternal grandmother had 'never worked . . . she was just a housewife, unemployed all her life', but her husband had started up a small painting and decorating business with Reg's father. When that collapsed, with the death of Reg's grandfather, his dad had found employment on the railways for five years and had then spent the next sixteen years with a firm of tyre manufacturers. It was never established whether it was cutting up the rubber which had left him with severe bronchitis (he had never smoked), and besides he suffered from arthritis of the spine and hands. He had been forced to take early retirement and receive a state invalidity pension but no compensation from the firm because he had never made a claim against them. In Reg's words:

'He worked from being fourteen years old to forty-eight years and never had a day on the dole and only about two weeks on the sick. He never missed a day even in the winter when his chest was bad... He's too old for a job now, being fifty odd and with his arthritis he'll never get a job. He still looks in the Jobcentre...he never fails to go to the Jobcentre. But when he goes for a job he gets told he's too old.'

Reg and Carol Ann joined his parents in a weekend bus trip to Jersey in the summer of 1983. Carol Ann teased him by saying that he did not seem to go anywhere without his parents and he readily agreed. The young couple returned home, laden with presents for both of their families and their friends. Carol Ann came back with over a thousand cigarettes, four hundred of which she gave away to her mother, Fenwick and others. Reg similarly distributed the booze he brought back.

Reg and Carol Ann both left school at the age of sixteen. Reg sat eight CSE exams in subjects ranging from Biology to Film Studies but he neither knew the results nor cared. His school had sent him a letter telling him that he could collect his exam results but he had not done so. The school had then sent him a record of his results but he had lost it. Carol Ann had difficulty remembering the names of the eight subjects she had passed at CSE level, although she thought she had been awarded a grade I in three of them. Both of them experienced about four months of unemployment before being placed on WEEP schemes for six months, Carol Ann in a large department store and Reg as a storeman in a small paint wholesalers. Both were kept on when their schemes finished.

Carol Ann was placed in the food department and thoroughly enjoyed the social contacts with the other shop assistants, especially their joint attempts to diet and to give up smoking. In May 1982, she was paid £182 nett a month and with annual pay rises she was earning £260 nett a month by August 1984. Her hours were at first 8.45 am until 5.45 pm every day (later changed to 7.30 am until 4.30 pm), and she worked Saturday mornings. Her pleasure at having a job was short lived, however. She soon 'got wrong from the D.M.': she was ticked off by the Departmental Manager who, Carol Ann was convinced, was picking on her. This woman supervisor criticized Carol Ann's clothes, her work, even on one occasion her hair when she had been caught in the rain. Carol Ann slowly learned how to stand up for herself, and once she snapped back at her superior, 'If you think I'm the worst dressed here, it's a lie'. Within sixteen months she was 'sick' of her job and her initial keenness evaporated. As she was on her feet all day serving customers and under the eagle eye of the supervisor, she began to find her job both exhausting and unsatisfying. The atmosphere, she reported to us regularly for the next year, had been soured, but she searched in vain for another job. She was eventually given the responsibility for her own counter, ordering, stocktaking, and assessing wastage; she was later moved to other departments to learn the workings of each. When promoted posts became available, she did not even apply, being content to stay with her friends. Carol Ann only began to enjoy her job again, however, when the strict supervisor left.

Carol Ann had grown up wanting to be a nurse but now ideally wanted to run her own small business. She had begun to feel more confident and self-assured since leaving school because she knew she was good at her job and enjoyed being given Christmas and birthday presents from some of her regular customers who were lonely old people. Initially, she felt:

> 'I'm below other people because I work in a shop. It isn't as good as an office job. I used to feel silly telling people I worked on a food stall . . . I though they'd look down on me.'

She had since changed her mind as she saw what few jobs were available to people of her age.

Reg was much happier in his employment, although he never received any formal training nor was he sent on day-release courses. He had grown up wanting to become a policeman but had not pursued that ambition. The boss of the small wholesalers who first employed him treated him well and even before the end of his WEEP scheme, was paying Reg several pounds a week more than the basic MSC allowance of £25 to encourage him to stay on. Reg's gross wage was £49 and after tax and insurance he took home £37. He commented that this was £5 more than a young woman who did the same job, and who had been there four years longer. Reg thought this was right because he considered that he worked harder; he served at the trade counter, made up orders, sent them out and checked deliveries. This experience stood him in good stead when in October 1982 he applied for another job at a wholesalers round the corner from his home. Reg explained that he went for his interview straight from work and was filthy from head to toe. He also had to fill in four pages of an application form in contrast to his previous job where he had just had an informal interview. He was offered the new job and took it because the pay was said to be double: he now hoped to come home with between £80 and £90 a week. The basic wage, however, was £43 and even after putting in an hour's overtime a day and three on Saturday mornings, he was only clearing £60 a week. When large orders arrived, he did occasionally earn as much as £103 a week but then the hours were from 9 am on Saturday until 10 pm without a break for dinner. Reg once said of his old boss that he was 'a great bloke, more of a friend than a boss to me', but after he left, the man passed him on the street without acknowledgement. Reg was the only man in the whole study who went from one job to another.

Reg established good relationships with his new workmates and bosses and was particularly tolerant of one who became very irritable while waiting for his divorce to be finalized. Over the time we knew him, Reg was told off for wearing earrings, dyeing his hair, not shaving, refusing to wear his glasses and poor handwriting; he took it all in good part. When Frank asked Reg if he had removed the earrings or rinsed out the dye from his hair, he replied, 'Did I, shite!' By August, 1984 he was enjoying the responsibility of 'cashing up' every night and the takings varied from between £400 and £800 per day. For this he was receiving £70 gross and £57 per week nett (or 42 per cent of the national average weekly wage at the time). Reg did appreciate, however, five weeks paid holidays per year, a free Christmas meal and hamper and a twice yearly bonus which had been as much as £300 in the past. We met him once during his two-week summer holiday and he had been into the store four times that day; 'he can't stay away from it', Carol Ann commented.

Reg did not attempt to disguise or hide his strongly held opinions; he was against blacks, gays and trade unions and was not prepared to listen to counter arguments. At school he had acquired the reputation of a fighter, of being 'the hardest lad' who had fought when challenged; but generally his reputation prevented trouble. He was also very clothes conscious, wearing futuristic shirts, fashionable jackets and trousers and black suede boots. His taste in modern music was wide, although he particularly liked electronic groups such as Kraftwerk and Japan; he and Carol Ann attended concerts given by The Police, Toyah, Depeche Mode, and Garry Numan. Reg paid for the tickets which cost up to £8..50 each. At home he had an electric organ, a synthesiser, an accordion and an electric piano which he had recently bought for £300 and was paying for at £4 per week.

Reg was also interested in video nasties and in hard core porno movies and magazines. The local ice-cream man sold pirate and porno videos from his van and Reg made a profit by charging his friends, brothers and uncles for admission to watch them.

There was another, very different side to Reg. He and Carol Ann quickly established a thoughtful and loving relationship and we witnessed numerous small acts of kindness and tenderness from both of them. He bought her singing birds in a cage, for example, and chose videos that *she* was keen to see when she had become tired of his films, like *The Zombie Flesh Easters*.

Reg took some stick from his male friends over his gentle behaviour towards Carol Ann: they thought he was being 'daft and soft'. Although she gave up seeing her girlfriends as soon as she began going out with Reg, and so drifted away from Fenwick, her closest friend since early childhood, Reg continued to see his mates regularly. Indeed, Carol Ann began to be treated as one of the lads; on one occasion, they all travelled into Newcastle for a big night out in the town. The group spent £40 on drink as they went on a pub crawl. On their way home, the lads had 'mooned' passers-by on the Tyne bridge and then urinated over it in full view of her. They referred to her as 'The Missus' or 'the little lady'. Reg, who remembered only a few years before following the group in matters of dress or activities, now stood his ground and refused to treat Carol Ann in the way his mates behaved towards their girlfriends:

> 'they've no respect for lasses . . . laugh at them . . . won't listen to them. They'll see a lass one day, then not see her for a while and then ring her up and go on like that.'

Their own courtship followed a different pattern. At first they had gone out frequently to the pictures, to concerts and to their favourite pubs. Then, as their relationship developed and they began to count the cost of an evening out, they took to staying at home in the evening, decorating a room together or watching television in Reg's room and going out occasionally for a drink. Within a short time, even the odd trip to a local pub stopped and they did 'nowt'. Differences over, for instance, Carol Ann's smoking came out into the open. When Reg went down with chicken pox, Carol Ann seized the opportunity to go out for the evening with Fenwick, but she laughingly told us she had her 'instructions to be back home by 10' from Reg. Shortly after they began living together, Carol Ann took on the housewifely role, doing the cooking and washing while Reg watched television. Reg helped at times by doing some hoovering and cleaning the windows but Carol Ann took charge of the domestic chores. She found that his frequent changes of clothes created extra washing and ironing for her and there were quarrels when he would not carry the wet clothes to the spin drier to let her watch a favourite TV programme. It became unusual for them to go out.

Their engagement party was a large, informal, friendly and joyful occasion. Reg had to be sent home by his employer the morning after his stag party because he was still drunk. He had arrived outside his sister-in-law's without his shirt and had fallen in the front door when it was opened. Carol Ann also held a party ten days before she was married: she drank fourteen Martinis within three hours and had to return home.

They celebrated their wedding with a traditional service in Church; the bride was in flowing white and the groom in a formal suit and grey tie with a plum coloured tint in his hair. Reg and Carol Ann were deluged with presents, including a tumble dryer from Reg's boss. Over seventy guests (including an uncle Carol Ann had not seen since she was a toddler) attended the wedding reception, followed by a party that roared on into the night. The formal proceedings were recorded on a video film which caught the obvious joy which spread from the couple to the whole company.

2 Picture of a Group

Some of the young adults we knew lived on Marlow Dene, a small council estate of well-kept houses and flats built in the 1960s on a spacious site, three miles south of Hillsborough town centre. To the east, the estate joined with Benditch, a much older area with its own strong identity, and to the west, the houses came to an abrupt stop at the edge of the Dene, a wooded gully which provided a natural play space for local children and adults alike. The only amenities on Marlow Dene were a row of six shops and one pub. There was a working man's club nearby and Benditch offered corner shops and a lively high street just over a mile away. It was a 40 pence bus ride one way into Hillsborough itself.

The first young people Sarah (Marshall) came to know in the area were all lads who lived within yards of each other on the Marlow Dene estate and who had come together at this time, in the autumn of 1982, because they were all unemployed. Regular weekly contact with this 'natural group' was maintained over a year, but the members of the group came and went as they variously got jobs or schemes or as the rhythms of life on the dole changed. This natural ebb and flow was heightened by the fact that Sarah most regularly met the lads on a fixed day each week. The Tuesday meetings were therefore only a window through which we were trying to view a whole panorama. Gradually, as the fieldwork developed, more people came into view and this picture of the lives of young people in and around Marlow Dene was pieced together.

A significant aspect, at least in retrospect, was the invisibility of young women. At first, we hoped to meet women in the area through the lads. Early on we learnt that nearly all of the men were either married or had a regular girlfriend, but although Sarah and Chris (the youth worker who helped us to make initial contact) constantly encouraged the lads to invite their partners, it was as if they did not give them a second thought when it came to our meetings. Consequently it was seven months before we met one of the women. By the end of the year, good relationships had been established with three of them, but not before Sarah had started to have meetings with four young women from Benditch whom she knew through the local youth project. These were set up precisely because the continued contact with the lads' group did not look as though it was going to lead to meeting any women. In the event, it did, but it took nearly a year.

At the end of a year's contact, the relationships established between

35

Sarah and the Hillsborough group felt like real friendship. Over a second year, it was possible to drop into their homes for a chat when in the area or arrange a reunion when most of them would turn up. As in Shipton and Milton there was a degree of self selection: those who became involved in the research were extremely likeable and friendly.

Knowing a small, localized group in their home area led over time to a picture of some of the social networks alive in the neighbourhood. The diagrams below show these networks as we came to understand them. This chapter concentrates on the core of six lads and their female partners whom we came to know best. Brotherly connections link them to two other all male groups: the 'young un's' and the drinking companions. (The four women in Benditch, although they knew the Marlow Deners, feature independently in other chapters as we contacted them separately.) The following is a chronological account of the group over two years; a final commentary highlights themes that emerged during the fieldwork.

Autumn/Winter 1982-83

Most of the lads whom Sarah first met (see Figure 1) had known each other for years. The eldest, Al and Troy, had been to the same school ten years previously. Gary and Kaffy were brothers, as were Morrow and John. Like Rick, Alan and the lad they called Pidge, they had all gone to Pinewood Comprehensive and all left when they were sixteen. John was the newest to the dole queue, after leaving school in July 1982. Flyn

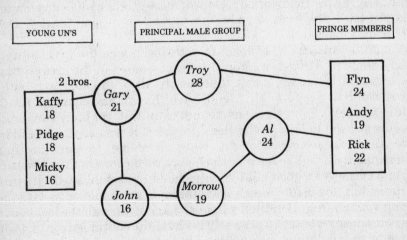

Figure 1: September to December 1982: Marlow Dene (Ages on first contact)

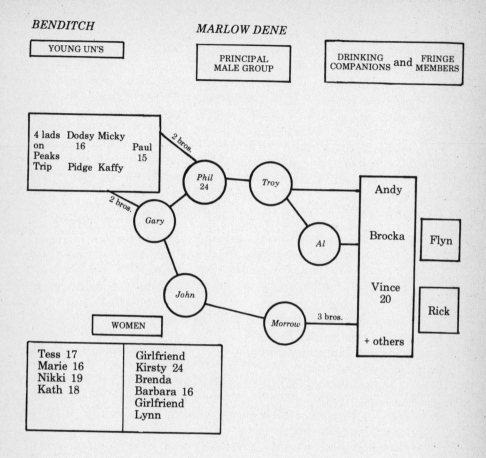

Figure 2: January to August 1983: Marlow Dene and Benditch (Ages on first contact)

was nearer in age to Al or Troy, but as a Catholic, he had attended Saint Theresa's. The lads were together as a group in the autumn of 1982 because they were all unemployed. Since February 1982 they had been meeting in their local community centre on Tuesday and Wednesday afternoons: they simply wanted to be together and to get out of the house. No one could quite remember how they came to ask for the sessions, except that they had become aware of the unused space at the centre: even the rickety pool table and old-fashioned record player seemed better than nothing for entertainment at the time. When asked if they played cards, Al replied 'No, we should do really. But it's no fun unless you've got money and we haven't got any'. Initially, they decided on Tuesday afternoons for the 'young un's' and Wednesdays for the over eighteen-year-olds, but by their own admission this proved pointless because there were so few of them anyway: in practice, the sessions were open to all of them. At least, this was the case until November 1982, when the management committee of the community centre banned them for two weeks because, they said, the lads had not been paying their 10p subs for the sessions, they were using the premises unsupervised, and the letting-off of a fire extinquisher was attributed to them. They were banned as a group, although Morrow and Kaffy were both helping out with the centre's junior disco and football team. Flyn and Troy complained that they were told what to do rather than asked, 'except if they want something done'. Morrow felt particularly upset by the ban because he and some of the others had recently helped to doubleglaze the windows, saving the centre at least £40. He thought the committee members too readily forgot their good deeds in the light of their minor misdemeanours. The lads generally were so resentful of the ban that they boycotted the centre altogether, and never reinstated their sessions, although occasionally one or two of the 'young un's' returned for a game of pool.

At eighteen, Kaffy and Pidge were 'young un's', although John, at sixteen, was not. The label was not applied rigidly according to age, but rather it was a term which the core group used to denote a felt difference between themselves and other lads with respect to general outlook and perceived maturity. Despite his age, John was never a 'young un': he got on better with men in their early twenties than with those of his own age and everyone accepted it.

When the lads were stopped from attending the community centre, the struggle to survive unemployment was resumed. Gradually we learnt more about their different means of survival. One or two were luckier than others at this time. In mid-October, Gary started a six months TOPs course in car body maintenance at an MSC Skillcentre eighteen miles away. In the six years since he left school, he had had two-and-a-half years' employment doing furniture repairs in a factory before he was made redundant. Since then he had been unemployed. The prospect of getting to the Skillcentre on time for 8 am and having to adapt to a working routine appeared daunting to Gary the week before he started. He joked about the excuses he could make for taking days off – a dentist appointment, an interview for a job – and commented that he felt he had enough to do maintaining his own body, never mind old cars. In the event, Gary attended the course regularly for the six months and learnt panel beating and various welding techniques in the process. At the beginning of November 1982, Andy started a five years apprenticeship as a fitter and turner. He had to travel eight miles, but got a lift both ways and Troy commented 'It could be a job for life'. Andy had, however, 'lost' the year's apprenticeship he had completed in joinery before being laid off at nineteen.

November also brought employment for John – at sixteen, his first ever. In October he was interviewed at the delivery firm where his girlfriend's dad worked and heard two weeks later when he was to start. The job was temporary, eight-week employment over the busy Christmas period. John said he liked the company. He especially liked the money: there were a couple of weeks when he brought home over £100 with his overtime: he worked eleven-hour shifts: 7 am to 6 pm and Saturday mornings. He finished on Christmas Eve. He saved £300 with which he bought an N registration Ford car from a neighbour. In the New Year, on the dole, he felt the pinch of poverty harder than before: '£37.80 for two weeks. It's crap'. While Andy's apprenticeship and Gary's MSC course took them out of circulation, John's job was so short term that after Christmas he became unemployed again like Flyn, Troy, Al and Rick. Flyn, after five years apprenticeship, was a time-served steel fabricator. He had been unemployed since the summer when, with a mate, he had gone south to look for work. Flyn reported that on the first day all he had eaten was an apple, on the second a banana and on the third a pie. Finally, they did get work and Flyn's savings were helping him through his unemployment during the autumn. Troy, who was twenty-eight, had been unemployed for four years. He was married with a five-year-old daughter call Mandy. Rick, twenty-two, and Al, twenty-four, had different but special experiences which occupied their time.

In October 1982, Rick's wife, Angie, had given birth to their first child, a baby girl, giving them extra cause to celebrate their third wedding anniversary. They were delighted. We met Rick when he joined the lads for the first night out in three months. He had been at home with Angie all this time. Once their daughter, Linda, was born, he found even less time, and less money, to see the lads, apparently sharing the care of the baby with Angie, grinning when asked about changing nappies, and claiming that he could do anything. Neither of them were employed. When in February, 1982, we bumped into Rick pushing Linda in her pram, he seemed very happy. He explained that they had moved from Hillsborough and were living nearer Angie's parents. When Rick had left, Chris, the youth worker, wondered whether he would be interested in one of the trips coming up. One of the lads said 'He's a family man now', as if this summed up everything.

Al's preoccupation at this time was of a completely different sort. Before December he went into hospital for treatment to his hand which he had injured after falling over a wall outside the pub one night. While he was there, the doctors also turned their attention to an old leg injury which Al had suffered in a motorbike accident a year before, but which had left him with a slight limp. He was in a convalescent hospital for weeks. He came home most weekends, sometimes to the flat of his girlfriend, with whom he had started to live and sometimes to stay with his widowed mother to whom he was very close. Whichever home he went to, he would join the lads on Sundays.

The Sunday evening drinking sessions, which involved an extended group of friends, were an institution. Long ago, these lads had changed their main evening out to a Sunday night because 'It can take twenty minutes to get served at the bar on a Friday'. Mainly through Troy and Al, Sarah heard a great deal about this group, but never came to know them well. Some of them were working. One was posted in the army (which gave them a good excuse to celebrate every time he came home to the Dene!), another was a pitman and a third, Vince, brother to Morrow and John, got a job in the shipyards. Once Andy had started his apprenticeship, he was only ever seen on a Sunday. Al commented that the lads who had jobs would finish drinking early because they had to get up the next morning. At the time, he felt great because he did not have to, but soon the feeling wore off and he felt worse beause he had nothing to get up for.

Al was a sensitive man, acutely aware of what affected his life. The first factor was his long-term unemployment, aggravated by constant comparison with other men in his family who, he thought, had 'done better' than himself. It was made even worse by the knowledge that his unhealed injuries would probably prevent him taking a job even if one were to come up. The second was the unsettling situation with his girlfriend. He was frequently unhappy with their relationship and deliberated over it for months, moving regularly between his lass' house and his mother's. A third, complementary factor appeared to be Al's concern over and loyalty to his family. He worried about his elder brother's health and circumstances when he moved back to live with their mother. Al also cared a great deal for his mother who had recently undergone tests and been diagnosed diabetic. In the New Year of 1983 he saw her onto the train when she went down to Cornwall to visit her youngest son and grandchild for the first time. With all these concerns, Al was only too pleased when occasions for physical activity offered themselves, like helping out a friend collecting junk with a horse and cart or accompanying an uncle who was redecorating the house of an elderly relative. He also worked voluntarily for a youth project on two weekend camps, overseeing teams of younger workers. Al attended woodcarving evening classes once a week and became more skilled at turning and shaping wood than he had ever been, deriving a lot of satisfaction from what he was able to produce. Al came to our meetings almost every week until the beginning of the summer 1983. There was no clear reason why he stopped attending. One or more of his constant preoccupations took the upper hand and he devoted his time and energy to these instead.

Of all the group, Troy's circumstances changed the least during our early months of contact. Before his four years on the dole, he had been a trawlerman, a farm worker, a painter and decorator and a labourer. He said 'I like to work' and he still helped when he could on the 'cobles', the local fishing boats. Fishing and the sea were the loves of his life and every year he signed up with the local club to go on their regular summer fishing trips to the Yorkshire coast. In the winter, there were less opportunities for fishing and Troy spent his time out and about, drinking at weekends, helping his wife Brenda to look after Mandy, watching the video shows on a Monday afternoon at the club, maybe with Al or another mate collecting coal for the fire. Sometimes they scoured the beaches for sea coal, but most often they went to the tips where they knew exactly how to retrieve the biggest pieces. Troy never appeared worried about his life in the way that Al obviously was. Morrow did though.

Morrow was nineteen and he had been unemployed for nearly a year when we met him. Before that he had been kept on after his goverment scheme on the docks, but was made redundant seven weeks afterwards. Although he had a gentle, friendly manner, he always seemed under stress. He never appeared to relax and he was the first young person we heard who admitted how depressed he was at being unemployed. Matters were made worse for Morrow when not only his kid brother, John, got a temporary job, but their older brother, Vince, suddenly started as a labourer at the shipyards after being on the waiting list for three years. Troy remarked that he had been on the same list for two years, but he doubted he would get a job: 'It helps if you know someone there'. Vince and Morrow's dad had laboured there for fifteen years.

Morrow's situation appeared to change for the better when, in January, he began to work two-and-a-half days a week on a MSC Community Programme (CP) scheme. He had heard about it through a friend of his dad's. At the interview, the assembled applicants were asked two questions: 'Are you disabled? What size boots do you take?' Two months into his scheme, Morrow said that the only reason he took it was to get out of the house. The labouring however turned out to be every bit as depressing and soul destroying for Morrow as being unemployed. He was one of a team of twenty who were clearing an area of wasteland to make a car park. The 'landscaping' involved such heavy work that within two weeks Morrow's gloves were worn through and his hands covered in blisters. One day he and another lad were given pickaxes at 8 am and told they had until 3 pm to destroy some cement foundations (which to Morrow looked perfectly sound). They 'grafted and grafted', missed their dinner break, and finished the job by three o'clock, only to be told that the new cement would not be arriving until the following Monday, four days away. Morrow's shift meant that he could no longer come to our meetings. Whenever we bumped into him, setting off for work in the pouring rain or actually on the site, one of a chain of labourers heaving stones from one spot to another, it was obvious that his lot was not improving. He still had ten months to do. What filled the rest of Morrow's week, apart from playing for several football teams, was setting up house with his girlfriend, Lynn. They still lived with their respective parents, but had been allocated a flat and spent all their spare time decorating it.

The core of the group we came to know over this period consisted of: Troy, Morrow, Gary, Al and John. We began by seeing a lot of Andy, Flyn and Rick, but they dropped out completely after the New Year. Gary's brother, Kaffy, only appeared a couple of times: one of the young un's', he had distinctly different friends, like Pidge, who lived next door to Al's mum. Pidge seemed to spend all of his time with his girlfriend, walking her to and from school and meeting her at dinner time. Another lad, Micky, came along once or twice, but we saw no more of him until the summer. This was also when we met Phil and the women.

Spring/Summer 1983

At the end of March, Sarah met John's girlfriend, Barbara, for the first time. Although we had known John for over six months, it had taken this time to learn that he in fact lived with Barbara at her parents' home. John continued with our weekly meetings, but it took until June, when Phil came on the scene accompanied by Kirsty before we saw Barbara and John as a couple. Over the spring, we mostly saw Troy, Al and John. Their age differences, twenty-nine, twenty-four and seventeen, bothered no one. They were all unemployed and seemed to appreciate meeting every week, even if it was not to do very much. The best meetings at this time were when we drove out to the country in John's car and went fishing. A conversation Troy and Al had on one of these trips was all about the 'battlin' ' one of their party had been involved in on the previous Saturday night. John listened to their story with interest. When he asked why they had not pitched in, Al commented that the others were bigger: 'It'd have been over with in two seconds!' but this was less the reason than an unspoken understanding of how to behave during a fight between two individuals. Al admitted that he had 'felt like joining in, but it wasn't on' and John agreed. The lads recounted the tale with excitement and amusement. After long experience, the lads were not afraid of fights, but neither did they seek them. If one happened, they knew what to do: usually its most lasting effect was as a topic of conversation.

The lads appreciated escapes into the countryside. On an early trip across the moors, Morrow turned up the melody 'Bright Eyes' playing on the car radio, commenting it was 'good for this scenery'. He also explained that he had taken his brother to see the film and thought it was excellent. When we reached the river John put on his fishing gear. He described the fly fishing he so loved as 'a gentleman's sport', but was quick to differentiate between himself and the well-heeled fishermen he had seen in Scotland: 'With them big hats, you know, Troy', he said, indicating a wide rim.

Gary finished his TOPs course in mid April. On his last day, he left at 11.15 am, along with a lad who got sacked and whom Jim described as 'useless. He did what I did when I went: worked for ten minutes then off to the toilet for fifteen'. Once he had disappeared there for nearly an hour. Now holding his TOPs certificate in car body maintenance, Gary had nothing to do. He went to the benefit office on his first day of unemployment for six months and was told to come back on Wednesday. Ten days later he was informed of his income: £23.65 per week, but his first giro was docked £8.11p. because of his last TOPs allowance. Gary found that he was getting up at about 7 am every day 'cos I'm used to it', but that he was then 'bored stiff'. Various plans to renovate cars for friends and acquaintances never seemed to come off. He had the skills now to repair his mate Bob's mini, but he could not afford the £25 it was going to cost for the new shell–nor could Bob.

In May, Gary began to drop out of the Tuesday meetings. At his house his father informed Sarah that he was 'With Bob–taking something apart down at the scrap yard . . . he has a chance to be on all day'. The next time we called he was outside his house working on his own M registration Cortina bought 'with a loan from a finance company'. He was still there when we passed nine hours later. He had replaced the offside wing and fitted a klaxon horn. Bob, his lass' brother, had a job at the time, so Gary was working on the car single handed. When it came on to rain, he said he thought he's just build a garage over the car, in the street outside his front door. He and Bob had been looking for premises with no luck. Even if they found some, a car repair business would be uncertain in Marlow Dene where car ownership was a third below the average for Hillsborough.

At the end of June, Gary was in court for non-payment of his fine, which in turn was for non-payment of hire purchase on his moto-cross bike. While he was at the Skillcentre, his brother, Kaffy, had been going down for him, to pay the fine off weekly. Several weeks previously, Kaffy had been informed that the debt had been cleared and there was no need to call again. It turned out the administration was wrong. Gary believed he would either get two months inside or a £500 fine. He said if his explanation was not accepted, he would 'rather go down – I'm not paying for their mistakes'. His dad told him that a similar mistake had been made by the court when *he* was eighteen, but he had still had to pay a fine.

We saw no more of Gary later in the summer. Troy reported that he thought Gary might be doing some work with his dad because he had seen them getting a lift down the mile to Benditch one morning about 6.30 am. Nearly a year before, Gary's dad, at forty-three, had been made redundant from his manager's post in a local manufacturing firm. In November 1983, we learnt from Kaffy that Gary had applied for a labouring job at £38 a week, but had not heard any more. Gary was still courting the same girlfriend, but according to the lads, most of his time was spent with Bob, her brother.

We were not to see Al for two months over the summer. The last time we met him was on Troy's twenty-ninth birthday in June, during an evening session with them both and John. Al had got two commissions for his woodcarving: they were from friends and 'just for pints', but he was obviously pleased at his progress. He was not going to run the craft stall at the local college though, because, he said, he would 'feel daft' and John agreed with him. Someone talked about insurance on the wares if they got nicked: 'And they will be', retorted John. This particular evening turned into a long one. Having met at the Jubilee pub in Marlow Dene – Troy arrived only after he had watched *Coronation Street* – we later moved on to the Lord Nelson. Although well over a mile away, this was the lads' preferred pub: the Jubilee only served the estate and was quiet.

The three lads talked about whom they had seen: Morrow had joined them the previous Sunday, but Vince had dropped off coming in recent weeks. They debated how they could visit their friend Brocka in Durham prison: he had not even sent his wife a pass. Brocka was twenty-six and had never been without a fine in the last ten years. The longest he had stayed out of trouble was six months. One night the police broke into his house through the door, but found nothing they were looking for. The next time Brocka saw the CID drinking in the Lord Nelson, he tripped on a step and went crashing into them, 'gin and tonics went flying all over'. The lads were friendly to Brocka, but even they had difficulty explaining all the trouble he got into. He provided 'good crack' though.

Al reported on his insomnia. He was staying awake most of the night, falling asleep about 7 am, not getting up till one o'clock: he thought everyone believed he was just dossing. Troy then commented dryly that the watch he had received from his wife as a birthday present would soon be in a pawn shop – two or three had recently reopened on

Benditch high street. Everyone passed round the baccy tin for roll-ups. John was looking forward to his holiday with his lass and her family. They were going to their caravan at South Shields for the Bank Holiday weekend. Despite Al's repeated attempt to get everyone to continue the celebration at his place, we went our own ways at the end of the evening. Al, though, did not reappear until the end of August. It seemed that at long last his life might be settling down with his girlfriend, across town from Marlow Dene.

In June, a camping trip to the Peak District was arranged through Chris and the local youth project. It was originally planned for those lads who were involved in our research, but in the event, of those we had met, only John came. It was at this time, however, that Phil appeared on the scene. He joined the trip and the rest of the group was made up of 'young un's': Dodsy from Marlow Dene and four others from Benditch.

Phil was twenty-four and had lived all his life in Marlow Dene. Over the months, Sarah had heard the lads mention him, but had never actually met him. When she asked John about him after his first appearance, he said: 'Wey, a topper lad . . . I thought you knew him'. Although unemployed, Phil had never attended any of our meetings because he had been spending all his time with his girlfriend, Kirsty. He had been out fishing with John one Sunday when John pursuaded him to come on the trip to the Peaks. From this time on, Phil attended the meetings every week, and later we met Kirsty.

There were five young un's on the trip. The eldest was eighteen, but the others were sixteen and had just left school together. Some had rarely and others had never been away from Hillsborough. In the mini-bus on the drive south, one of them remarked that if you whistled at a flock of sheep, it sent them running. They prompty whistled their way down the country and hardly stopped for the next four days! On the first night after everyone had gone to bed, from her tent Sarah heard one of the young un's comment: 'You want to see the stars, there's fucking loads!'

Conservations over the days covered topics from pets (all had great admiration for the ferrett Gary used to carry round with him in his pocket) to tattoos (when Chris asked John if he had tattooed his arms himself when at school, John straightaway replied that he had: 'in Maths.'). All the lads on the trip had tattoos. They talked of friends who were skinheads who had 'Made in Marlow Dene' tatooed across their chests or backs. This led to a discussion with John about the time he wore Doc Marten boots and sported a skinhead haircut. Apparently Gary used to as well, whereas Troy was a Hell's Angel in his day. When Sarah asked John when and how he had stopped being a skinhead, he replied, 'I just let my hair grow'.

One incident on the camp highlighted at once the male ethos of the young un's group. The lads found some steep rocks which plunged straight into a lake. Chris established that the water was deep enough to jump into safely, and the lads then jumped twenty feet and more off the tops of the rocks into the deep, cold, black water below. The rock faces were grey and sheer and it was obvious that the lads had to pluck up the courage to jump. From the dinghy below, Sarah witnessed their bravado in supporting each other one minute, egging each other on the next and either jumping or 'bottling out' (backing out) the next. In the end, they all jumped several times and could tell the tale of their daring feats once they returned home. The young un's were in fact more certain about jumping twenty feet into dark water than they were about making scrambled eggs at the camp.

On their return from the Peaks, Sarah learnt from Dodsy, who had been on the camp, and from Kaffy that their friend, Micky, had been thrown out of his home in Marlow Dene. Dodsy's family took him in after he had been sleeping rough in a tent in the Dene for three weeks. Micky's family had for years been known to the local Probation Office and Social Services department and he himself was still subject to a care order. In the winter, he had attended a couple of our Tuesday meetings, but no more. Sarah had often seen him around the estate, but he remained with the group of young un's we only came to know at a distance. At the end of the summer, we learnt that with the help of a local community worker, Micky had got a bedsit in Hillsborough town centre, although not before the landlord had the DHSS girocheque for rent in his hand.

Two weeks after the trip, none of the lads from the research group were around the Dene, so Sarah called at the house on the nearby Peel Road estate, where John was living with his lass' family; her mother, Mrs Kane, invited Sarah in. Barbara was at home because she was on the 'works holiday' from the shipyards where she was doing her second YOP placement in an office. Everyone sat in the comfortably furnished, small front room and chatted over mugs of tea. Barbara and her mum shared the knitting of a sleeveless jumper and showed Sarah the wool they had bought for £3. John remarked that a similar jumper would cost £12 in the shops.

When Mrs Kane asked Sarah what holidays went with a university job, John laughed, 'It's all holiday'. 'What about you, John, you're on it permanently', Mrs Kane retorted, with a more helpless than malicious tone. With Barbara joining in, she talked animatedly about their dog and the stray cat they had given a home. John took more notice of his tea and the television than the conversation. The fieldwork took a dramatic turn from this moment on. Suddenly, after nine months out and about with the lads, we were in a domestic setting where the women held sway.

The next time Sarah met Barbara was a month later when they chatted on her doorstep. John was away with Chris, the youth worker, and a party of others. Barbara wondered what clothes he had taken with him as she had been looking in the cupboard and nearly everything was still there. She explained that her dad was just taking their old three-piece suite round to her grandfathers who had plenty of room to store it. Her parents were going to throw it out, but she commented quickly that she would like it for when she and John set up home.

It had been in the spring when, on the way home from a fishing trip, John had announced in the car to Troy, Al and Sarah that he was going to get married and did they want to come? The couple had met at school and had been courting for four years, since they were thirteen, and now John was as much a son to Barbara's parents as he was to his own. He certainly saw more of them. He and Barbara were already looking to the future together.

It was in August 1983 when Barbara announced to Sarah on the phone, 'Did you know we're getting married ... Well, I'm going to have a baby'. She was very excited. They had intended the wedding to be the following year, but now it was just eight days away. Mrs Kane said that her uncle Sammy could not believe the news when he heard. He was employed where Barbara was on her YOP scheme and he had just put in a good word for her: there was a good chance she would have been kept on, but Barbara commented that she was still not sorry she had left. She had not enjoyed the scheme at all. Her mum went with her to the DHSS office: since leaving the yards three weeks before, she had signed on twice, but had still not received any money. Mrs Kane remarked that it was not right.

The wedding was at the end of August. John and Barbara were married at the Town Hall in the morning and celebrated with their families over a buffet lunch. In the evening, at least a hundred guests filled the social club managed by John's uncle. Andy's brother ran the disco and everybody did the can-can, while Mr Kane filmed them, aided by the arc light held overhead by Morrow, the bridegroom's brother and best man (even though they had hardly seen each other for months). Barbara was obviously very proud of John in his new pale grey suit and matching tie: she commented it was the smartest she had ever seen him. She also confided that she had been relieved to get out of her wedding dress because it had felt so tight. For the evening, she was in a simple, pale blue loose-fitting dress.

The Kane family sat together near the entrance, greeting the guests as they walked in the door. The women who followed Sarah and Chris into the room thrust their present into Barbara's hands saying it was

'From the cleaners' and with much hilarity headed straight for the bar. Mrs Kane commented that if the evening 'do' went as well as the day had gone, it would all have been worth it.

John's family were dispersed around the room. Morrow greeted Sarah and Chris with a big grin, relieved at the end of his duties as best man, and introduced them to his girlfriend, Lynn. They were sitting with two other couples. Morrow said he felt really happy for John and Barbara. He also told the story of how, that morning, the car in which a friend was driving him and John to the Town Hall, had been in an accident. No one was hurt, but the car was badly damaged. A passing motorist stopped and when he learnt of their plight, promptly took them to the garages he owned nearby and chose an expensive car in which he drove them on to the ceremony.

Shortly, Phil and his girlfriend, Kirsty, joined Sarah and Chris at their table: it was good to see them as two days before, they were not sure if they could afford to come, even though drinks at this bar were relatively cheap. As we sat, it was Kirsty who talked about the people in the room: who was who and who belonged to which family. She was not from this side of town, but having courted Phil for over two years, she knew his circle of friends well. She pointed out John and Morrow's brother, Vince, at the bar and some male friends of John with whom, she said, he used to go to nightclubs. For obvious reasons that night, Barbara did not dance a great deal, but John was on the dance floor quite a lot, including two or three times with his male friends. The couple did, however, take the floor on their own for the traditional first dance.

The wedding party brought together some of the lads we had not seen for months. Flyn was there with a group of his football companions, lads his age in their mid-twenties. He was still unemployed, but he looked fit: his mother said he was never in the house. Andy was with yet another group. Troy did not turn up, but we learnt later it was because he had started a job some distance away from home and had arrived back too late to attend. We never learnt why neither Gary nor Al made it. When Sarah and Chris came to leave, Barbara was sitting with her family who were all as bright and breezy as ever. When they asked where John was, she explained he was getting some air. They said goodbye to John outside where he stood, smiling, propped up against a wall. The bar had done good business all night.

For their honeymoon, John and Barbara went to the Kanes' caravan for a few days. They left on a Friday; on Saturday John telephoned Phil to ask if he and Kirsty would join them. Kirsty confided that at first she did not want to go, after all, it was their honeymoon, but in the event, Phil's dad drove them to Shields the following day. Mr and Mrs Kane also made the trip for the day and everyone had Sunday dinner together. It was hardly any different from previous Sundays which John had spent there with the Kanes. After Barbara's parents went home, John and Phil proceeded to fish and shoot in the woods together as if they were back in the Dene. Meanwhile, Barbara and Kirsty, who had only ever met briefly before, were left to their own devices. In the evenings, the couples went to the local pub together, but during the day, the lasses sat in the caravan. Kirsty said that she thought they would have gone mad if they had not found a pack of cards, and over the few days they smoked well over a hundred cigarettes between the two of them.

Kirsty was twenty-three. While they were both unemployed, she and Phil had been spending all their time together. Kirsty, who had four CSEs and one O level, had given up her job two years previously because she was fed up with it: 'clerical, dogsbody, cleaner: they had me doing everything'. Phil had done one week of an apprenticeship on leaving school, then worked in a slaughter house ('I'd feel all the blood running down the back of my neck') and later he did three years' in a warehouse in the same factory as Gary. He got the sack, but we never learnt why. Altogether, in the seven years since they left school, Phil had been unemployed for three and a half, Kirsty for two.

In July 1983, the couple were allocated a flat in Marlow Dene, just up the road from Phil's parents, and after a week spent redecorating it, they moved in together. Kirsty brought her belongings from home over several bus journeys. They furnished the flat with help from their families and, soon after moving in, Phil bought a kitten which promptly settled in with the couple.

The last weekly meeting we had in Marlow Dene was at the end of August 1983. It was unique among all the meetings because it brought together the different groups observed during the previous year. Women and men were present: John and Barbara and Phil and Kirsty sat on one side of the table. On the other side, Al and Troy sat with a cohort of their Sunday night drinking friends. One of the young un's, Micky, joined us for a quick drink and another, Kaffy, was just outside, at the door of the pub. Later in the evening, Gary and Kaffy's dad joined us and talked at length with Troy, and Al left with the older lads to go to the Lord Nelson.

September 1983 – August 1984

After twelve months of intensive fieldwork, relationships were well enough established to enable easy-going visits to be made from time to time to the area on the invitation 'have a dodgeround' – in which to catch up on everybody's news. Interestingly, in this second year of more intermittent contact, the focus developed on the female partners of the lads and on the lads as partners in a couple rather than together as an all male group.

We had known Troy, for instance, since the first meeting in September 1982, but it was not until September, 1983 that we had our first-and last-full family conversation with him, his wife, Brenda, and their daughter Mandy, whom we had only ever met at the door before. After four years' unemployment, Troy had been taken on as a labourer with the last firm that he worked for. He had been out working at all hours because the job they had on at the moment was on the sea shore and depended on the tide. After living with a wife and five-year-old daughter on £65 a week social security, he could now bring home about £150, but only after working a 98-hour week. Brenda commented that one week Troy came home with only £40 and that they were better off when they were on social security: she had recently applied for Family Income Supplement.

At a later meeting, when Brenda was on her own, she was nevertheless still delighted that Troy had a job, although she found she missed his company and was visiting her parents on the nearby Peel Road estate a lot more. In fact, she wondered if they weren't getting a bit tired of her being there all the time while Mandy was at school. She said that she used to go out with her brother's wife, but he seemed to resent this and he put a stop to their meeting. Brenda worked before she was married and used to go out with the lasses, but had not done so for years. She was friendly with one or two neighbours, but described the others as 'stuck up' and anyway, she was not the sort to be interested in getting 'to know everyone's business'.

Originally, Troy believed his job would finish soon after the summer. He never knew from day to day where he would be or how long the jobs would last. In the event, he was still with the same firm a year later, in August 1984, but he had to travel to wherever the firm secured contracts. In December, Al gave Troy's apologies for not turning up to our Christmas celebrations, but he was working in Yorkshire all week, coming home only at weekends. He said that Troy had already been banned from two pubs and there were only five in the village, so he was trying to be more careful!

In the spring, when Sarah visited Brenda, their flat showed the signs of their new income: they had been able to replace their worn carpet and a colour television stood where the old black and white one used to be and Brenda had ordered a wall unit for the living room. Mandy had her first new toys in years. Troy had been saving his lodgings allowance thanks to having bought a £100 caravan with a friend. They lived in it all week and got a lift back home at weekends. Brenda, though, said that she was 'lost' with Troy no longer at home and she knew that Mandy missed him too. She went to the Jubilee pub every night at 8 pm to receive his phone call. For Mother's Day, Troy bought her a shopping trolley, needed now because he was not there to help carry their weekly groceries.

When we last saw Troy, in August 1984, he announced that they had moved from their Marlow Dene flat to a house with a garden in Benditch. He said Brenda was 'over the moon' with it. It was council property and needed modernising, but he was doing what he could to it at weekends. They also had a telephone. At this same meeting, Al remarked on Troy's change of fortune in the last year. Nothing so positive had happened to him.

Over the year, Al had become a little more settled with his girlfriend who was now expecting their baby, but he seemed to remain as uncertain about their long-term relationship as he had ever been. He was still unemployed and in the New Year had had to return to hospital for an operation. He was new getting arthritis in his injured joints. He had managed to take on an allotment in Marlow Dene, however, and had chickens, ducks and a goat on it with a guard dog to check the livestock were not stolen. He had sold some chicks and called the whole venture 'something to do'. He had kept up with his woodcarving as well as Sunday night drinking with the lads, but when we last saw him, he described his future as 'very bleak'. He was twenty-six.

We saw nothing of Gary in the second year, but heard about him from the others and his brother, Kaffy. Gary was courting the same girlfriend and was supposed to be getting engaged, but had never got round to it. According to the lads, he spent most of his time with her brother, Bob, working on cars. He had passed his driving test and he still called at the Jobcentre, but in the sixteen months since completing his TOPs course he had never found a job. In October 1983, Kaffy, at twenty, started a twelve-month CP scheme because he was about £10 a week better off on the £31.67 allowance, rather than on the social security rates which had recently been cut. He also qualified for the scheme having been unemployed for over a year.

Morrow, having completed his twelve-month CP scheme in January 1984 was, however, no longer eligible for one. He discovered this in the months after his scheme when trying to find a job of any kind. He had become increasingly depressed. He had hated the scheme, but he felt worse now. He paid off his debts as soon as he received his giro, then in a few days was broke again. In his own words he felt trapped in 'a vicious circle'. Every month, he reported, he was called for interview at the Employment Office and every month, he was asked the same question: 'Why are you not working?' At first he accepted this, but one day burst out in reply: 'Don't you read the fucking newspapers?' He kept as busy as he could, especially training for and playing football: 'That's all I've got in my life just now'. He finally moved in to the flat with his lass and her little boy, but after about six months it did not work out and Morrow was back at his parents' house. He and Al were alike in their depression about their continued unemployment and unsettling personal relationships.

In the second year, we saw the most of the two couples we knew best. November 1983 saw Phil and Kirsty married and the birth of John and Barbara's little girl, Joanne (a boy would have been called John). John had been present at the birth. They still lived with the Kanes at that time: they had been waiting for the baby to arrive before applying for a house, otherwise they knew they would only have been offered a flat. When we visited just before Christmas, they had moved to a house less than half a mile from Barbara's mam and dad. Friends and neighbours gave them most of the furniture, the cooker was provided by the DHSS and John had plans for a potato patch at the end of the garden which looked onto the playing fields of their old school. Not long after they had settled in, however, they were burgled. No one was caught and none of their possessions retrieved, but as soon as they could, they arranged an exchange of council property and moved to their new home: a flat directly opposite the Kanes' house.

Thanks in particular to the support of Barbara's family, the couple appeared to adapt well to being parents. Barbara confided to Carol (Borrill) that she had concealed her pregnancy as long as she could, saying 'I hoped it would go away', but in the end her mother had asked her directly and, on finding out, had simply taken the siuation in hand with 'We'll have to see what we can sort out'. Barbara seemed quite happy being a mother, and John helped with nappy changing and enjoyed playing with Joanne.

The Careers Office still contacted them. John said, 'I've told them I'm married now - a scheme's no good'. In the New Year, after a year on unemployment benefit, the couple went on to Social Security: Barbara commented, 'We're always filling in forms'. In August 1984, they had their rent paid and £53 a week to live on. They saved regularly to pay the gas and electricity bills and managed to keep something by for going out together when they could; Mr and Mrs Kane would babysit for them.

Phil and Kirsty had a registry office wedding and a small party afterwards. Their parents paid for a bedroom carpet for them rather than a reception. They were pleased with their flat and Phil in particular seemed a real home-maker, saying on one visit that they wanted 'a better picture' than the print of a leopard they had hung over the fireplace. They seemed to have regular visitors, especially Phil's brother, Paul, who was fifteen. One day when Sarah was at the flat, Paul came in to ask his brother for help after his motorbike had been stolen.

At Christmas 1983, the couple had their rent paid and were living on £87.60 Social Security a fortnight. Then, in March, Phil got a part-time job through the local youth project, working four afternoons a week on outdoor activities. Kirsty described the job as 'just what he wanted'. When he received his first wage packet and adjusted girocheque, they were worse off than they had been on social security: the DHSS said this would be amended over time. It did not help the day they found out, however: Phil had bought a pair of workboots for £29 from his first wage only to discover the following day that their giro had dropped from £87 to £25. That fortnight they only just managed to make ends meet.

Commentary

The fieldwork in Hillsborough highlighted certain aspects of the lives of young adults. For instance, our approach of trying to meet the female partners of men already contacted was fundamentally at odds with what the all male group was about. When contact was established with some of the women, it was their isolation in the community which became clear, their lives being so defined by those of their men. A graphic illustration of this was the story of John and Barbara's honeymoon.

The three male friendship groups were strongly single sex, based on male traditions of survival: hardness ('battlin''), bravado (the rock-jumping incident), drinking (the Sunday sessions) and solidarity. Their comradeship was evidenced in their refusal to admit women to their meetings (Sarah was an anomalous outsider) and in their togetherness in the face of adversities, like poverty (passing round the baccy tin), trouble with the law (visiting Brocka in prison), trouble with family (solving Micky's homelessness) and unemployment (using the community centre).

In the face of poverty and unemployment, they fell back on means of survival traditional in their working class community. Troy, Al and others collected coal for fuel. In 1937 George Orwell wrote (1962, pp.91 and 93):

> In the 'dirt' that is sent up from the pits there is a certain amount of broken coal, and unemployed people spend a lot of time in picking it out of the slagheaps . . . Technically it is stealing but, as everybody knows, if the coal were not stolen it would simply be wasted.

Technically, undeclared work is illegal too, but as the lads knew, it was usually their only means of eking out their employment benefit and of keeping skills and self respect alive. The various jobs on the side which they worked have not been referred to in the main account for reasons of confidentiality, but a majority occasionally had small undeclared earnings. As the effects of unemployment settled harder on the community, however, there was less money available to pay for windows to be cleaned or gardens dug. With the onset of the miners' strike in 1984, the competition for undeclared work became intense and bitter.

The opportunities offered by the local job market were well known by those we knew. Most were unemployed. Most of the women stayed at home. Among the drinking companions, one lad was a pitman, another in the merchant navy, another a labourer at the yards. Among the young un's, those who had recently left school debated the options open to them: a govvy or the dole. (Only one lad we knew of, Barbara's younger brother, who left school in the summer of 1983, found an alternative. He got an apprenticeship with a small local firm of joiners.) Even having contacts in the area was of little help when the area happened to be an unemployment blackspot. Some effects of the employment that was available can be seen in the case of Troy. He had no problem adapting to a job again after four years on the dole, and his home soon showed the signs of his improved buying power, but his wife and daughter only saw him at weekends. The advantages of being employed again had to be weighed against the cost to family life. Al and Morrow's continued stressful states were also evident signs of the struggle for self respect that comes with prolonged unemployment.

On a different, lighter note the mention the older lads made of how they used to dress (John as a skinhead and Troy as a Hell's Angel) contrasted with their ordinary appearance when we knew them, suggests that, for them at least, style had been of transitory importance only.

Other themes we picked up from this fieldwork concerned the stereotypes of young adults held by older ones (at the community centre, for example) and the artificiality of strict age brackets imposed by officialdom (at seventeen, when still subject to a Local Authority care order, Micky was the same age as John who was a married man with a wife and child).

Finally, the issue of power, both individual and structural, raised itself over the months of contact. From the personal level (Barbara becoming pregnant; the lads boycotting the centre) to the structural (two out of twenty-seven getting long-term jobs while we knew them), the factors that controlled the lives of the young adults in Hillsborough, as in Shipton and Milton, were many and involved. The following chapters attempt to unravel some of their complexities.

Section II
In and Out of the
Labour Market

Introduction

This section of the book finds the young women and men seeking, but denied, the opportunities brought by an independent income and the status of worthwhile, full-time employment. The plight of young adults struggling to gain a foot-hold in the labour market is no new phenomenon. First and foremost, we wish to stress the historical continuity of the problem. R.H. Tawney, writing in 1934 but drawing on research completed in 1909, could be describing the experiences of young people in the mid-1980s after the Youth Opportunities or Youth Training Schemes (YOP and YTS) when he argued:

> The havoc wrought by casual labour, the prevalence in certain industries of 'blind alley' employment, the systematic exploitation of cheap juvenile labour by firms which take on successive relays of children, employ them 'for their immediate commercial utility' and dismiss them, when they demand higher wages, to make room for another batch, which will be dismissed in its turn – all this is an old story. (pp.4–5).

Tawney's arguments (1934) and those of Jewkes and Winterbottom (1933), and retrospective essays such as Horne (1983) and Rees and Rees (1982), contain detailed accounts of the main problems encountered by young people of fifty or eighty years ago which have a very contemporary ring to them: substitution of older workers by juveniles, the poor makeshift of juvenile instruction centres (Training Workshops by another name), and regional inequalities (60 per cent of all the young people in Great Britain unemployed in 1934 were found in the North East, the North West and Scotland). The parallels are many and striking and extend to the very terms of the public debate and of governmental responses, despite all the changes that have taken place since the 1930s or the early 1900s. Then as now, government programmes were designed to increase the employability of young people and to prevent their demoralization, as Rees and Rees (1982) have made clear. The concentration on the unspecified needs of industry rather than on the abilities or needs of school leavers, the power of industry to have its explanation of the crisis accepted (the so-called failure of schools), and the very real failure of much of British industry to provide training of any kind for young workers – all these themes have been part of the historical record for close on a hundred years.

The experiences of fifty young adults in the labour market become more understandable when it is recognized that these have always been typical of their class. Since the late 1970s, school leavers have frequently spent their first two or three years moving in and out of the labour market. And increasingly, as this market has contracted and they have become too old for initial youth training programmes, their choice between jobs, government schemes and unemployment has become ever more closely centred on the last option, thus questioning the whole notion of 'occupational choice', as presented in the psychological literature (Super, 1981).

The bottom fell out of the job market for young adults over the period of our study and there was a corresponding rise in placements on MSC government schemes. We wish to convey some impression of the size of the problem by quoting some regional statistics.

When our fieldwork ended in August 1984, the MSC were running a campaign to focus attention on the problems of youth unemployment in the North East where nearly 50,000 young adults aged between sixteen and twenty-four had been out of work for six months or more (*Employment Gazette*, July 1984, p.300). In September 1984, the total number of unemployed in the region was 244,009, one in five of the workforce.

The women and men we knew shared the overall fortunes of their class, their age group and their region. Their opportunities in the labour market were different, however, according to their sex and to the specific area in which they lived. To reinforce these points, women and men are considered separately in the following chapters as are the three areas. Having visited the distinctly different areas of Shipton, Milton and Hillsborough, we felt it important to look at them separately, or there is the danger of losing the subtle but vital point that the specific area in which an individual lives has consequences as real for day-to-day living as the region in which s/he lives does for long-term life opportunities. The need to protect the identities of the areas and of our sample means that we are not able to describe the structure of opportunities offered by each local economy. In addition, during the fieldwork, we were refused interviews by as many employers as we were successful at interviewing others. Nevertheless, the importance of local area factors is hinted at with figures taken from the 1981 Census data. In 1981, when the national average male unemployment rate was 10.5 per cent, the rate in Milton was 18.9 per cent and on some estates it was as high as 30 per cent and 45 per cent. Similarly, in Hillsborough at the same time, when the borough average was 16.7 per cent, the estates of Benditch and Marlow Dene were suffering levels of 25 per cent and 20 per cent. By 1983, the figures had reached 31 per cent and 29 per cent, and on other nearby estates 43 per cent. Regional, never mind national, statistics iron out such local pictures.

A final comment needs to be made with regard to the language of 'work', a language that confuses more than it clarifies. Dinstinctions need to be drawn between alienating labour and creative work, between official and unofficial labour (e.g. jobs on the side), and between paid and unpaid labour (e.g. housework). The term 'work' tends to be used loosely to refer to all these different categories and its use is deeply engrained in our culture: we found it difficult to eradicate the imprecise uses of the word 'work' from our *own* writing and thinking. We have been careful to distinguish between jobs and government schemes, for instance, as the young adults usually did themselves, referring to 'shit jobs' and 'proper jobs' as against 'govvies'. We have also tried to keep to the following usage:

1 Jobs/Employment/Proper jobs=Official paid labour
2 Housework/Voluntary work/Creative use of time=Unofficial unpaid labour.
3 Undeclared work/Unofficial work/Work on the Side=Unofficial paid labour.
4 Unemployment/The dole=Without official paid labour.

The collapse of jobs and the hesitant moves to alternative lifestyles have highlighted the inadequacies in the ordinary usages of the word 'work'.

3 On the Dole

> People say to me, 'How can you afford a car on the dole?' but, I mean, that's all I have. I don't go out, I don't drink, but I get my enjoyment from driving you see ... Everybody's got to have some form of escape. To get out of their normal routine.   *Winnie*

> I'd have taken to drink if only I'd had the money.   *Karl*

> If the government gets its way, there'll only be YTS for us. There may be some fiddle jobs. There could be FE ... There's always suicide.   *Joe*

As we launched our research project, youth unemployment hit the headlines and became the dominant issue in our discussions with the women and men in our study, most of whom were recent school leavers trying to find a job. Their comments reflected the frustrations and futility of searching for non-existent jobs. This was made worse by the insistence of the Jobcentre or Careers Service that they should make frequent visits, even threatening to stop their social security if they did not attend. The majority of young adults, at least in the early stages of each period of unemployment, looked at adverts in the local paper and visited the Jobcentre regularly. Karen, for example, called in daily while in town shopping and said that it was so crowded, 'You got sick of pushing people out of the way'. Troy commented wryly of the Jobcentres, 'All the cards in the window are faded by the sun!'. Women and men soon discovered, however, that there were next to no jobs, schemes perhaps, but no proper jobs. Simon claimed to have written to over a hundred different firms in his attempt to find employment and Winnie commented, 'I write for loads and loads of jobs and you never hear anything ... About ten in the last few weeks. I got two interviews and then they never bother saying anything again'. A further problem people faced, however, was that even when there were jobs on offer, they were either too young or lacked the experience or the qualifications necessary. Sharon had become so accustomed to the dearth of proper jobs that when she received a phone call from the Jobcentre informing her of vacancies in a local firm she thought it was her boyfriend playing a joke on her!

As our sample moved in and out of the labour market the number who were in jobs or unemployed at any one time changed constantly. There was a steady overall increase in the total number of unemployed in our sample, but this rise does not reflect the shifts in and out of the labour market or on and off schemes. For example, in January 1982, four of the six lads in Marlow Dene were on the dole, Gary was on a scheme and

John was in a job. In January 1983, the figures were the same; four lads were unemployed, one on a scheme and one in a job. By this time, however, Gary and John were both unemployed and it was Morrow who had a scheme and Troy who was in a job. Phil and Al, therefore, were the only two who were unemployed for the whole time between January 1982 and January 1983. Though the total number of unemployed in our sample frequently changed, many people's circumstances remained constant for months; they were the long-term unemployed.

Lengths of long-term unemployment varied from just over a year to five years. Almost half of our sample, twenty-three young people out of the total of forty-eight, experienced periods of unemployment officially defined as long term (fifty-two weeks or more). By August 1984, nine women and three men had still never experienced a proper job. Young adults like Winnie had left school and been on various government schemes (in her case, two six-month YOPs and one CP for a year) and had still not been able to find permanent employment. Others among the long-term unemployed, like Kirsty, Pete, Stewart and Al, before we met them, had been in employment for a while after leaving school, but had been made redundant, or given up their jobs, and had been unable to find employment since as the recession deepened. Others like Karen, Hal, John and Mark had all experienced short periods of temporary employment – usually as hiccups in long periods on the dole. John, for example, found a ten-week job during the Christmas rush in 1982, and Hal was employed for a few weeks in a sauna in the summer of 1983, and later had a temporary eight-month job.

Being one of the long-term unemployed was not entirely hopeless. Troy, after four years on the dole, suddenly landed a job; and Joe was acccepted into the navy in September 1984, and so started his first period of official employment at the age of twenty-two.

Poverty

> I'm sick, just depressed, this unemployment and no money.
> *Morrow*

> What's the worst thing about being unemployed?
> Not enough money, 'cos you can't do very much with dole really. *Stephanie*

When we first knew the young people in Shipton and Milton they were all on government schemes receiving £23.50 a week, which soon after rose to £25. The majority managed to make ends meet, though with some difficulty, and for those who had recently left school, this first income of £25 seemed reasonable. One of the younger lads in Marlow Dene argued that having £25 'all of your own' was a good reason for taking a scheme, and was certainly better than £16 social security. One by one people finished their schemes and, if they could not find a job, registered as unemployed. They all experienced an immediate drop in income. Those under eighteen-years-old in 1982 received social security of £18.90 a week. The majority gave £10 to their mothers for board, leaving them with £8.90, which had to provide them with everything else including trips to the Jobcentre, entertainment, clothes, cigarettes drink, newspapers. This amount, by the summer of 1984, was not even enough to buy one pair of fashion jeans which were priced at between £14 and £20. In April 1983, those under eighteen received £15.80 per week as the housing allowance of £3.10 was removed from the benefit by government policy. When they reached eighteen they received £23.65, but in April 1984 the housing allowance was also cut from this figure which reduced the weekly social security payment to £20.55. Those on the dole also received a small increment each year. Joe commented sarcastically:

> I'm getting an extra 15p a week! When I went down last week they told me. 'You're getting good news, you're getting a rise!

The men and women found it increasingly difficult to manage on their social security as they got older. They continued to give their parents £10 for board which did not cover the whole cost of food and housing. As their clothes wore out they found it difficult to afford replacements. During one meeting the lads in Marlow Dene discussed the prohibitive cost of shoes. Al was anxious about losing the trainers he had left in the van as they were all he had to wear. Phil said that he had bought himself two pairs of shoes in a sale, setting him back £15, but ensuring that he had decent footwear for the next twelve months.

One way of buying clothes was through a mail order catalogue:

> And I've got a catalogue, and I usually get some clothes out of the catalogue every so often and I pay three quid every two weeks for my catalogue. . . *Jimi*

Many women and men in our study bought their clothes on credit through catalogues as this was the only way they could manage one large, single payment for items such as shoes and trousers. Others used 'the club' or 'provvy' cheques which enabled them to choose clothes and other goods they needed from their local shops. These were the only forms of credit available to young adults on the dole, but they paid dearly for them. Items bought through the catalogue were between 25 per cent and 30 per cent more expensive than in the shops, and people using 'the club' paid up to 35 per cent interest.

Most of the people in our study lived in their parental home so they had a roof over their heads and sufficient to eat even when unemployed. Existing on a low income, however, presented them with two major disadvantages: they lacked the money to occupy themselves during the day; and, more important, they could not participate in the social world of people in employment. The most relevant definition of poverty is not an arbitrary figure which covers the cost of the bare essentials of life, but Peter Townsend's (1979) notion of including in poverty those who lack the resources to participate in the customary activities of their communities. When unemployed, the women and men were in danger of becoming isolated because they could not afford to contact others of their own age. Working as we were with young adults when they were both employed and unemployed we could contrast the differences in their activities at these different times.

A recurring theme during contact with the lads in Marlow Dene was how they could afford various activities. If we wanted to arrange an evening meeting in the pub or a special trip, we had to inform them well in advance so they could save up, and on a number of occasions we were told that lads had stayed away from the meetings because they could not afford to come. In Shipton, where we also met in pubs and cafes, almost without exception when they were unemployed the women and men would accept only one drink, or none at all if they could not afford to buy us one in return. We were willing to buy them drinks, but we learnt from the lads in Marlow Dene that our willingness only brought their poverty home to them. On one occasion Al muttered to Carol that he found it 'humiliating' being bought drinks by Frank when he could not reciprocate. As researchers who had only occasionally experienced periods of unemployment, it was difficult for us to appreciate fully the embarrassment and humiliation that prolonged lack of money could bring. On one occasion Sarah observed,

> When Fred popped into the community centre to ask if we wanted to go to the pub for lunch, the lads said 'lunch?' and he amended this to 'Okay, bevvies' and the lads all declined. After Fred had gone there were obvious groans among the lads as basically they could not afford to go to the pub.

Initially we were puzzled by young adults' apparent inability to manage their money week to week in what we considered to be a planned and controlled way. We were told repeatedly by the majority of those when unemployed that they had spent their girocheques within a few days of cashing it; for example:

Jimi: If I waited for my giro, I wouldn't be able to go out on a Friday or something 'cos I get me giro on a Saturday. It's like borrowing a fiver on a Friday.

Carol: Off whom?

Jimi: Off me mam usually, and then I pay her it back on the
Saturday . . . If I have, say, a few nights out on the trot then
it means the next week I can't go out. It makes no odds 'cos
I'm still okay for eating and that.

The pattern that emerged was that young adults spent their social
security within two or three days. They then borrowed from their
families until their next giro arrived out of which they paid their debts,
and so ran out of money even sooner during the next fortnight. Their
behaviour could have been interpreted as fecklessness, but further
discussion with them showed us the central importance of having one
or two big nights out, spending and socializing on a par with those in
jobs. This was one of the many tactics the young adults used to
maintain their self respect; they felt the need to participate in the
customary activities of the community for two or three days a
fortnight, and for this it was worth being broke for the other ten days.

'Doing nowt': how young people spend their time

Half past ten, nearly eleven o'clock, quarter to eleven I got up,
washed, had me breakfast and then sat in the house for a bit. I
watched the tennis for a while–went to see Eddie, came back about
four. I had me dinner before I went to see Eddie. Got there about two,
came back down about four. Then watched tennis again until I
came out to see you.   *Jimi*

This was how Jimi described a typical day in his life while unemployed;
this was 'doing nowt'.
Karl commented:

. . . you've definitely got no money, like, and you've got nowt to do
through the day. It's worse in the winter. It's not so bad in the
summer when it's nice weather, but it's terrible in winter: There's
nowt to do, especially when *The Sullivans* isn't on!!

How many readers have seen or even heard of *The Sullivans*? As this
programme was broadcast at 12.30 p.m., probably only pensioners,
those who have been unemployed or stay at home with young children.
During our contact with Karl and others, watching *The Sullivans*
became a recurrent joke, a shorthand way of referring to activities
typical of young people when unemployed.
    It took us some time to find out what women and men were doing
when on the dole because, when we asked, they all tended to reply
'nowt'. One day Scotch, for example, gave this response and then
shortly afterwards revealed that he had in fact spent all afternoon

decorating his uncle's house. Until we knew them better and could pursue the topic, the response 'nowt' was a standard ploy which effectively ended the conversation on how they spent their time. This was a delicate issue and saying 'nowt' kept insensitive, prying older adults at bay.

We did eventually collect detailed information about women's and men's activities and routines during their periods of unemployment. It became obvious that many spent long hours each day completely alone, though they still saw their friends. They were deprived of the social contact of the office or factory and could not afford to go out regularly with friends who were also unemployed.

There were sex differences in how young adults spent their time. In broad terms, most of the women were absorbed into family life; domestic commitments became their primary concern. Rocky said of his girlfriend, 'Me lass is expected to do the washing up, the ironing, all the housework. She doesn't like being a woman and being forced to do this housework'. Men were more likely to spend a large part of their day away from the home and so have routines which were more public and visible, though these were not necessarily as purposeful as the women's. As Jackson (1984, p.116) commented 'the daylight realm is peopled with busy women, growing toddlers-and lost males, drifting, ill, killing time, expended'. At various times we all observed men huddled in public libraries or wandering the streets in our three areas, presumably forced out of the house during the day. Many men in our study, however, spent most of the day at home, but they were preoccupied with model making or painting and not concerned with housework. Some reported that they helped more in the house than they had when at school or in a job. Al, for example, said 'I get the coal, do the garden', as this made him 'feel more useful'.

Routine

In the early days of each period of unemployment both women and men spent their time catching up on sleep, and generally enjoying the feeling that they were on holiday after the rigours of a shit job or a boring scheme. Many like Karen reported that they wanted to have a rest before starting to look for employment. After periods which ranged from two days up to three or four weeks, they then actively began looking for jobs at the Careers Service or Jobcentre and in the newspapers. They also began to feel bored.

During these early weeks of unemployment the impression young adults gave us was that they all filled in the time in a fairly leisurely way. Watching television and videos, going into town, doing housework, decorating, gardening, swimming and visiting friends were all activities mentioned which helped to keep boredom at bay. As the length of their unemployment increased, some women and men began to develop regular routines and activities within the limitations imposed by their poverty. Some, more than others, seemed to be consciously trying to fill their day. These routines were no substitute for employment but they did help to structure their time.

Shipton

The women

Only four out of the twelve women in Shipton, Poppy, Karen, Winnie and Fenwick, were unemployed for any length of time. With the exception of Poppy they all spent much of their time at home and saw little of their friends. Fenwick commented, when reflecting on her experiences on the dole, 'I never let myself get bored'. She got up around ten o'clock observing, 'To me that's midday over'. After that she would, 'Either just help my mum or laze about or go to the shops . . . listen to music, that's what I like. I mainly just live day by day'. She reported that she hated the dead time of mid afternoon and even at weekends used to think 'Oh God, another day–even though I never got bored'. Winnie and Karen spent their time running the home for their working parents: cooking, cleaning and shopping. Winnie's parents helped her to buy a car after which she picked her mother up from her work place each day. She also spent many hours watching the family's video.

Poppy, in contrast to the other women, spent very little time at home. During each period of unemployment she kept herself busy seeing friends, looking for a job and helping a friend of her father's. On one occasion she studied for 'O' levels, on another tried to set up her own aerobics classes, and another spent all her time with her boyfriend who had just returned from a trip to Europe.

The men

Seven men in Shipton experienced long periods of unemployment. Joe made the most obvious effort to structure his day in order to avoid what he thought was the rut that others got into: staying in bed until mid-afternoon, getting up, going to the pub, and then going back to bed. He was very critical of those who got bored, stating very emphatically that there was no reason for this as there was plenty to do. He commented, 'You've got to keep your mind active, you've got to keep busy'. Joe woke early most mornings and went for a run of four or five miles. After breakfast and tending to his four chickens, which he kept in the back garden, he spent his day making model aeroplanes, visiting the

Jobcentre, seeing friends, reading the newspaper and watching television. He occasionally went out with mates in the evening to the pub, using this opportunity to develop his local contacts which from time to time led to temporary jobs.

Smiler lay in bed until late morning and then went to the pub at dinnertime to play pool. He was one of the few who said that he was able to spend more time with his friends while unemployed because about three quarters of them were also on the dole. Smiler bought a Citizen's Band radio and stayed up talking on it until the early hours. He spent as little time as possible at home and reported that he never gave any help with housework.

Scotch, Jimi and Gordon followed similar routines: staying at home in the morning, going out in the afternoon to see friends at their homes or hanging around the streets,and then returning home in the evening to watch television or videos. Their social activities were restricted to Friday and sometimes Saturday nights out with friends.

Hal was different as he was one of the four people in our study who consciously used his time to develop skills with an eye to creating his own income in the future. He did a three year correspondence course in massage, financing himself completely, and voluntarily helped at the local swimming baths to gain experience. This eventually paid off when he found his temporary post at a health farm.

Milton

Routines and activities

In common with young adults in Shipton most of the women and men in Milton felt a sense of relief when they first became unemployed. The major difference, however, was that with the exception of Stephanie's one week of employment, *none* of the women had experienced a proper job. Initially they found being on the dole preferable to attending the Training Workshop, as did the men. The young adults in Milton also kept themselves busy with activities such as shopping, decorating, seeing friends and so on. These were, however, less varied than the activities of the women and men in Shipton as those in Milton were restricted by lack of facilities, and the cost of transport could be prohibitive.

The women

Stephanie described her routine in October 1982 as 'Help mum, watch telly...sometimes clean up...come down the town'. More specifically she reported starting her day by watching breakfast television after which she went into town every morning and bought bits and pieces for herself and her mother. In the afternoon she did household chores and watched television in the evening. Sometimes in the afternoon she visited her grandmother. Six months later her routine had only altered in that she reported getting up later, 'There's nothing to get up for'.

Clara reported that her routine revolved around the home. Her widowed father made breakfast for the younger children in the family so she did not have to get up early-usually between 9.30 and 11.00. After her own breakfast Clara tidied up, did the washing, cleaned upstairs and then ironed, by which time her brother and sister arrived home from school. She babysat at a friend's twice a week and went into town on a Thursday night. Any spare time she had during the day was spent popping in and out of her neighbours' houses and her housework was often interrupted by visits from the women who lived locally.

After her marriage, Theresa was also kept busy with housework, making and receiving visits from her neighbours, and also spent a lot of time at her mother's house round the corner. She, too, rarely ventured further than the local shops.

Sharon spent most of her time at her boyfriend's house where they watched television and videos, helped his mother and decorated the home-twice in two and half years. She returned home once a week to see her own mother and do her washing.

The men

Ben was the only person in Milton who did not spend a long period of time on the dole. By the summer of 1984, Stewart had experienced a total of five years out of work, Pete three years, Charlie two years, Mark eighteen months, Jack and Max eleven. Stewart's four consecutive years on the dole was the longest continuous period in the Milton group.

Charlie reported that he stayed at home in the mornings, sitting upstairs in his bedroom while his unemployed parents sat together downstairs in the kitchen. He read the paper or listened to music. After his dinner at midday two or three friends called for him and they went 'up the street' to spend the afternoon killing time in town, sometimes being moved on by the police. Charlie and his friends occasionally played pool in the local sports centre, but despite concessions for the unemployed this was too expensive to do often. Four evenings a week Charlie pumped iron at home with his brother, following a strict programme of training. He rarely went out: he could not afford it, nor was he supposed to drink while in training.

Mark described his routine as getting up around eleven o'clock, having a bath and washing his hair. He went out around 12.30 to his grandfather's and spent the afternoon there. He met his girlfriend from school and walked her home, remaining at her house until around midnight. Mark was one of the many young adults who when unemployed used his time to develop further his relationship with his partner.

Pete used his time practising his drums and playing with a band. He hoped eventually to make an income playing gigs with a group. He also pursued his interests collecting bottles and old coins; valuing the bottle collection he shared with his father at over £1000.

Hillsborough

Routines and activities

When they were unemployed the women and men in Hillsborough complained of boredom and depression and their poverty was a constant reminder of their problem. They did not give the impression, however, that they suffered the anxieties experienced by those in Shipton about filling their time. They lived in communities where the majority of people were on the dole and where there was a long history of unemployment, so consequently there existed a well established set of responses. One example of this was witnessed by Sarah. She spent a long, sunny afternoon sitting on a fence with John and Phil watching a group of the young un's on holiday from school. Sarah watched the younger lads riding their motorbikes over the waste ground near the Dene. John and Phil occasionally had a ride as did Phil's father. The young un's were spending time with older companions as if on an apprenticeship for unemployment: they were learning how to do 'nowt'.

The women

Brenda, Barbara and Kirsty lived the life of the traditional wife and mother, staying at home to do the housework and, in the case of Brenda and Barbara, taking the primary role in caring for their children. For all three, the most contact outside their marriage was with their parents. Between taking and collecting Mandy from school, Brenda walked the mile and a half to her parents where she spent most of her time once Troy was back in employment. Barbara appreciated the support of her mother who lived over the road and visited her with baby Joanne while her husband John was out and about. When Ben started his part-time CP scheme, Kirsty would call into his parents' house at the end of their road for company.

All three women's lives seemed to revolve around their men; their time at home was controlled by the appearances of their husbands and the provision of meals.

In Benditch, Marie, Tess and Nikki were immersed in the social life of the estate. Marie's house was always full of visiting sisters and their children. She was kept busy joining in 'the crack' in the front room or 'running messages' to the corner shop. 'That's all I do from morning till night: shop, shop, shop', she commented. At quieter times she would sit on the front doorstep and enjoy the street life, 'I know practically everyone'. When not on their schemes, Tess and Nikki's days became extensions of their normal activities: helping with the youth project, socializing in the street, cafe and pub and, sometimes, courting.

The men

For all their talk of boredom the lads in Marlow Dene always seemed to be busy, and it was often difficult to arrange day trips or meetings because of their various commitments. All the lads spent much of their time out of the house, but they still fulfilled family duties, for example, Troy, Rick and John looked after their daughters if their wives had to go out. Many lads helped out their parents and relations with tasks like moving furniture, digging the garden and repairing cars. John spent many hours building a fireplace for his parents and later for his brother. The lads had interests of their own: Troy and John went fishing, Al started to breed dogs and began to cultivate an allotment. He and Troy were involved in voluntary work with a local youth club. John and Phil took their air rifles over the Dene, and Gary was kept busy doing up cars, an activity later taken up by John. The lads also played pool together. Contacts in their neighbourhood gave them information about possible employment and also provided opportunities to make some money in unofficial work. Typically one of the lads would disappear for a short period and it would be rumoured that he was doing work on the side. He would appear back on the scene and no comment would be made. These men were understandably cagey about their undeclared work.

'I don't let it get on top of us': reactions to unemployment

The discussion of the three areas shows that unemployed young adults developed activities and commitments which gave a regular pattern to their lives. Each day was much the same, but at least some sort of structure was imposed on their time which made life more tolerable. The monotony of their lives was underlined to us by their excited anticipation of special events such as eighteen or twenty-first birthdays and the anticipation of the occasional parties and days out which we arranged, and by the fact that these events were then discussed for months afterwards since nothing else of note had happened to them.

Despite boredom always being close at hand, many women and men, when we asked, said that having plenty of time to do what they wanted was one advantage of unemployment. Some also said that not having to get out of bed until late was an advantage. We discovered, however, that the time they did get up varied constantly. After an inital rest period during the early days on the dole most people got up early on in the morning, but during periods of despondency or staying up late watching the television or videos, they slept in until late morning. Young adults therefore gave the responses which reinforced the stereotype that unemployed people lie in bed, but in practice did not always live up to this stereotype themselves.

Some long-term unemployed young people gradually became less anxious about their routines: 'I just please myself' Joe said. It seemed that the longer they were away from the imposed structures of school, scheme or job, the less effort they made to create their own time structure. Jimi, for example, when asked how he coped with unemployment replied, 'Okay, very well, in fact *very* well. I've never known anything different . . . It takes a hell of a lot to get me bored'. As their length of unemployment increased some young adults seemed to be less concerned to prove that they were busy and using their time constructively. Others found more to occupy themselves as one activity led to another. Some simply spun out a small task to fill the whole day.

Initial responses

> I love it, I love being on the dole, I do. *Poppy*

Poppy's comment was made in November 1982 after she had voluntarily left her shit job and had been unemployed for five weeks. The sentiments she expressed in the early days of unemployment were shared by the majority of young people when they first started signing on. Though actually unemployed and available for employment, government legislation made young people ineligible for Social Security benefits until the September after they had left school (or June if they left at Easter). They therefore felt that they were on holiday, rather than unemployed. This was also true of young adults when later they finished a government scheme or job which they found boring. Karen, for example, reported that she spent the first few days after her job ended lying in bed until late in the morning catching up on her sleep. The women in Milton all expressed a feeling of relief and sense of freedom when they left behind the restrictions and petty regulations of the Training Workshop. Thus, when they first became unemployed, like actors between jobs, the women and men said that they were enjoying a 'rest'. Many also said that they wanted to wait before they started looking for further employment. This cheerful outlook did not last for long.

Coming to terms with unemployment

> I'm just fed up and I get bored and things like that ... My mam gets at us. *Stephanie*

> Too much time to think when you're on the dole – it makes you depressed. *Al*

> I had got into a rut. Couldn't be bothered to do anything. I wouldn't get up, wasn't bothered about work, lost interest in everything. I got really depressed. I got sick of sitting around, m'n. I couldn't sleep, couldn't get to sleep until 3 or 4 [in the morning]. *Smiler*

Annie, the Milton woman from a family of travellers was the only person we knew who enjoyed being able to choose how she spent her time and so never looked for a job. Jimi from Shipton commented:

> Na, I'm not bored like. It's quite good, you know, do what you fancy during the week anytime you want, you know. Working inside an office or something in this weather, you know – but there again I would like the money. As I say, I'd like a job for money basically, not just because I would like a job.

These two people in our study were the only ones we encountered who claimed to enjoy being unemployed, though in fact, one month after he announced his lack of interest in getting a job, Jimi started a temporary post doing shifts at a children's home, and a year later was planning to attend training courses to qualify as a residential worker. He was one of many people who did not discuss his deeper feelings about being unemployed with us. He indicated his sensitivity when he told us how much he hated being asked if he was still unemployed because 'the answer's always the same'. And yet he claimed to enjoy not having a job. Jimi and others hinted at their deeper feelings, but only talked in detail when they were again employed or on a government scheme. For example, when Fenwick answered our questions on unemployment she said 'I enjoy it but I never let myself get bored'. Half an hour later she replied to questions on employment, basing her responses on her experiences on a scheme. Only then did she admit that when on the dole, 'I felt guilty about not working – others could be calling me a lazy person ... I felt I let my family down'.

We have quoted some typical reactions after a few weeks or months of unemployment and yet we suspected that all of these young adults wanted a job. Our suspicion was confirmed over and over again when they finally found employment and described themselves as 'over the moon' or 'chuffed to bits'.

Reactions to being on the dole varied, however, quite markedly. At one extreme were people like Poppy, Smiler, Morrow and Al who admitted to feeling bored, depressed and at times completely demoralized. In addition Morrow and Al experienced difficulty sleeping at night. Poppy, Smiler and Karl all admitted to drinking excessively when they could afford to, as a temporary escape from their predicament. At the other extreme were Winnie, Theresa, Annie, Sharon and Jimi, all of whom claimed to have come to terms with their unemployment. In the middle were people such as Karen, Clara, Stephanie, Scotch and John: they wanted a job, experienced periods of depression and found it difficult and frustrating to live on Social Security. At the same time, however, they had developed activities and routines which filled the day and gave them some feelings of purpose.

Many of the young adults, however, moved constantly in both directions between the two extremes from utter dejection to positive acceptance. Poppy's feelings about being on the dole gradually worsened during each successive period, particularly as most of her friends were in jobs. Morrow became more depressed when his family and friends around him began to get employment and he was left high and dry on the dole. Sharon, however, gradually became more and more resigned and settled as her length of unemployment increased. We found no clear link between reactions to unemployment and personal characteristics such as employment history, motivation or age. Women suffered as much as the unemployed men in our study, some even more as they became increasingly isolated and felt restricted by housework and childcare.

The stigma of unemployment

We asked our sample why they thought there were high levels of unemployment in Britain. Many like Reg explained by saying 'Nee jobs' and could not elaborate. Some like Poppy volunteered:

> Cos of Government policies–no money put into industries for proper jobs. Instead they waste it on Training Schemes that don't have prospects.

The men and women varied in their ability to articulate the reasons for high levels of unemployment, but in general they believed that the world-wide recession combined with government policies were the major causes.

Initially we were surprised, therefore, at responses to our written question, 'Why do you think *you* are unemployed?' Stephanie replied:

> Because I haven't got qualifications and that, the experience, and there's not many jobs around . . . and then you go for an interview, you have to have a school education and the qualifications and that . . .

This sentiment was shared by Jimi who explained his unemployment as being 'because I've got nowt, you know. I've got no 'O' levels or anything'. Fenwick said she could not find a job because, 'I don't know the right people . . .'. Young adults blamed themselves for their joblessness even though they were aware of some of the structural factors responsible for high unemployment.

During one discussion with Jimi, Carol pursued with him the apparent illogicality of blaming himself. He replied:

> I always seem to start blaming myself. But they put it to you like that when you go to the Jobcentre. 'Is that all you've got? Have you tried doing this?' . . . It's often the case, they put it to you, therefore you believe in it, you know.

Even those in Marlow Dene, who lived in an area of traditionally high unemployment, felt personally stigmatized. Another written question we asked those on the dole was how they thought other people regarded the unemployed. Joe's comment was typical: 'The majority regard you as a scrounger'. He said that he belonged to 'the social class of the unemployed'. Karen gave another typical response, 'A lot of people who are working think that unemployed people could get work'. Morrow reported that his parents thought he could get a job if only he tried harder. Others, such as Clara, Fenwick and Jimi, thought that the unemployed were viewed as being lazy. They knew that there were exceptions, however. Al commented:

> People who've got unemployed people in the family under-stand – others think they're dole wallahs.

There was some agreement that their grandparents' generation were more sympathetic as they themselves had experienced a recession and high unemployment. Jimi remarked, 'Yea, they understand it because they've been through it all before'.

Contact with official agencies

Almost without exception the payment of Social Security benefit was delayed at the beginning of each period of signing on the dole. We were told of waiting periods of between three to six weeks. Young adults' first experience of unemployment, therefore, was of poverty and enforced financial dependence on parents. Scotch reported that his payments had been delayed for three weeks because he had filled in the form incorrectly. Karen waited four weeks because she had been given the wrong form to complete. When she did receive her benefit she was overpaid and as this was not discovered until months later when she was again unemployed. She had to pay back what she owed at £2 a week out of her benefit which at that time was £23.65.

Rocky's social security payments were delayed for so long that he did not receive them until after he had started his job, and when he was paid he did not agree with the assessment. Karl found signing-on a depressing experience:

> Gan to sign on, gan in that bloody queue, miles long. Bucketing down with rain, it always seems to be raining on a Thursday morning when I gan doon to sign on.

Some felt that they were badly treated by the staff when they went to sign on. Theresa reported that when she was first unemployed the staff made her feel like a scrounger. Jimi described in detail one of his experiences:

> They're sitting behind the desk and you go up. If you're a few minutes early, you are told to go back. It you're a few minutes late, you've got to see the supervisor. They send you back to wait until it is your proper time. They canna get job satisfaction, I canna see it . . . There was one bloke. I went in ten minutes early. He says, 'Oh, you're too early, you'll have to wait a bit'. And I sat there for ten minutes and nobody came to sign on. I could have just been signing on. The thing was in front of him. He could have just bunged it out.

Joe was particularly incensed by his treatment. He had waited six weeks for his social security to arrive when he first became unemployed. He was often kept waiting at the office, and he reported that they 'went on at him' for not finding a job. On one occasion Joe was kept waiting for twenty minutes. He was shown into a back office and interviewed by a supervisor who told him that his attitude was 'all wrong'. Joe countered this by saying, 'I'm only a number on a piece of paper to you lot' and made his point by asking the supervisor if he knew his name, which he did not. Joe was offered the services of a social worker which angered him further. This interview was followed up with a visit from a DHSS inspector. Joe attempted to get back at the system with a symbolic gesture. He never took his own pen when he signed on, but pointedly asked to borrow one which he then kept, breaking it outside the office in full view of the staff as he left.

By the end of our study the majority of the people in our study were nineteen or twenty and some were thinking about leaving home and setting up in a flat. We were told that for those on the dole this move to independent accommodation was made very difficult if not impossible by the Social Security office. Poppy commented:

> I went to see about it, cos, like, I could be getting a flat in a fortnight's time. The dole's supposed to give you the deposit and the rent, but you've got to pay first and then get it back ... You've got to say you've been thrown out of the house before you can get your rent back.

A further bone of contention for some was the insistence of the Careers Office (who have statutory responsibility for young people until they are eighteen) that they visit them regularly. Until his eighteenth birthday, John received a series of letters from the Careers Service: they threatened to stop his benefit if he did not visit. Gordon and Jimi also reported getting similar letters. The principal objection to visiting the Careers Office was that it cost money to get there on the bus, and since no jobs were on offer and only schemes, it was a complete waste of time and effort. Gordon did in fact go to the office regularly for a while and it cost him £1.28 each time. He mimicked his exchanges with the staff:

> 'Hello Gordon. No job yet Gordon? Sorry about that, Gordon. Goodbye then, Gordon. Make sure you come back next week' ... A complete waste of time, m'n.

When they reached the age of eighteen, women and men started using the services of the Jobcentre which many seemed to find more convenient. At first, they were impressed by the number of display boards covered in cards and thought that there was a greater variety of job advertised there, but soon discovered that they were ineligible for anything but schemes. Jimi commented:

> They try and help, like, they seem pretty good so far ... They try quite hard. He was really helpful the bloke the other day, the one who got me the application form for the course [a CP scheme].

Effects on relationships

There is substantial evidence in the literature (See Madge 1983, McKee and Bell 1984) that unemployment can have adverse effects on family relationships. This issue was only touched on by the young adults in our study and so, though some women and men reported family tensions while on the dole, we could not draw definite conclusions about whether unemployment was a main or a contributory factor.

We asked specific questions about their relationships with parents while on the dole. There was a general feeling that being unemployed had led to tensions. Karl commented, 'It did at first, I was getting on top of them being in the house all day'. Poppy said, 'At first it was tense, then we talked about it and settled down a bit'. Stephanie commented, 'There's always arguments at home' and Clara said that she and her father 'fell out more'. Asia, Morrow and Smiler reported rows about their efforts to find a job. Smiler said 'We didn't get on. We had arguments. They didn't think I was looking for work'. In contrast, Fenwick was able to spend more time with her mother while she was on the dole and believed that as a consequence their relationship improved. She commented, 'I was closer to me mum when at home than now'.

The opportunity to spend time with their partner also had a beneficial effect on many young people's relationships with boyfriends or girlfriends. Mark, Phil and Kirsty, Karen, and Sharon and Steward all spent as much time as possible with their partners. Being on the dole could, however, also lead to strain: Jacki and Bernadette both reported rows with their boyfriends about money. Both these women were employed and consequently had a higher income than their male partners who were on social security. Jacki and Bernadette complained of having to subsidise their lads: buying them clothes and paying when they went out. The two men accepted this financial assistance, but they also resented and were humiliated by their dependence which was in sharp contrast to the traditional role of the dominant, supportive male. Further tensions arose in Jacki's relationship when she began to go out on her own, arguing that if she had earned her money, she wanted to be able to go out and enjoy herself: being a wage earner gave her an independence from her partner which he found unacceptable.

Some positive features of unemployment

There seemed to be three possible benefits of being unemployed. First, though they often found time hanging heavy on their hands, women and men did appreciate having the freedom to choose what they did, albeit within strict financial limits. They also had time to themselves which was not available when in a job or on schemes and the opportunity to develop interests, as long as these did not cost money. Second, young adults had the time to develop relationships with their partner and to be more involved with their children, if they had any. Third, being on the dole allowed them to return to education. This was an option only taken up by Poppy, Hal and Jack, however, as most had been completely alienated by their earlier experiences at school.

The majority of women and men had an inner strength and resolve. Even though unemployment was often a depressing and demoralizing experience, most were determined that they were not going to be totally overwhelmed by it. 'We have our pride', the lads in Marlow Dene told a newspaper reporter, and this sense of self respect was conveyed by many others. For example, the Marlow Dene lads would not let us buy them drinks, women and men insisted on a cheaper drink than they usually had, or they made a pint or a half last a whole evening. Also on the odd occasions when we loaned them money, it was always repaid.

We believe that the unwillingness of our sample to talk about their experiences of unemployment also reflected their sense of self respect. They did not want to admit to feeling bad, or being unable to cope as this might have reflected adversely on them as a person.

Though women and men slipped into despondency much of the time they kept themselves busy and organized. Some, like Joe and Charlie, engaged in activities that gave them a definite sense of progression and purpose. Joe's running not only kept him physically fit, but also provided something to aim for. He included the local park in his daily run as this also gave him the opportunity to eye up women! Charlie's body-building also gave him a sense of purpose. He was one of the few people who talked in terms of what they would be doing in one, two or even three years. He discussed his planned progress, and hoped that eventually he would be able to earn money displaying his muscles in the local clubs: body building had become his career. Clara derived a similar feeling of purpose from organizing the family home and caring for her younger brother and sisters, and when Theresa and Barbara became mothers the child became the major focus in their lives; they had found something or someone worth devoting time to. They had found a career.

In February and March 1983, Alan Bleasdale's drama *Boys from the Blackstuff* was broadcast. The drama made heroes out of the unemployed and the young adults identified with this positive image of themselves because, as Joe commented, usually the media emphasized 'all the bad points first'.

Giving up hope of a job

After months on the dole, fruitless job searching, and in the face of ever-increasing national and regional levels of unemployment, some young adults gave up hope of ever getting a job. They still wanted employment, but they thought their chances too remote. Al, Sharon and Charlies were examples of people who appeared to have given up hope. Al, still in his mid twenties, commented on his job prospects:

> I feel sad for them – the young ones especially. It's all over for me now, but at least I've had a chance.

Charlie reported that he had given up looking for a job, had stopped going to the Jobcentre or looking in the paper. He said 'There isn't any point', because he knew relatives and friends who were getting laid off all the time. Sharon, after eighteen months of unemployment, said that she had stopped looking for employment, 'There's no point because there's no jobs'. She felt there was nothing to be gained from sitting around feeling miserable. 'You've just got to accept it and get on with life'. Ironically she was not getting on with life because she and Stewart were not prepared to marry until one or both of them found permanent employment.

Survival tactics

We have summarised the responses of young people to unemployment under a number of survival tactics and longer term strategies. When on the dole young adults struggled to maintain their self respect and to keep boredom at bay. Our fieldwork suggested a number of tactics which they used to achieve this. The aim was always the same: to maintain physical and mental wellbeing in adverse conditions. Some of these tactics were also used by young adults to help them survive shit jobs and govvy schemes. We have identified six major tactics used by young adults; these are not mutually exclusive and commitment to each varied markedly.

1 *Routine*

It seemed important, especially in the early months of being unemployed, for young adults to structure their time, fill in the day, and to give themselves a sense of purpose. All this helped to imitate the structure previously imposed on them by school, a govvy or a job. Most important, however, as time went on, the activities helped to combat boredom. Those people who lived in communities where high unemployment was the norm had an established network of contacts which they could utilize. As the length of unemployment increased, many people became less anxious about maintaining a strict, active routine. Some seemed less concerned to prove that they were busy and using their time constructively. Others found more to occupy themselves as one interest led to another.

2   *Spending patterns*

Most young adults spent their social security soon after receiving it, preferring to spend their money on one or two big nights out every fortnight, rather than eking it out and spending a little every day. This made sense in human, if not economic, terms. Friday and Saturday nights out drinking with friends are part of the traditional culture of the North East. Young adults wanted to be part of the ordinary life around them at least for a short time and this made it worth being broke until the next giro arrived. In addition, these brief excursions into the social whirl of their working contemporaries provided a welcome relief from the monotony of their daily routines, and for some the numbing effect of alcohol was a break from the suffering of unemployment.

3   *Relationships*

One of the major problems facing unemployed young adults was the ever-increasing sense of isolation. Many, particularly women, spent their days in the home and both they and the men could only afford to participate in a few of the evening social activities with their working friends. Some people, however, had friends who were also unemployed so they spent part of their day together and could share with them their common feelings of despondency.

4   *Subemployment*

This describes young adults' movement in and out of the labour market as they went from jobs to schemes and on to the dole. Until recently it was possible for young women and men to give up a job when they could not stand it any more, have a breathing space, and then move on to another. As the recession deepend in the 1980s, however, the dearth of employment has denied people choice, even between shit jobs. Until they were too old for youth employment schemes, young adults were able to use subemployment as a tactic to help them cope with unemployment: if it becomes intolerable they knew they could go on another govvy. As they got older, they graduated from YOP or YTS, and worked their way through WOC, TOPs and CP; then schemes ceased to be an option and with jobs almost non-existent, there were no choices left, only the dole.

5   *Work on the Side*

This provided a welcome increase in income and periods of useful activity while on the dole. For generations of working-class people, unofficial jobs have been a vital means of defending self respect, maintaining a basic income and preserving existing skills in times of unemployment. It can also be a way into a more permanent, official job. For some who have never had a job, work on the side may be their only way of gaining valuable experience in the labour market.

6 Defence Mechanisms

Some young adults simply would not talk about being on the dole and the feelings this generated. Some women and men said they avoided the topic deliberately – with us, and with their friends. Going out drinking was a means of forgetting about unemployment, not a forum for discussing the experience and its implications. This partly explains why young adults replied 'nowt' when we asked what they had been doing. Perhaps they judged their activities to be 'nowt'; marginal and without purpose, in contrast with what they judged to be the constructive activities of a job, and therefore not worthy of mention. Many were also aware of the image of the unemployed as 'scroungers' and 'layabouts' and perhaps they did not want to admit to anything which would reinforce this stereotype. Far safer to say 'nowt'. These six tactics were adopted as short-term, fairly *ad hoc* means of surviving the dole. Some young people had, however, begun to develop more *long-term strategies*. They had accepted that they had little chance of finding a job through conventional channels and were looking for alternatives.

Long-term strategies

1 *Skills*.

One response was to develop skills in an attempt to improve their employment prospects and perhaps generate an income. Some people on the dole used their time to develop abilities which gave a sense of progression and also had the possibility of more permanent employment in the future. One lad, for example, started to do bodybuilding at home. Another lad hoped eventually to make a living out of his music, while another studied massage and hoped to set up his own business. A fourth started breeding dogs, and another took a course in carpentry one day a week.

2 *Giving up hope of a job.*

Some young adults in our study seemed to reach a point where they

decided that there was no hope of them ever finding a job. For those on
the dole, accepting that they would never find employment meant that
they were no longer being faced with the continuous disappointment of
being turned down or of their letters not being answered. Giving up
hope of finding employment made psychological sense because it
protected their self esteem from receiving one damaging blow after
another. Some long-term unemployed young people lowered their
hopes and expectations and retreated into themselves to prevent
further damage.

Commentary

Youth unemployment is no stranger to the North East. Witness a
speech of the Lord Mayor of Newcastle upon Tyne made in 1937:

> In this area there are thousands of young persons of both sexes who
> are now attaining the age of twenty without ever having done a
> day's work. They see no prospect of employment . . . (quoted by
> Horne, 1983, p.314)

Most writers agree (see Jahoda 1979, Watts 1983, Warr 1983a and
Roberts 1984) that unemployment has adverse effects on adults. But
there is still a debate about the effects of being on the dole on young
people who, it is believed, are at 'the most vulnerable age emotionally'
(Ridley 1981). Jobless young adults, Roberts (1984) argued 'lack
relevant aims and motives' and their mental health has been shown to
deteriorate. Jackson *et al*. (1983), for example, found that compared
with those in jobs, young adults on the dole are 'less satisfied with life,
have lower self esteem, suffer greater depression and anxiety, and have
lower social and family adjustment scores'. Additionally, Roberts
commented there are fears that the lack of an 'adult wage' at sixteen,
which until recently compensated those who had failed at school, will
lead to young adults rejecting society. There is concern that the
consequences may be an increase in crime, policing problems and
'embittered young adults, available for mobilization by extremist
political movements' (p.72).

Roberts' discussion of the effects of unemployment on young people
also considered the alternative argument 'that unemployment is far
less devastating for young people than adults'. This view is shared by
Watts (1983, p.103) who argued, 'some school leavers who have not
experienced much occupation socialization, and who are not impressed
by the employment opportunities open to them, will not be as adversely
affected by unemployment as most older adults'. Warr's (1983a, p.308)
comments are in the same vein:

> Teenagers who are unemployed tend to have fewer financial

problems than other unemployed people, for instance because they may be living reasonably cheaply with parents. They carry forward from school a network of friends and leisure activities, and the social stigma of unemployment may be less for them than for unemployed middle-aged people.

Our fieldwork challenges the ideas of Roberts, Watts and Warr on a number of points. We found that unemployment tended not to be seen as a problem by young people when they first left school, and so as Watts and Warr suggested, they were not adversely affected at that time. But this was *only* during their early days on the dole. As periods of unemployment lengthened the women and men in our study began to experience real and substantial financial problems, particularly if they took on the financial responsibilities of marriage and children. The majority of young women and men in our study did 'carry forward from school a network of friends', but at most they could afford to socialize with them once or twice a week when on the dole and often tended to sink into social isolation. Rather than the social stigma being less for unemployed young adults we believe that they are doubly stigmatized: not only are they on the dole, but they are also in the no man's land of adolescence without the status accorded to either adults or children.

Roberts (1984) presented additional evidence to support the idea that 'young people can cope' with unemployment. First, he suggested they have families who can support them and, as it is now more usual for young women and men to remain financially dependent on their parents, 'adult independence can be achieved without wage-earning status'. Our fieldwork suggested that families would have difficulty supporting young adults indefinitely. Parents should not be expected to, nor should the young be denied the opportunity to become financially independent. How can full adult status be achieved while women and men depend on their parents to buy their clothes and pay for their entertainment? We wish to add to Robert's suggestion that young adults no longer see the dole as charity. Those in our study who received Social Security benefit saw it as their right, but they still felt like scroungers because of their treatment by older adults, Social Security officials and the media.

Roberts also reported that young people suffer less while unemployed because they have 'no occupational identities to shatter, and . . . their personalities cannot be assaulted in quite the same way as life-long steel workers and dockers' (p.73). We believe their position is much worse than this suggests: young adults who never have had a job have no occupational identity at all – they are not even an unemployed shop assistant or joiner, they are simply *unemployed*.

We do not hold much faith either in the argument put forward by

Roberts that young adults can cope with unemployment because, by virtue of their youth, they can 'realistically expect their prospects to improve'. A more accurate scenario for the future was painted in *Economic Prospects for the North* (Robinson, 1982, p.123) where the conclusion was reached that:

> Some of the older members of the workforce are clearly destined never to work again and some young people may never work.

Finally, Roberts suggested that young people can adapt to unemployment particularly in areas where it has persisted throughout the 1950s and 1960s. The trend, he argued, is for young adults to get used to being unemployed and to cope rather than to 'fester and eventually explode' into political action. In addition, survival skills that have been passed down through generations can be taught to young adults by their parents: how to claim their rights and how to survive on low incomes. It is also in areas of persistent unemployment, Roberts claimed, that leisure activities and social contacts are usually available to help pass the time.

We found some evidence to support these arguments. The women and men in our study were not involved in political action as a response to unemployment, and a few young adults seemed to have given up all hope of finding a job. But we would agree with Hirsch (1983) who commented that it is a mistake to view passive *acceptance* of unemployment as an indication that people judge their unemployment as *acceptable*. We want to stress that unemployment was reluctantly and gradually accepted by young adults – because there was no other option available. This acceptance, however, did not always occur in areas where unemployment was most persistent. Some of the young adults who suffered the most lived in such areas.

Roberts' discussion of unemployment considered evidence which supported two opposing views: that young adults in unemployment suffer either more or less because of their age. Our evidence suggested, however, that attempting to discuss one global reaction to unemployment is unproductive as young adults' responses varied considerably: the young unemployed are not an homogeneous group, self-contained and hermetically sealed off from the rest of the population. For the same reasons attempts at isolating the psychological characteristics of the unemployed are doomed to failure. There is no sharp division between the employed and the unemployed. The most common pattern followed by school leavers and young adults in our study was to move from government scheme to unemployment, then back to government scheme, and on to a further period of unemployment with occasional breaks when in a job.

We were left in no doubt after our two-and-a-half years of contact with young adults who were regularly on the dole, that with only the one exception we mention they all wanted employment and were prepared to take almost any kind of proper job. We were also left in no doubt that much of the time most young adults were adversely affected by unemployment, but there were exceptions. We found that their reactions varied, and moreover an individual's feelings about being on the dole changed markedly during a single period of unemployment.

Our evidence suggested a complex interaction between individual factors such as abilities and character and other moderating variables identified by Warr (1983a) and Roberts (1984) such as family support, finances and social contact. Our extended period of contact with them, however, has emphasized the extent to which all these factors can change with time. The detrimental effect of unemployment does not, as Warr (1983a, 1983b) has suggested, simply increase the longer a person is on the dole. Changes such as the government deciding to reduced social security by £3.10, or quarrels with parents about moping round the house or friends finding employment were all likely to increase young adults' suffering, but such changes occurred to different people at different times during periods on the dole. Other changes, such as meeting a new partner or finding a job on the side, made being on the dole more tolerable.

We found no simple connection between duration of unemployment and young adults' reactions to being on the dole, and therefore question Breakwell's (1984) very specific finding that young women and men become depressed around their sixth week of unemployment. This would seem to us to be an artefact of the questionnaire methods used rather than a reflection of either the variety of reactions *among* individuals or the variations *within* any one individual. The evidence discussed above also leads us to raise questions about the findings of researchers such as Powell and Driscoll (1973), Harrison (1976) and Hill (1978), who claimed that people go through the following clear stages when they become unemployed: shock, optimism, despair and finally resignation. While some young adults in our study *did* seem to give up hope, this response changed dramatically when they finally found employment and easily fitted into a full-time job.

We found that young adults blamed themselves for being unemployed. This has been confirmed time and again by researchers such as Norris (1978), Stirling (1982), and Cashmore (1984). Why was it that young adults blamed themselves even when they were aware that there were over three million unemployed and a scarcity of jobs? There were a number of interconnected reasons that reflect the way young people viewed society and not just their attitudes to the specific problem of unemployment.

Young adults (and presumably many older adults) did not make the connection between national statistics about the recession and their own subjective experiences, nor were they used to talking about their own lives except in personal terms. In addition, the young adults lived in a society where the political atmosphere sought to divide the populace–no longer into biblical sheep and goats–but into high fliers and lame ducks. In endless exhortations to individual effort and individual competition in the so-called enterprise society provoke intense feelings among those who lose (as some must) and are then invited to consider their failure as a personal one. The widely-held assumption is that, if young adults cannot find a job, then they have only their own lack of skills or lack of effort to blame, particularly if they have been introduced to all manner of job searching and interview techniques on a government training scheme. The media and conservative politicians alike perpetuate the myth that all can succeed through hard work by publicizing stories of the infrequent individuals who move from rags to riches. As a consequence, British society is prone to view unemployment as a personal trouble rather than as a public issue, to use the terms of Wright Mills (1970).

Two general themes emerge from this discussion. First, our evidence suggests strongly that we need to move from individual, psychological explanations of mass phenomena like unemployment to more sociological and collective interpretations. Second, the constant harping of the character or ability of those who happen to be unemployed is a good example of the fallacy of individualism. We use this term to refer to a general principle whereby young adults explain social mobility, financial success and failure, employment and unemployment by exclusive reference to the characteristics of the individuals concerned. We would agree with Richard Jenkins (1983, p.132) who made the further point that 'power and inequality become transformed, as a result, into the expression and reflection of real differences in the qualities of individuals'.

In addition, Kelvin (1984) has pointed out that the very language we use in connection with unemployment stigmatizes people. For example, the unemployed receive 'allowances' and 'benefits' rather than payments which can be considered as rights, and these and other terms such as 'dole', 'assistance' and 'relief' are 'all redolent with images of charity to the inadequate' (p.419).

One of the main observations of our research is that the unemployed are not a discrete group. As this chapter has illustrated, it was the same young adults, approximately half our sample, who during the relatively short period of two-and-a-half years when we knew them, had been in and out of shit jobs, on and off govvies and the dole. The present crisis of youth unemployment cannot be explained by a sudden decline in the standards of schooling nor by a lack of employable skills among school leavers; it has been caused more than anything else by the virtual collapse of the job market which never showed much interest in training young adults anyway. The figures for Newcastle make the point: in 1974 80 per cent of all school leavers found full-time employment, which nine years later in 1983 was obtained by just 16.6 per cent. In Gateshead in one week in September 1982, more than 4000 young people aged sixteen to eighteen, who were either unemployed or on government schemes, were chasing the twelve jobs known to Careers Officers and Jobcentres. Such figures make nonsense of any attempt to establish the personal characteristics of the unemployed. We examined our own data to see whether – in a particular month – we could differentiate between those in a job and those who were not. Neither educational qualifications, nor physical attributes, nor enthusiasm for employment, nor any other personal quality that we could think of explained the difference. Having relatives, friends or local connections who notified you in advance about possible vacancies explained more of the variation than any other factor.

While youth unemployment is no stranger to the North East, long-term unemployment for young adults is a new phenomenon and no one as yet is sure what effect this will have on the present generation of school leavers. How will they feel in the year 2000 when they look back on sixteen years of unemployment and look forward to a further thirty plus years of unemployment before 'retiring' at the ages of sixty or sixty-five? If we are to see the emergence of a new sub-class of young adults who are state pensioners from the age of seventeen, then political discussion must turn from the provision of a minimum *wage* to the guarantee of a minimum *income*.

4 Shit Jobs and Govvy Schemes

Letters from Poppy

Extract from Letter-January 1984.
Well, I got the job as a receptionist!! The pay's not very good at the moment 'cos I'm on three months trial, but it gets better after that!.. . It's a dead responsible position-I do all the cash and organization so if things go wrong it's on my head!!! I'm starting to settle in now though and don't make *too* many mistakes so life's looking up at last-I feel much more contented now and part of the human race once again!

2 March 1984

Hiya Carol,

It's bad news I'm afraid-well, (deep breath. . . .) I got the sack!!! It was exactly 2 weeks before my three months trial period was to end and my good pay rise to start! I was totally devastated to say the least ... I felt as though someone had kicked me in the teeth. It was last Saturday when Tony (the manager) told me ... he was really embarrassed and told me the decision had nothing at all to do with him as he thought I was really good at my job and had built up the appointment book well! Really Carol ... I loved that job and worked damned hard at it but there's not a thing I can do about his decision. The reason the proprietor gave was that he needed someone either engaged or married with a settled outlook-what a load of shit!!! Anyway, his decision was final and on Monday morning I trudged back to my second home (the dole). Once again I'm a useless bloody number! However I was dead surprised when Tony (the manager) phoned my house on Monday evening to say that he was really sorry the way things had turned out and that there had been dozens of receptionists before me who they'd sacked after only a few weeks! He felt really awful about it and said that if it hadn't meant his job-he would have risked telling me a little sooner! So I felt loads better after that!!!

After one week I'm dead bored. I can't even get my job back at the Cock and Bull cos they've cut the staff's hours by ½. I've been to the Job Centre every day at 9 a.m. but there's nothing going! It's the first time for ages I've been really depressed!

I haven't been seeing much of Steve lately-him and his best mate have decided to go into business together. Terry was working for the Council in the offices and Steve packed in college. They're going into the music business-promoting local bands and things. I'll tell you more about it when I see you again!!!

Well, Carol, just as I thought my life was beginning to look good I've
been pissed on again!

See you soon (I'm gonna cheer up now cos its off my chest!?!).

Loads of love

Poppy

Poppy was in and out of employment, on and off schemes more than
any young person in our study. Her experience therefore bridges the
two chapters in this section. It epitomizes the choices open to young
adults which in their own words were: shit jobs, govvy schemes and the
dole. Poppy illustrates the fundamental point that the women and men
who were in employment and on schemes were the same women and
men who at other times were unemployed. The picture is a constantly
moving one because the people who are the statistics move. Some
individuals had relatively permanent jobs and feature in this chapter.
Others were long-term unemployed – which is officially defined as
being continuously without employment for fifty-two weeks or
more – and appeared more in the previous one. These young adults
represent either end of a continuum while those like Poppy run up and
down the whole length, moving in and out of the labour market. Her
story therefore runs as a thread through these two chapters which are
about the *same* group of people at *different* periods of time.

We were able to chart the employment histories of forty-eight young
adults. None of them had permanent jobs for all the time that we knew
them. Fourteen, from Shipton, by the end of our study were in full-time
employment. They featured towards one end of the continuum. At the
other end, eleven from Shipton and Milton, never experienced a proper
job. The majority, twenty-three from all three areas, were in the same
boat as Poppy: in and out of employment and on and off government
schemes, all to varying degrees. This was not by choice. Most of the
jobs were temporary or only seasonal; part-time ones were rarely
financially viable as the wages affected Social Security payments. All
the schemes were of fixed duration, anything from twelve weeks to
twelve months.

The vitally important differences between proper jobs and youth
training schemes are considered at the end of this chapter. For now,
govvies are considered alongside jobs because the experience of each
varied little. Whether they were 'trainee' or employee, young people
talked about dangerous conditions and the carping criticisms of
supervisors as well as of having good fun and learning new skills at
work. Their accounts highlighted the poor quality of their jobs and

schemes. Our long and close contact with the women and men also emphasized the lack of choice or opportunity they had in the labour market. It is these two points that the following pages illustrate.

Whereas the low status and repetitive tasks experienced on jobs and schemes were common to all the young adults, the structures of opportunity were different for both sexes and again in the three areas. We therefore consider the women and the men separately in Shipton, Milton and Hillsborough. First, however, we look briefly at the employment history of one of the Hillsborough lads. At twenty-eight, Troy was the oldest in the sample. His story helps to locate those of the younger women and men in time and establish a sense of continuity.

Troy left school with no qualifications in 1970 at the age of fifteen. He got a job straightaway as a painter and decorator for £13 a week. He left this to work as a labourer because it paid £40 a week. Later, he went out to sea on the trawlers and later still worked for 'a canny farmer'. Troy stated 'I like to work', but he had been unemployed for four years when we met him the autumn of 1982. The following July he got his first job in four years, as a labourer for the contracting firm where he had last been employed in 1979. They were cleaning out sewers along the coast. Troy said it was 'Funny, but you get used to the smell'. The gaffer was a friend of his and one Monday he told Troy he had better bring his cards in as he was being taken on full time. He was chuffed at being taken on officially as he had been working with the firm a few weeks already. At first he was away long hours, sometimes doing a 98-hour week which brought home £150 (in 1983, the national weekly average of males working 40 hours), but later, when the jobs took him out of the North East to the Midlands and Yorkshire, he could only come home to his family at weekends.

Throughout the early 1970s, therefore, Troy followed one traditional working-class pattern of a constant variety of unskilled jobs. This was before mass unemployment hit. In January 1983 the average period of unemployment in parts of Hillsborough was nine years, so complete had been the collapse of the heavy industry on which it was founded. Troy's experience of five years' unemployment was under par compared with many of those around him. Shipton and Milton did not have quite such high levels, but when our fieldwork began early in 1982, employment opportunities were shrinking fast and the early pattern of frequent job changes followed by Troy when he left school was no longer an option.

Shipton

We met the young women and men while they were doing WEEP, a government scheme under YOP, so initially all our information was about the experiences of trainees. As the months and years went on we built up an overview of their working lives. Just over half of them, fourteen, were in full time employment for most of this period, that is from the end of their last scheme. Nine of these were in fact kept on by the employers they were working for as trainees. The rest, seven men and four women, variously experienced a number of short-term jobs and schemes and long-term unemployment.

In the early stages of contact in Shipton, the young women and men talked a little about the types of job they would prefer, such as nursery nurse or joiner. None were outrageous or unrealistic in their expectations, especially when it came to what they considered a reasonable wage. At sixteen and seventeen, with few qualifications, they were prepared to accept around £40 a week (the wage Troy was earning ten years previously). In practice, for many, anything over £25 a week was acceptable.

Several months out of school, reality began to bite hard. Tony and Scotch each applied for about forty jobs, Reg on the other hand, for only four. Smiler hoped to get a job through his dad's contacts in the car trade. Fenwick kept in regular touch with the Careers Office and Jimi bought the paper early every day.

Initially all those who found jobs or were kept on, were delighted, with the exception of Bert, who was resigned rather than pleased. Earning between £35 and £45 a week after their £25 MSC allowance seemed like a small fortune and they all indicated a sense of relief that they were no longer among the ranks of the unemployed. Crucially, however, none of them had any *choice* in the type of employment they acquired: all were simply pleased to have the job offered them.

Gradually most of them became disillusioned. Although they acknowledged that most jobs had boring aspects, they were not prepared for quite the mindlessness that confronted them every day: endless filing and refiling, stacking shelves, loading wagons and putting up with awkward customers or, worse still, petty supervisors and difficult bosses.

The picture was not completely black: at least six of the young adults did enjoy their jobs. Although she was not keen on night shifts and worried about her exams, Shuk liked the fulfilment she got from nursing and also the company of her workmates. For a long time, Jane found the same satisfaction in her technician's job. Gradually, Jacki began to enjoy using the skills she acquired in the betting shop and looked forward to having the responsibility to manage one on her own one day. Fenwick, Winnie and Scotch enjoyed their schemes – while they had them.

The most general picture in Shipton overall though was one of frustration and leaden hours for most in employment, and even despair for some; Asia, Carol Ann and Bert all decried their lot at different times. Their jobs were full time and relatively secure, but low paid and endlessly boring.

The women

We knew twelve women in Shipton. Jane, eighteen when we met, was the eldest and Fenwick, at sixteen and a half, the youngest. Eight had full time employment and the remaining four were in and out of jobs, on and off schemes. The following histories illustrate the different experiences of three of the women in the labour market: Bernadette who was in an undemanding job, Jane who was in initially good employment and Poppy who was in and out of both.

(a)   Bernadette

Bernadette was delighted when she was kept on with the Local Health Authority, even more so because she would no longer be in the office but out at various doctors' surgeries helping to run ante-natal clinics. She was also pleased that the £25 allowance on her scheme changed to a gross income of £47 per week, but was surprised and dismayed at the amount deducted each week for tax and insurance. She took this temporary post knowing that there was a possibility of a more permanent job at the end of it, as a woman was leaving to have a baby. Bernadette's hopes were realized and after a summer of speculation she was offered the new job two weeks before her temporary post ended. She said 'I was so pleased that I nearly cried', but her joy was partly overshadowed when she learnt that she would be on one month's notice. She also had to spend most of her time in the office and soon found the boredom almost intolerable.

In November 1982, Bernadette saw a post advertised working full time in the clinics. She applied and in January, 1983 was delighted to inform us that she now had a full time, permanent job. She was employed as a clerk at the clinics, travelling to a different doctor's practice each day. She sorted out files, doctors' notes and record cards in the morning and then assisted with the general running of the clinic in the afternoons. She said she enjoyed the social contact and was getting on well with the health visitors and other secretaries.

Bernadette's enjoyment of her job was short lived. Three months after starting she again complained of boredom with a weekly routine which never varied. At each meeting with us she made the same comments about her job, but usually added that she felt she should not complain because she was lucky to be employed. By August she had started to take days off because she could not stand the boredom any longer. She reported that a new clinic was opening shortly, and she desperately hoped that this new development would make her job more interesting. A year later, at our last contact, nothing had changed. Bernadette was still bored, and still taking unpaid days off to alleviate her boredom.

(b) *Jane*

With one 'A' level, Jane was the most highly qualified in our whole sample from all three areas. Her first scheme was on WEEP as a veterinary nurse. After two months she complained that all she was asked to do was clean out cages. 'They used to check on the cleaning...if I missed bits out I got told off'. She had been led to believe that she would gain some experience in laboratory work (her 'A' level was in Biology). The only other tasks she was given were measuring 'with an inaccurate measure and I counted a few pills'. When she was asked to clean windows, she refused as she did not consider it training for a veterinary nurse. 'When another scheme came up, I took it straight away – it didn't matter what it was'. At least the second one involved the type of work she wanted: it was in a research laboratory. She was able to show her competence: 'I got responsibility' and she was left in charge when another worker went on holiday. Then she landed her post as a trainee technician in a hospital. Jane learnt afterwards that she had been given a good reference as a steady, quiet worker. Her reason for going on a scheme in the first place was that 'It gives you something to talk about'. On a more personal note, she said, 'I've got loads of confidence – before I would never refuse to do anything, I always did what I was told to do', but her experience at the vets had taught her where to draw the line.

Jane's full-time post involved one day a week release to study for an Ordinary National Certificate (ONC) qualification. The college day was from 9 am until 8 pm and she was constantly revising for exams – which she always passed. She belonged to her trade union, but the only time she talked about politics was when she saw a poster one day on the noticeboard which notified staff of the expected number of redundancies to be made in the Health Service. At this point, Jane became aware for the first time of outside influences on her job. She also knew that graduates were applying for basic technicians' posts, so even after three years' study, she would not be as highly qualified. She explained too how, once qualified, it was likely she would earn less as there would no longer be the opportunity for overtime. One of her workmates had moved to Hillsborough to take an unqualified post because it paid more. Jane enjoyed her job though and persisted with her training. She just hoped that cutbacks in the hospital services would not directly affect her. Early in 1984, however, she was full of the changes that were happening in her job. She had always completed about six hours overtime a week, but this was being cut. She was being given less responsibility and her tasks were more boring. Worse still, the authorities were changing the conditions of her ONC course to the extent that even after three years' study, it was not certain that she would be fully qualified. With her colleagues, Jane tried to find out what their situation was going to be, but they could not get a straight answer from anyone. When we last met her, in August 1984, she was so fed up with her position that she was applying for other jobs.

(c) *Poppy*

Poppy, whose letters were quoted at the beginning of this chapter, left school in 1980 at the age of sixteen with four 'O' levels. Soon afterwards she started a YOP scheme working in an office. She did well and the firm wanted to keep her on, but the union objected and she finished at the end of her six months. She commented at this stage that she thought this was fair enough, considering older workers had more to lose than her.

Poppy's next scheme was at a post office. She hated it and left after one day. Poppy's first taste of unemployment followed. In June 1981, after four months on the dole, Poppy was interviewed for and offered a job as a trainee hairdresser in Shipton. She found that the heat in the shop gave her headaches and the hours were longer than she realized. After two days, she determined to find a better job, but there was nothing to apply for.

When we met Poppy early in 1982, she had started her third WEEP scheme, as a receptionist with a private Temping agency. She was led to believe that she would be kept on, but eventually told that there would be no job for her at the end of the placement. Poppy was furious because she had worked extremely hard, practically running the agency when the owner was away. She took her grievance to the Careers Officer who advised her to leave at once and she did.

In May 1982, the Careers Officer sent Poppy for a job as a clerical assistant in an accountant's office. She got the job, but very quickly found it boring. All she had to do was take photocopies, answer the phone and make cups of tea: 'I'm the lowest of the low'. In July, though, she felt brighter about her prospects as she was being given a wider variety of tasks, including using the computer on her own and supervising a lad who had started there on a WEEP scheme.

By August, Poppy had reverted to her original feelings about the job and was applying for new ones. She was eighteen now and went to the

Jobcentre which, she said, had far more jobs to offer than the Careers Service. She felt at this time that being eighteen had opened up a lot of opportunities for her. None of her interviews came to anything, however.

It was the general atmosphere in the accountants' office that affected Poppy even more than the menial tasks she had to do. She reported that no one was allowed to speak, not only while they were working but during their breaks as well. The senior clerk was a middle-aged woman who had been with the firm for years. She ruled the office staff with a rod of iron. Poppy responded to this atmosphere by avoiding it: she took days off whenever she could. She did not want to leave the job because if it was her decision, she would be ineligible for unemployment benefit for the subsequent six weeks. Neither did she want to be sacked because it might have affected her employment chances afterwards. But, in September, Poppy could take no more and handed in her notice. She said it felt like a weight lifting from her shoulders. On her second to last day, the senior clerk told her she could not come into the office dressed as she was. Poppy explained that she was dressed as she always had been and had one full day left to do and so the long standing differences between the two women ended in confrontation. Poppy admitted to us: 'Well, I'll tell you what I told her. I told her she needed a good fuck'. She left the job with her pride and her dress sense, but suffered the penalty of six weeks with no income.

Poppy had been employed at the accountants' office for five months. After leaving, she was on the dole again for six months, until March 1983 when she announced that she had started what she called a WOC scheme. She did not know what the initials meant: we later learnt they stood for Wider Opportunities Course, one of the options under the TOPs programme. She heard about it through a friend of her dad's. It was for twelve weeks: 'I go every day to Brownwell Skillcentre' where she could try anything she wanted: motorbike maintenance, sewing, handicrafts, painting, basic electricals. She also went on two placements, one to a residential home and one as a receptionist in a local hospital. At the end of the twelve weeks, though, Poppy was back on the dole and said she felt worse than before and that it would have been better never to have done the scheme in the first place. Particularly, in the hospital, she considered she had worked harder than anybody else, but after paying her bus fares, she had come home with £23. This was less than she had been getting in unemployment benefit.

Poppy undertook her WOC course in the belief that it would improve her chances of getting a job. The MSC leaflet describes Wider Opportunities Courses as follows:

These courses are open to men, women and unemployed young
people who either cannot get the job they would like or want to try
something different and are unsure of what sort of work would suit
them. Under guidance, they try themselves out on a number of skills
to identify what they like and do well. They are also taught social
skills, such as applications for jobs and conduct at interviews.

Poppy had, however, already succeeded in interviews, had landed jobs
and schemes with no problem and subsequently worked well at them,
but she had not been given permanent employment. She knew from her
experience what she liked and did well. She knew what sort of work
would suit her, but it was simply not available, at least not in any
secure or well-paid form.

The men

We knew thirteen men in Shipton, Joe was the eldest, at nineteen when
we first met, and Bert the youngest at sixteeen-and-a-half. Their job
and scheme experiences were broadly similar to those of the women in
Shipton, although fewer men (six) had had permanent full-time jobs
and three had never had a 'proper job' (as against one woman). The
four others followed the in-and-out, on-and-off pattern already typified
by Poppy.
   Four of the six full-time wage earners got their jobs through their
YOP schemes. Reg was kept on as a storeman at a wholesalers, Bert as
a storeman at a light manufacturers and Tony gained an apprenticeship as a welder and fitter with the construction firm with which he did
his six months Work Experience. Tomma graduated from his scheme
with a building firm to an apprenticeship with them as a bricklayer.
The other two employees were Rocky and Simon who got their jobs as
civil servant and storeman respectively through answering advertise-
ments.
   The three men who never had official full time employment while we
knew them were Joe, Gordon and Scotch. The remaining four, Karl,
Jimi, Smiler and Hal, all had jobs at different times, but they were
nearly always temporary and when they were not, like Karl's job at a
local printers, it was redundancy that brought them to an end. Karl had
been made redundant at the age of seventeen.
   The following accounts show Rocky, who was over-qualified for his
clerical post, and Tomma who enjoyed his apprenticeship as a
bricklayer.

(a) *Rocky*

In November 1981, Rocky, after getting nowhere with job applications
to banks was interviewed for the civil service and accepted. He did not
start, however, until the following May. His scheme had been with a
chemical firm where he enjoyed learning 'something new every day'.
When there, he saw his own post advertised. Rocky checked up with his
workmates afterwards to learn that the lad who had been appointed
seemed no different from himself. Rocky had worked hard on his
scheme there and he had the necessary qualifications (seven 'O' levels,
including Chemistry). He did not understand why he had not been
taken on. The firm's handling of the whole affair still rankled with
Rocky months later, especially as he came to dislike more and more his
job in the Civil Service.

At first, he had enjoyed being a Clerical Assistant, especially the
company of his colleagues, but as the months went on, the endless
filing and processing of letters wore him down. Occasionally there was
the satisfaction of sorting out a particularly complicated claim, for
instance, but Rocky's main comment was: 'Anybody could do my job'.
He complained that it was nothing like he had been led to believe on
reading the booklets in the Careers Office. He said the 1982 literature
made claims about promotion in the Civil Service which were simply
untrue. He was over qualified for his post from the beginning, but every
level was affected in the same way. He had hoped that after a year, he
would be in for promotion, but learnt straightaway that this was
unlikely to be before eighteen months and then, if he was accepted, it
would probably be a further year before he could find a post to which to
move.

Rocky explained to us that he took the job because it was supposed to
be steady and because he wanted to go into clerical work as he was not
very practical with his hands. He earned about £67 for a basic forty
hour week.

In November 1982, Rocky had extra paperwork to do while a
computer was installed in his section. He commented that, in the long
run, this would mean less jobs in administration. At this time, too, all
the interviews for promotion were stopped for a further six months
which depressed Rocky even more as his prospects were now put back
at least a year. At our meetings, he voiced his frustrations at his under-
employment. It perhaps spurred him on in his involvement with
helping to set up meetings for a local youth group: over the months, it
was this, not his steady, mindless job, that stimulated him and
engaged his organizing abilities.

In May 1983, Rocky received his assessment and was told there was
little chance of promotion, but he could probably change to a different

section if he wanted. He did this as he could not bear the thought of twenty years in the same office, even though he enjoyed the company. In August 1984, he was still there, increasingly frustrated at how much his steady job had let him down.

(b) *Tomma*

At seventeen, Tomma was taken on as an apprentice bricklayer after a six-month WEEP scheme with a local building firm. Despite often stating that he was 'sick of work', he seemed to enjoy his job, recounting tales from the workplace, often at length and with much amusement.

He did not, however, enjoy his day-release study once a week, 'it's a good day for college as no one feels like work on a Monday morning'. At one of our meetings, when his girlfriend, Jane, was preoccupied with her ONC exams, Tomma almost forgot to mention that he too had sat several papers the previous week. He much preferred the practical, physical graft on site.

Tomma enjoyed being a member of a team and the contact with older workers who initiated him into the ways of the workplace. One day, one of the managers came into the hut when they were having their 'bait' ten minutes earlier than they should have been. Tomma only just managed to pour away his tea and push his sandwich in his pocket in time. He described how whenever they got the opportunity, they would play football and have 'a bit carry on for a laugh'. As the youngest one there, he was on the receiving end of many practical jokes, like the day he opened his bait box to find a dead mouse in his sandwich. He enjoyed the fun, but was quite relieved when a new 'can lad' appeared in the form of a new apprentice.

Gradually, Tomma gained experience and status. After his first year, he expected a £5 rise, but in fact got £16. He was then, in April 1983, earning £57 a week. He took his lead from his workmates who would, for instance, exercise an unofficial go-slow on the site if they felt too much was being expected of them in a day or if they had a quarrel about overtime payments. When we first met Tomma, he had not joined a union because he thought they 'did nowt' for their members and anyway his boss was openly against unionised labour. Towards the end of the second year of his apprenticeship, however, the firm's owner sold up to a national building concern. At this stage, Tomma did join a union because some fellow workers he knew had been laid off. He felt pleased that he had when, with two others, he was caught leaving early one day, at 5.25 pm instead of 5.30 pm. Their shop steward accompanied them when they were called to see the manager: Tomma was relieved when nothing more came of the incident.

Under the new management, so many foremen had appeared on the site that it was difficult for the brickies to get their traditional weekly game of football in before getting their pay on a Thursday. Then when they came to collect their wages, they were taken aback at the new payslip, 'it was ten foot long!' and having to sign four separate sheets, 'all colours', where one used to do. Tomma soon adapted to the new regime, however, and was still on his apprenticeship when we last saw him.

Milton

The training workshop

Initially, all twelve young people we knew in Milton were attending the Training Workshop. It was one of about two hundred such workshops set up nationally under the MSC's organization of Special Programmes. Potential trainees had to be aged between sixteen and eighteen-years-old and to have been registered as unemployed for six weeks or more. They worked a 40-hour week and no overtime was allowed. Staff had to be recruited from the unemployment register.

The MSC (1981) described Workshops as 'providing basic training and work experience for young people in a productive environment under experienced supervision' and saw the main aim as training young people in a range of adaptable skills that 'will develop their potential and improve their prospects of finding permanent employment'. Trainees attended for a maximum of twelve months during which they were supposed to receive induction training and attend a 'Life and Social Skills' course. The MSC also stipulated that the range and level of work experience should relate to local needs and occupations. Young people were also to be provided with 'adequate support, supervision and personal advice in the course of their day-to-day experiences in the workshop'. Comments made to us by both the staff and the young people at the Milton Training Workshop indicated a wide discrepancy between the organization and procedures stipulated by the MSC and the realities of the local provision.

When we first visited the Workshop, between thirty and forty young people were receiving training for periods lasting up to a year. The options were divided between what was considered appropriate for each sex. The young women learnt catering skills in the canteen, sewing at industrial machines and assembly work on a production line. One or two, usually those who had already acquired typing skills, were trained in reception duties. The young men learnt painting and decorating, woodwork, basic metalwork and printing skills. Young people were referred to the Workshop by the local Careers Office or applied in person on the recommendation of friends. In common with many Workshops, Milton had problems recruiting young people, and the numbers were often below capacity.

From time to time, trainees were sent on placement: the women to a local light manufacturing firm, Toulons, and the men to a nearby builders or to the leisure centre. They all criticized these industrial placements. Mark described his weeks with a contract builder:

> 'slave work . . . I do nothing but make tea and carry chipboards up ladders.' His friend commented, 'In ten minutes, he was up and down the ladders at least twenty times'.

The women described the working conditions at Toulons as 'awful' and reported that they were forced to go on placement there under threat of dismissal or with having their 'wages' docked if they refused. Any money they made from extra work went to the fulltime staff. Theresa claimed that during her three weeks in the factory canteen, she spent the whole time washing up. The only cooking she did was making ten pints of semolina. The incentive in being there at all was supposed to be the chance of a permanent job. A few months after we first met the women, though, they protested about the conditions at Toulons to MSC representatives and as a result were allowed to choose whether they went there or not. Shortly after this, however, the length of their breaks at the Workshop were cut and they claimed it was because they had made a complaint.

Another occasion when they showed some resistance was on protesting about having to attend an open-air baths which, they said, were cold and dirty. This was on the afternoon each week when they were expected to do sports, although they were also expected to pay their fares to get to the leisure centre and their entrance fees. After their one refusal to use the baths, the sporting afternoons were stopped altogether. Sharon declared triumphantly: 'We're gannin nowhere and we're not bothered neither'.

Such occasions were rare, however. Docking allowances appeared to be the major form of control used by the staff. The young people lost a percentage of their weekly £25 for missing days without an adequate excuse, for being late, for wasting time at the Workshop, for refusing to go on industrial training placements or on the 'Life and Social Skills' course, for being 'cheeky' and at one time, we discovered later on to our dismay, for refusing to participate in our research. They were stopped from smoking and the women were not allowed to wear nail varnish or jewellery. All the young people considered that the discipline at the Workshop was too strict, especially in view of the low remuneration. A few times, they asked us about the legal position concerning restrictions, but whatever we replied, they felt powerless to effect changes. They feared getting their money docked even further if they protested. Generally, they seemed to have good relationships with their supervisors who complained as loudly as they did about the inadequacies of some of their accommodation. The premises were cramped and suffered extremes of temperature, the walls were cracked and daubed with graffiti. There was insufficient space for more than a few to work on the benches and lathes at a time.

The women and men had most criticism for the manager, Mr Long, and his secretary. One of them commented: 'they treat us like bairns' and we were aware, from our first meeting with him, that Mr Long referred to them as 'children'. He went on to describe three particular young women as 'wrong un's' and one lad as so badly behaved that he would 'end up in a mental home'. Of another young woman who was in the care of the Local Authority, he stated that she would have to leave the residential home she was in when she was eighteen and 'be put into the wide world where she'll become a prostitute within a month'.

Mr Long attributed these young people's behaviour to their family backgrounds. He said he knew all about them because he had such a network of contacts in the local area. When he was informed that a particular young person was coming to attend the Workshop, he would telephone one of these contacts to get what information he could about them. 'Then I hit them across the head with it when they come in'. Mr Long considered his approach helped him to maintain discipline because it made him appear all-knowing.

During our contact with the Training Workshop and even afterwards we heard a great deal of criticism of young adults from Mr Long. He described all those at the Workshop as 'low ability' and claimed they lacked the motivation to acquire permanent employment.

We asked Mr Long how he would select young people for the pilot YTS scheme at the Workshop. His criteria were that the young person had to be clean and be able to hold a conversation. He commented that he had interviewed three young people for an hour each and had taken none of them on. Later, though, when commenting on the full implementation of the YTS scheme, he said: 'We have to take anything now'.

On one occasion, Mr Long said of the young adults with whom he came into contact: 'all they care about is surviving'. He was referring to what he saw as their lack of drive and initiative. When at a later date, he commented they had not 'got a hope in hell of surviving the wide world', he seemed to be dismissing them all as failures. He maintained however that they benefited from the Workshop because they were always treated 'with courtesy and respect – they come back to visit because they've been treated with courtesy and respect here'.

The claims of both the MSC and Mr Long rang hollow as we followed what happened to the young adults. The overwhelming effect of the Milton Training Workshop on those we knew was the sense of relief they felt once they had escaped it: the lads referred to it as 'a prison camp'. The escape was both physical and mental. Pete said of the premises that he could not bear to be in a place with no windows. The relief of no longer being there lasted in some cases for years. Although she had not been employed in the two years since leaving, Sharon reminisced in April 1984: 'It was like going from one school to another ... Mr Long would be nice to you one minute and turn on you the next, but some of the supervisors, they were the worst ... we were *told* to volunteer for your discussion groups, you know'.

The women

We came to know five women over two years. Stephanie's single week at the factory, described in Chapter 1, is the sum total of the experience of the labour market held by all five women in this time, and this in the area which reputedly provided more female employment than either Shipton or Hillsborough.

A sixth young woman, Pat, with whom we lost contact after she left the Workshop, had had some experience of employment, in a packing factory, but it was only temporary. She got it because several of her friends worked there. Later, we heard she had a job in a supermarket in Runswick.

Two of the women, Sharon and Annie, were unemployed from the time they left the Workshop. Annie was the only person in the whole study who said she did not want a job. She kept herself busy though: she helped her boyfriend's dad with his mobile shop. Stephanie, Clara and Theresa were on and off schemes, mostly off. Here, we look at Clara and Theresa who both found their schemes empty experiences.

(a) *Clara*

Clara's scheme at Notex typifies the worst aspect of both shit jobs and govvies. Some months after her mother's funeral and an episode when her father threw her out of the house, Clara was settled enough to call at the Careers Office once more. In fact she asked if she could go back to the Training Workshop because at least it was somewhere she knew and where there might be vacancies. She was told that there would only be a place for her if she was handicapped (we never learnt why), and instead she was offered a scheme placement at Notex, a light assembly factory not far from where she lived. She started in November 1982, working from 8 am until 4.30 pm on the assembly line, piecing together small bits of wire. Clara did not seem to know what the end product was other than something electrical. Her eight-and-a-half hour working day included a ten-minute teabreak in the morning, half-an-hour for dinner and 'we're supposed to get another break at three, but we have to work through that one'. She was paid £25 a week.

When Sarah visited Clara after she had been at Notex two weeks, she explained that she could sometimes earn overtime by working late on a Friday night or from 7 am to 12 noon on a Saturday. She would then bring home £33 for the week, but she confided that she was often quite relieved when there were no Saturday morning shifts to be worked because 'I like to watch television then with the little ones'.

At this meeting, Clara had a large bandage on her hand. She had sprained her wrist at the factory that day. When she took the bandage off, it revealed the little cuts all over her fingers: 'they sting a lot'. Sarah asked if there was a nurse on hand. Clara replied that there was, but she wasn't very helpful. 'She just said "I don't know what your rashes are", and there are never any elastoplasts or headache tablets'. Sarah asked if she was getting headaches: 'I think it's the light and the dust'. On another occasion, Clara described to Carol how she had worn the protective gloves she had been issued, but the solder had gone straight through them. It also got behind her goggles because they were such a bad fit. At Christmas, the management would not allow any decorations 'for safety reasons', but the workers smuggled in a little tree which they tucked away in a corner. Clara had been placed with the lads and she missed the companionship of her female friends. They had all exchanged Christmas cards, but one lad who she described as 'a bit soft, but canny' had received none: he said even a birthday card would do, with the wording changed, and Clara took it upon herself to buy him one.

Initially pleased about her scheme, Clara, as the weeks went on, talked less enthusiastically: 'I don't know if it's worth it really'. Her modest hope of advancement at this time was to move from the assembly line into the boxing department. She also looked forward to April when she would be eighteen and expected to go on to £45 a week, although she knew that higher wages brought the increased opportunity for them to be docked. A friend had assembled a hundred and fifty units incorrectly and had been docked £43.

Carol visited Clara at the end of April 1983: she had finished her scheme the previous Friday, having been given one week's notice, ten days before her eighteenth birthday. Clara said that before she heard formally, a friend had come up to her in the toilets because she had heard they were going to lay Clara off. Officially, she was told she was dismissed because she had not been working hard enough, but Clara could not believe this. She thought it was because there were not sufficient orders coming in. It may also have been because at eighteen she was due to be paid full wages. Clara subsequently joined the ranks of the long-term unemployed, getting neither job nor scheme in the following sixteen months.

(b)   *Theresa*

Theresa heard about her six months TOPs Hotel and Catering Course from a Careers Officer who visited the Workshop, after which she pursued it herself and was given an interview: fifty-four people had applied for just sixteen places. Theresa was told afterwards by a lecturer that she had got her place because she stood up to the interview panel. They were impressed when she expressed her belief that she should be present if they were discussing her personally.

Three weeks into the course, Theresa reported it was 'okay'. She was spending three days learning how to cook and two days preparing food for the college canteen. Her hours were from 9 am to 5.15 pm as well as three hours homework a day. Her allowance was estimated at £35 a week plus £10 for travel and food.

After two months, Theresa simply described the course as 'alright', but by the end of the third month, she found it repetitive and boring. With ten weeks left to go, she was already looking forward to the end of it. She obviously found the 'Life and Social Skills' course a waste of time, commenting in her wry manner one day that they had been learning 'how to communicate'. She did however learn useful information about DHSS benefits and felt secure that she knew what she would be entitled to if she could not get a job at the end of the course. She seemed to think all along that this would be the case because of her suspected epilepsy (the topic the interviewers had wanted to discuss in her absence). At the same time, this was the main reason that she did not look for a job, despite the tutors' encouragement to do so.

Theresa told us that she had engineered a change in her placement –to the large pub over the road from her home–which saved a lot of effort travelling and nearly £10 a week. On another occasion, she explained she had been docked £21 one month for three separate days she had off, two for legitimate visits to the doctor and one because of being given incorrect instructions as to where she was supposed to be.

Theresa finished her course in July 1983, taking exams on the final day. We met her the following week. She felt the course had got her nowhere and that she had not learnt anything new. In her usual dry manner, she remarked that the course was worth 88p a week: she had seen a job advertised and it gave the wages as 88p more for applicants with a TOPs certificate. She was going to 'hoy away' all her notes because she had come to hate the course so much. She had been keen on catering before, but the course had put her off it completely.

The MSC leaflet that describes TOPs courses states:

> ...It provides training for people who want to brighten up their job prospects by adding to skills they've already got or by learning new skills employers are calling for ...

> *A job after training*? We can't guarantee you one. But with your new or improved skill and the MSC's own job finding service, you've got a better chance.

The men

At first, we knew six young men in and around Milton. Pete was the eldest at nineteen-and-a-half, Mark the youngest at sixteen-and-a-half. We came to know a seventh, Stewart, who was Sharon's boyfriend. He was twenty-four when we first met him, and had been out of a job for two years. Like Troy at the beginning of this chapter, Stewart's experience indicated what was likely to be in store for the slightly younger men in the same area. On leaving school, he got a temporary job in a food factory. He later worked at a bookie's and described once how he had picked spuds, seven days a week for three months. He did a six month scheme with the local council, but after this, as for Troy in Hillsborough, came long-term employment.

As we kept up with the other six men over two years, it seemed they had about as much as Stewart to look forward to. Charlie was only just seventeen when we first met him, but by the end of the study he too, at nineteen, had been unemployed for over two years. Four others, Mark, Jack, Ben and Max were in and out of work nearly always for reasons beyond their control. Mark worked at Toulons as a labourer for a while, but was laid off the week before Christmas, 'in case they had to give me a Christmas bonus!'.

(a) *Ben*

Ben was unemployed for five months before he got a job through his uncle with a small employer who did landscape gardening. When we met him one week in May 1983 he had been laid off, along with eleven others, because the ground was too wet. He was being paid for that week, but doubted he would for a second week if the weather did not 'fair up'. After eighteen months, in the autumn of 1983, Ben was made redundant with just a week's notice. He was unemployed for four months, then he got a job as a storeman. He only stayed a month, however, because the opportunity came to start as a driver at his mother's workplace. The pay was better and the job more interesting. When we last saw Ben he was showing off his Ford Escort car which his new income had enabled him to buy on hire purchase.

(b)   *Pete*

Pete had left school with five CSEs, had a job with a builder for two years and had been unemployed for a third before doing six months at the Workshop. He was subsequently unemployed for fourteen months before starting as an estate worker, a job he heard about through a friend who was giving it up after eight months because it was so physically hard: ten hours a day clearing woodland, five-and-a-half days a week. Pete did not get the chance to give it up though before he was made redundant. He was the only one in our sample to try his luck in London. He spent six weeks there looking for a job, sleeping on the floor of a friend's room in the hospital where he was employed as a porter. Pete got nowhere: at one interview when an employer heard his accent he asked Pete how much he drank because 'all Geordies are alcoholics'. He returned to the North East and, although he had once said he would 'never go on another govvy, even if there was one available', he started a scheme which paid £54 for a twenty-eight hour week. He knew there was no chance of it leading to a full-time job: 'it's a scheme for the supervisors as well', but at least the short hours gave him time to practise with his band. At our last meeting, Pete confided his thoughts:

> I've ended up being sick with everybody . . . sick with govvy schemes. They just stop people getting proper jobs. Firms are getting work done for nothing. I blame the government for these schemes. They'll not be able to stop them schemes now . . . now that local firms know they can get labour for nothing. There's no chance of labouring jobs now . . . they're all done by people on the schemes.

Hillsborough

The women

The experience of the seven women we knew in Hillsborough echoed that of the women in the other areas, most specifically Milton, as most experience was of govvies and unemployment rather than of proper jobs.

We met Barbara, Kirsty and Brenda in Chapter 2: by the end of our study, they were all married and unemployed, although they were not registered. The other four women had been on a mixture of YOP and CP schemes.

Marie, Tess, Nikki and Kath all left school at sixteen with no qualifications. Marie, the youngest, was unemployed for six months after school before she did a three months MSC Basic Skills Scheme at a college in Hillsborough. Her main memory was how much it had cost her in bus fares. She was subsequently unemployed for over a year.

Tess did two schemes of six months each, working as an auxiliary first in a primary school and then in the physiotherapy department of a hospital. Once Tess was off work with a dislocated jaw, injured when playing sports with some of the handicapped. Her gran commented on her being on the sick so soon after starting her scheme. Tess replied 'Two weeks off does you no harm'. She completed her twelve months then signed back on the dole.

Nikki, who was nineteen, enjoyed her year as a CP worker at the local youth project. She had far worse memories of her WEEP scheme as a machinist with a small family business. They took four young people on schemes, then sacked the cleaner and asked them to do her work. Nikki commented 'there were definitely too many chiefs' and said that now, if she was asked to do someone else's job, she would tell the manager where to go. She explained she had not at the time because she was only seventeen and she never really knew what was expected of her on her scheme anyway. Like most of the young workers we knew, she was sent to get everyone's dinners. She did not mind this too much because it gave her the opportunity to skive off a little and to join up with Kath who had a 90-minute break at midday on her scheme and 'nowhere to go'. They used to sit on a park bench. On Fridays, after work, Nikki went to help Kath with all the chores she was expected to do on her placement at a family-run 'Bed and Breakfast'. Kath was overwhelmed with the tasks: cleaning and tidying as well as cooking and serving and looking after the proprietors' three-year-old daughter. We saw the least of Kath who, when she became pregnant, spent all her energies on setting up home, getting it ready for her boyfriend's release from borstal.

The men

As we saw when we met the lads in Chapter 2, most of them were unemployed for most of the time. Only occasionally, a CP scheme or a TOPs course came their way. Whether because of their age or locality or both and unlike those we knew in other areas, the lads never talked of specific job aspirations. It seemed irrelevant when friends, such as Flyn, were time-served in apprenticeships – qualified and jobless. If there were any vacancies in the local pit, they would know about them and also know who would be in line for them, someone from a pit family. Vacancies in the shipyard were equally remote when their names had been on the list for two years already and 400 voluntary redundancies had just been called for.

When one of their number did venture, through sheer desperation, into the only legitimate labour to be had, like Morrow on his CP scheme, the stories he brought back of shifting large boulders by hand and having the tea hut declared out of bounds, were hardly incentive for the others to follow suit. They were hardly incentive for Morrow himself to stick with the scheme, but in the end, the £10 extra each week won the day. There was the added consideration that at the end of the scheme, he would qualify for unemployment benefit as against the lower rate of social security, so he did the twelve months.

In contrast, Gary said that he enjoyed his vehicle body repair TOPs course, but the 'better chance' of a job afterwards offered by the MSC brochure never materialized. The skills he had learnt required such specialist equipment that he was not able to keep in practice although he was constantly working on his own old car. After the course, Gary remained unemployed and even more frustrated than before because he was unable to put newly-acquired skills to use.

In many respects, Troy's eventual job was a shit job because it was insecure, dirty work and hundreds of miles from home. On the other hand, he had always been prepared to do labouring; it lasted for much longer than he expected, it was legal, and it brought home over twice as much as he had received on social security. With all this to recommend it, it felt good, especially after four years on the dole. It perhaps felt better for Troy though than for Brenda and Mandy, his wife and daughter at home, who, although they appreciated the improved income, missed Troy's company and support.

Commentary

Jobs and schemes have been considered together in this chapter because they offer young adults similarly unattractive opportunities, both in terms of experience and future prospects. The similarities are basically qualitative and examples such as the treatment by seniors and conditions in the workplace help to explain why, for instance, Breakwell *et al.*(1982) found that the psychological effects of jobs and schemes were similar. The differences between jobs and schemes are fundamentally structural and relate less to institutional factors and more to government policy.

Similarities of shit jobs and govvy schemes

Low Pay

Both jobs and schemes paid badly, but there was a sex difference. The training allowances while on a scheme were at fixed rates for both sexes and were more fair to women than the local job markets where women employees were on lower wages than the men. The level of MSC allowances was so low, however, that neither women nor men could do much more than eke out an existence on them.

At the beginning of the study, the youth training scheme allowance on WEEP and at the Training Workshop was £23.50 for a forty-hour week. In February 1982, it went up to £25. At the time of writing, in autumn 1984, an increase to £26.25 has recently been agreed. Since the inception of youth training schemes, therefore, allowances have increased by less than 12 per cent, representing in real terms a substantial depreciation over a period of six years. The allowance has always been inclusive of £4 weekly travelling expenses. If trainees incurred more than this for their travel, they were entitled to claim extra.

We now discuss the young workers' incomes more fully, noting Fraser's point (1980, p.173) that psychologists 'should not become so engrossed in the study of self esteem that we ignore starvation'. Let us begin with one particular case which makes a number of general points. In 1982, the Young Workers Scheme that Julie was on paid £40 a week at a time when the average gross weekly earnings of sixteen-year-old females was £52. The small factory where she worked as a wages clerk received £15 subsidy from the Department of Employment as long as her wage did not exceed £40. Had her boss thought to raise her pay to between £40 and £45, the subsidy would have been halved to £7.50. A study by the Institute of Manpower Studies reported in March 1983 that nationally only about 16,300 young people were in jobs as a direct result of this scheme and estimated that about 6,500 older workers had lost their jobs as a result of the subsidy to young workers.

After one year, at the end of the Young Workers Scheme, the firm kept Julie on at £1.10 an hour for a forty-hour week. She was by then drawing-up the weekly wages of all the workers and personally making up their wage packets: she was responsible for approximately £17,000 a week in wages–£884,00 a year–and described it as 'a lot of responsibility for a nineteen-year-old'. In the summer of 1984, therefore, Julie let it be known that she was looking for another job. She was promptly given a pay rise, to £2 an hour. She had been working for the firm for two-and-a-half years and had just spent her two weeks' annual leave in Shipton because she could not afford a holiday of any kind. On their TOPs courses, Theresa and Gary received approximately £45 a week. Morrow and Kaffy received about £31 for their two days a week CP schemes and Stephanie £43 on her five-day one. These schemes paid the hourly rates agreed by the appropriate unions;

however, to keep the overall cost down, the hours were fixed by the MSC at a reduced number and there was no opportunity for overtime.

It was only these slightly higher paid schemes that included National Insurance and so made the participants subsequently eligible for unemployment benefit. This benefit was slightly higher than the basic social security to which trainees on £25 a week were entitled at the end of their schemes.

The employed women we knew earned less than their male counterparts. Jane and Shuk, both in training and on £50 a week, were the highest paid, but the two highest male wages, at £150 and £107 including overtime, were over twice theirs. The next highest wages were men's (£80, £78 and £67). All the other women and men in employment brought home less than £37 for an average of forty hours (a few of the men could bring this up to between £40 and £50 if they did overtime). Jones (1984, p.19) has shown that the wages of both males and females who were kept on after WEEP schemes were far lower than those 'who had obtained their jobs in other ways'.

Poor wages were bad enough, but the £25 allowance on schemes was worse in its denial of the right to pay state contributions and consequent ineligibility for higher benefits in unemployment. On the other hand, in this respect the schemes that did pay those contributions were more worthwhile than the lowest-paid shit jobs.

In the year to April 1984, average adult earnings went up to £159.30 a week. In the summer of 1984, it was reported that 'a low pay target of two-thirds average earnings (i.e. £106.20) is being increasingly adopted in wage bargaining' (*The Guardian*, 30 July 1984). The young workers we knew at this time, however, had wages of between one third and one half of the national average. The majority brought home under £50 a week, thus falling short of the low pay target by more than £56. Unequivocally, they were low paid.

The argument that young workers have priced themselves out of the labour market is principally based on the finding of Wells (1983, p.230) that 'the employment of young people under 18 years of age appears to have been reduced by increases in their average earnings relative to the average earnings of adults. . .'. Wells himself urged that his results should be viewed with caution because of deficiencies in the data and the finding has not gone unchallenged. Comparative evidence from West Germany where the first-year apprentice earns 25 per cent of the adult rate would appear to add some support to the argument. The fact, however, that 94 per cent of the skilled apprentices in the Ford Motor Company of West Germany 'will have to be content with the offer of an unskilled production job' (Reardon, 1983, p.7), shows that there are more factors operating in the youth labour market than wage levels.

Our own evidence, admittedly based on a very small sample, suggests that unemployment has already driven down levels of pay for young people - at least in the North East. And their willingness to accept a job that earned them around £40 per week, if only they could find one, puts them on a par with the much larger representative samples of international studies. An OECD article states (as quoted by the Network Training Group, 1983, p.9):

> Most studies show a small minimum wage effect on youth unemployment: the Minimum Wage Study Commission concluded that on average a 10% rise in the minimum wage led to an increase of less than 1 percentage point in the teenage unemployment rates. When the Commission updated many of these studies, they found that the unemployment effect virtually disappeared.

Conditions in the workplace

Again, conditions in the workplace were similar in both jobs and schemes, but there were marked sex differences.

The first was a perpetuation of the traditional types of workplace for female and male: whether employee or trainee, the women found themselves in shops and offices, the men on building sites, in forests and warehouses.

The second sex difference was the attitude to conditions, due partly to these different places of employment and partly to what concerned female and male workers when there. Jobs in offices, shops and clinics, for the most part provided women with relatively clean and safe conditions; exceptions were at Toulons and Notex, the factories in Milton. The women talked more about social relations in the workplace.

Both Clara and Poppy, for instance, complained that they were not allowed to talk with workmates, and we collected evidence that, at certain times, some women were subject to sexual harrassment. Bernadette had problems in knowing how to tell a persistent young doctor that she did not want to go for drives with him. On one of her scheme placements, Karen was made to feel uncomfortable about working in a small room with one other male clerk as others made up stories about them. Jane was expected along with other female colleagues to endure the pranks of the male technicians who squirted syringes filled with saline up their skirts.

The men, on the other hand, subject to far harder physical conditions, often seemed to enjoy describing the faulty machinery they had to use or the gory details of accidents witnessed. The lads recounted their tales of danger in the workplace less to shock than to make something exciting and positive out of something which was neither, or at least which offered few other rewards. They gained a manly sense of worth from hard graft. As Willis (1979, p.196) wrote:

> Difficult, uncomfortable or dangerous conditions are seen, not for themselves, but for their appropriateness to a masculine readiness and hardness.

> Though it is difficult to obtain stature in work itself, both what work provides and the very sacrifice and strength required to do it provides the materials for an elemental self esteem.

A particular form of masculinity on the one hand and lack of alternative job opportunities on the other combine to explain the lads' outlook on physical labour. Apart from these differences, the tediousness of the tasks undertaken by both women and men was the same. Whether they had formal qualifications or not, most of them were under-employed. Whether in jobs or on schemes, the tasks were so basic that the only quality they stretched was their patience. The few who did find their employment rewarding enjoyed it because of the opportunities to learn and practise new skills; like Jacki, for example, in the betting shop and Gary at the Skillcentre; and also because they were given responsibility, like Reg in the warehouse and Poppy for a short while, on her scheme at the Temping agency.

For most, though, jobs and schemes consisted of boring, repetitive tasks, numbing to both brain and body. In the face of this, the reasons that kept them going were their pay, despite the low levels, good company and the spectre of the alternative, the dole.

Status as workers and treatment by seniors

Whether trainee or employee, the young workers began, as to be expected, at the lowest levels in their respective workplaces. Over time, a few of the employees raised themselves a little (literally, in the case of Carol Ann who was gradually 'promoted' from the basement to the top floor of the department store where she was employed), and later some had responsiblity for the younger workers on schemes, but generally they were all at the bottom of the hierarchy within the labour market. What they did have in common was the treatment they received from their supervisors.

Most of the older adults who were sympathetic to the young workers were in fact colleagues at the same level, like Reg's workmates at the warehouse and Winnie's at her placement in a nursery. Some bosses and supervisors were also friendly and supportive. Far more common, however, were adverse comments from the young adults about those immediately above them in authority. This may be the usual relationship between those in power and those subject to power; it was accentuated, however, by the very youth of the women and men we knew. Smith (1970, pp. 198-9) noted:

> The peculiar status of adolescence in Western society encourages the development amongst adults of a stereotype of adolescence as a category which is typified by its irresponsibility.
>
> ...Stereotypes frequently relate to readily observable criteria such as clothes and hairstyles, since these simplify the process of categorization.

We learnt of these processes in action, from Poppy's arguments in the accountants' office to the treatment received by all those at the Training Workshop. In addition, Mr Long sought information about the trainees from local sources, even gossip, and from this proceeded to divide the women and men into two simple categories: 'good workers' (clean, deferential, punctual) or 'wrong un's'. His views were more often than not based on incorrect information; nevertheless, he made the decisions to take individuals on at the Workshop, to recommend them for jobs, how much to dock their allowances, and when to terminate their training. In this way, however stereotyped or biased were the views of employers and supervisors, they had, as Jenkins wrote (1983, p.105) 'the power to make their models of reality count as the major reality'.

Trade Union involvement

Out of eleven women and sixteen men who had more than one week's employment during the period of the study, just four joined unions. They were all in permanent full time posts. Jane at the hospital laboratory and Rocky in the Civil Service were approached by union representatives during the first week in their jobs and consequently joined straightaway. Tomma joined his union after nearly a year at work and Jimi joined NUPE when he was on temporary contracts as a residential worker. Other young employee's attitudes to unions were mixed. Reg and Carol Ann specifically chose not to join because they did not believe that unions achieved anything. Fenwick said she would join if she had a job.

Generally, there was widespread ignorance of the basic roles of trade unions, fuelled by the constant bad press given to unions nationally. Another influence on young adults' failure to join unions was the very insecurity of their position in the labour market. Not long out of school and struggling to survive, they did not consider action through trade unions as a means of protecting the status quo, never mind improving it. Part of this was what they saw as the inefficiency of unions to help their members anyway. Part was also the lack of opportunity to join. Several reported that their bosses would only employ non-unionized labour; paying any union dues when in casual or temporary jobs was to all intents and purposes a waste of money as far as the young employees were concerned. When on schemes, it never occurred to them to join and no one, neither the unions nor the MSC, encouraged them to do so.

Training and future prospects

In practice, there was little difference in the training received in jobs or on schemes: in either context, it was minimal. If anything, it was more evident in some of the jobs than most of the schemes. Jane, Shuk and Tomma, who were all in employment, received the most training, attending day-release courses and taking exams for higher qualifications.

Of the schemes experienced, the TOPs courses taken by Theresa and Gary seemed to involve the most training of practical skills, although Theresa did not think she had really learnt anything new. The young adults in Shipton all enjoyed the 'Life and Social Skills' element of their WEEP schemes, but were highly critical of the practical skills courses they had to attend as part of the training day away from the employers' premises. They considered the presentation an insult to their intelligence and found the sessions irrelevant to their Work Experience. Their jobs were so poor that they could be learnt on placement, in a few days if not a few hours.

The CP schemes undertaken by Morrow, Kaffy and Stephanie were replacements to the MSC's Community Enterprise Programme (CEP). In a report on the latter, Tucker (1984) concluded that:

> The lesson of CEP is that training within special programmes is unlikely to develop on any significant scale unless MSC is firmly committed to its development and provides financial and practical support to schemes to that end.

The CP programme that replaced CEP allowed training but, however, provided no specific funding or development strategy and it showed: none of the young adults we knew were involved in any training.

Finally, the training the Milton group received at the Workshop was only basic. Most left before they had completed the full year because, as well as disliking the atmosphere, they did not feel they were acquiring any new skills.

In sum, just three proper jobs provided practical training, and only one scheme, but although this provided Gary with new skills, there was subsequently no opportunity for him to sell his labour because of the depressed economy of Hillsborough; neither could he set up in business on his own as he could not afford the expensive machinery involved.

Grubb and Lazerson (1981, p.100) wrote of 'the dismal American experience with manpower programmes in the 1960s' and of the continued 'tendency to generate training programmes uncoordinated with the labour market and with the requirements of available jobs'. They listed the consistent criticisms of vocational education over the years (p.96): the tendencies 'to separate lower-class and minority youth from their white, middle-class peers', to provide neither long-nor short term advantage in the labour market, nor 'returns in either earnings or employment rates'. They further argued that for all the rhetoric about flexible and transferable skills, in practice, vocational courses become more and more specific and narrow. Finally, in their view vocational education is an essentially conservative strategy whereby schools or Further Education colleges are expected to produce results in terms of jobs that only industry and commerce have the power to achieve.

The MSC schemes in Britain in the 1980s seem to be repeating the same ineffectual pattens. Even within the range of programmes, some schemes appear to stratify the young workforce, with some such as TOPs or WEEP trying to attract 'higher ability' participants than others, such as Training Workshops. Vocational training therefore is currently sustaining inequality of opportunity as well as providing little prospect of future improvements in the labour market for individuals. The broad-based training followed by the MSC is no golden road to employment. As Jones wrote (1984, p.5): 'Describing skills as "transferable" does not guarantee that these skills will actually be transferred'.

None of the women and men we knew had job security. Even the sixteen in full-time employment had little or no prospects of advancement, although at the end of our fieldwork, Jimi was looking towards in-service training with his department and eventual promotion, and Reg was aiming to move from behind the trade counter into the office. Nine trainees in Shipton were kept on in 1982 after their WEEP schemes, but none of the other young adults who subsequently did schemes found they helped them to get jobs. This was less to do with the women and men themselves or even the quality of the schemes than to do with the local labour markets. Increasingly over the early 1980s, the successful placement rate of schemes was dependent on the buoyancy of local industry and commerce. For instance, even those on a good scheme in the North East would be less likely to find subsequent employment than those on a mediocre scheme in London.

The young adults talked very little about the future. In spite of their using the Careers Service, only three had any sense of career as most middle-class professionals understand the term. All that most of them wanted was a job and they could not even get this, nor were they likely to in the near future.

Differences between shit jobs and govvy schemes

Availability

> If you're sixteen to eighteen, you have the option of YOP or YTS courses. Between eighteen and nineteen, you're stuck and nineteen and over you can retrain on TOPS.   *Winnie*(18)

A prime difference between jobs and schemes for both the women and men was their availability. In 1981, when the youngest in the study left school, YOP schemes were more readily available for them than employment. In 1984, by the end of the fieldwork, their younger sisters and brothers had virtually no option but to go on a YTS scheme:

> Like, we get £21 something on the dole. Because they (the government) cut it down, they (younger siblings) get £14 or something and then that's cut down for living at home, so we are better off. They've cut the dole so low that they've got to go on these schemes   *Winnie*

Once aged eighteen the only schemes available to young adults were TOPS and CP, conditioned with criteria such as having to have been registered unemployed for twelve months previously, and the Young Workers Scheme. None of the women and men would have gone on schemes at any stage had they been able to secure proper jobs, yet all but the three oldest had done so: we knew forty-five MSC graduates, some with multiple MSC qualifications

Method of entry

Of the young adults in employment, those who were not kept on after their WEEP schemes got their jobs through answering adverts in the papers, or occasionally via the Jobcentre, but most frequently through time-hallowed word of mouth, via friends and relations. Some of them even heard about schemes this way, although they subsequently had to be interviewed by the official agency.

   All the schemes were entered through the Careers Service who sent letters summoning the women and men on their books to the office, even though they had nothing to offer but MSC placements.

Pay and Conditions

The collapse of the labour market for young adults transformed their status. The MSC and the government invented new terms and created a new status. Workers on YOP and YTS were no longer employees but 'trainees' and they were not paid a wage but a 'training allowance'. Although a trainee frequently did the same tasks and the same hours as fellow workers, she or he received usually less than half the employee's wage and was not entitled to the same annual leave.

> And you're doing a job that someone's getting £75 a week for, basic.
> I mean, for £25 we were doing that job and some of them were, with
> overtime, coming out with £80 a week. *Annie*

Trainees were, and under YTS largely remain, deprived of most of the benefits and safeguards that protect employees. They had no rights to statutory sick pay nor were they covered by the Health and Safety Act. From January 1984, YTS trainees were given full protection under the latter, although the initiative for the change did not come from the MSC but from the Health and Safety Executive.

Not being employed meant that those on schemes had no means of redress against their 'sponsoring agency' (the new status of employers under the MSC) in practically any sphere. For example, they could do nothing about their allowances if they were docked, about their training if it was inadequate or not provided, or about discipline procedures. Most drastically, they were not covered by Industrial Injury Benefit and in the last three years of YOP, nationally, there were seventeen deaths and over 9000 injuries to trainees (Finn, 1984, p.21).

In October 1982, the Employment Appeals Tribunal ruled that the Youth Opportunities Programme gave no legal protection against race and sex discrimination in the workplace (*The Guardian*, 28 October 1982) and placements tended to reproduce the biases of the ordinary labour market rather than introduce equal opportunities for women and ethnic minorities. YTS trainees are now protected against discrimination in recruitment to the scheme, but are still unprotected once they are participating.

Young adults were therefore more exploited when on schemes than when in jobs, even dead-end ones. In most respects, this was true of TOPS and CP schemes as well as YOP and YTS; and in its subsidy to employers to pay low wages, the Young Workers Scheme only reinforced the short deal dealt to the young by schemes.

Through MSC schemes, the government set the example of overtly denying young workers their basic rights. They offered a package full of promises which never came to anything. At least employers did not pretend to be offering anything else but shit jobs.

Section III
Relationships

5 Family and Neighbourhood

> There's me mam. There's her brother ... with two kids, they live next door. Me mam's other brother lives further down the street and he's got-one, two, three, four, five, six kids. And, er, two brothers are married to two sisters, and their mother lives in the middle of the street. *Reg* (19)

> The estate's got a bad reputation, but it's not so bad ... They make out that you couldn't sit in a pub like this, that you'd get bashed, but you don't . . . if they do fight, it's between themselves, not outsiders. *Tomma* (18)

All the young adults in the study felt an intense sense of belonging to their areas, their own street even; with only four exceptions, all were still living in the area in which they were born, which in most cases was the same area where their parents and grandparents were born and brought up. As Reg described it, he lived surrounded by his relatives. The majority of the young adults had aunts or uncles nearby and, when we asked, they frequently could not count the number of cousins they had. Their family histories were tied into the life of their local neighbourhoods and, in turn, their own lives were shaped by their family circumstances and the neighbourhoods to which they belonged. The young women and men were part and parcel of local culture; they came from it, lived it and, eventually, they would pass it on. In other words, they led the lives traditional to their areas and to their class. What sort of areas did they come from and what type of class?

At one stage, we asked some of them the question: 'Do you think you belong to a particular social class?' Four replied 'not really', Max describing himself instead as 'a normal, everyday person'; two more 'supposed' they were working class. Jane and Tomma were more definite in stating what they were, Tomma describing other classes as 'millionaires ... wish I was, like'; Jane said that class was defined by money, but also by where you lived, 'also the way you're brought up; if your parents are snobby, you are too'. Reg, Carol Ann and Fenwick tentatively thought they were 'round about middle class'. Joe and Scotch decided they were middle class, although Joe originally answered that he was a member of the social class of 'the unemployed'. Poppy said, 'I suppose I'm middle, I'm not dead rich', then 'middle, middle...mam and dad, do you mean? Middle, just average working, poor people!' Another exchange went:

> Asia: I'm middle class, but I'm no snob!
> Carol: Why do you think you're middle class?
> Asia: Well, all my friends are middle class and I seem to get on with them and they don't go out with any snobs or lower grades than middle.

The main impression we gained from the young adults was a lack of class consciousness in national terms, but an acute awareness of different social strata as experienced in their own areas. Scotch announced once: 'the police get up young people's noses all the time. The two groups hate each other – apart from the upper level'.

When Poppy's father went bankrupt in his taxi business, they had to sell their house in central Shipton. They moved to Shadwell Rise and the first council house they had ever lived in. Poppy described the estate:

> It's massive. The bottom end is the rough end and the top end's alright, so. . . on the bottom, when you come by on the bus, there's cardboard against the windows where the window things are smashed and they haven't put them in. And there's paint, spray paint, around by the doors: it's not very nice.

But she went on to say that her mother was much happier there because of the friendly neighbours: 'Where we used to live, people were snobbier. . . I think people think they're better than they are, don't you?' She then explained where she had spent most of her time: 'at the other end, like the council estate, that's where all my friends were'.

Jimi in Shipton told us about two areas he knew. He had moved the mile from Wentworth to Southwood when he was eleven and straightaway he noticed that people were less friendly. He believed this was because the people in Southwood were often those who had 'gone without and made money' and were now 'hard' as a result of having made good themselves. He described Southwood as 'posh' and Wentworth, with affection, as 'the funny farm': he always went drinking there and happily explained: 'The people are great. It's the people who make a place'.

At one Shipton meeting, there was a lengthy conversation about housing in the borough:

> Karl: You know when people are allowed to buy their council house now, wey, not everybody's bought one, but a lot of people think they're better, you know, when they've bought them, 'cos theirs is the only one in the street.
>
> Carly: No, *we* don't think we're better, Karl.
>
> Karl: No, but a lot of people do, like.
>
> Carly: A lot of them in ours don't, although they've had them stonefaced and all new windows in and archways . . .
>
> Winnie: The thing is when they try to sell, they get nothing for them. Nobody will buy them. People don't want to move to a council estate.

Next, the topic of a particular estate came up:

> Winnie: All the, like, bad people-you know what I mean by bad people, rogues and that-I mean, they [the authorities] always think, stick them in one place and get rid of them... At one time the buses or nothing would go through Hedge Croft after a certain time.
>
> Karl: It's obvious if you've got a lot of people who are, you know, supposed to have a bad name, in one area, there's gonna be more trouble.
>
> Carly: They think, stick them all together and get them out the way.
>
> Winnie: But I was working in Hedge Croft and there's some smashing families up there and they've been put there because there's nowhere else to go, but the first opportunity, they get out. I mean, there's some really nice families who'll do anything for you, then there's the real hard cases, you know. And people are worried about their kids, they say: 'Well, we don't want them growing up like that'.

Perceived social divisions were not therefore confined to different areas with specific reputations, but were known to exist within any one estate. It was the same in Milton and Hillsborough. Sharon described one part of the estate in Runswick where she lived: 'Anyway, the glue sniffers are on the roofs and that. You don't go there at night'. Once, the Marlow Dene lads reminisced about how gangs from north of the Dene used to battle with ones from the south. They laughed as they realized how small the whole estate was, as if in growing up, their horizons had broadened a little. A sense of 'us and them' still remained however. They joked about some of their friends' disinclination to open the door to callers. Troy always checked through the fish eye lens in his door to see who was there. He once missed out on the opportunity of free tobacco from a sales representative because he did not open the door to her, thinking that she was checking television licences. All the women and men knew of local people who 'shopped' their neighbours to the police or to the DHSS, although such types were in a minority. People in most areas were prepared to help out. One lad recounted how his street was full of glass fish ornaments after he and a mate had had two hundred to sell. They 'got shot of loads' to neighbours at £1 a time: 'they're in every window!'

Local Families

All the women and men had lived a long time in the same areas, most of them for all their lives. Jane, who had lived in Kent until she was ten-years-old, was not born a Geordie, though her grandparents were from the North. Tess was born in South Africa, but her family returned to Benditch. Jack's family also lived in South Africa for a while: originally from Hillsborough, they came back to settle in Milton. Max was born in Germany. All the others lived where their parents had lived most of their lives and in most cases, their grandparents too. In Marlow Dene, Phil who lived along from Al, Morrow and John, said there had only been two changes of family in their street in the twenty years since it was built. Long-standing residence was usual in all the neighbourhoods we knew.

All the young adults saw aunts, uncles, cousins and grandparents regularly. For a few, this was only for 'Christmas and birthdays', as Karen put it, but for most, bumping into family members was inevitable. Winnie often saw 'Aunt Milly on the bus' for example, and many homes received regular visits, like Rocky's unmarried uncle who came fortnightly for his Sunday dinner. The closest contact was frequently with grandparents. When we asked Julie about hers she explained they had lived in the area for thirty-eight years and then said that she did not visit them 'as often as I should, three or four times a month at the most'. Bernadette, Joe and Stephanie all had experience of their grandmothers living at home. Tess sung her Nanna's praises: 'She's not worn her teeth for twenty-five years ''cos they're uncomfortable, she's half deaf and gets her words all wrong, but she's geet canny... what a laugh!'

Mark in Milton and Fenwick in Shipton saw the most of their grandparents. Mark seemed to live with his grandad as much as with his mother and father. He walked the two miles to his house every day and spent every weekend, Christmas and the New Year with him. When Fenwick was unemployed and her grandmother was in hospital, she called every day to see her, from 11 am to 2 pm and from 3 pm until 5 pm. On one occasion, a doctor was rude and condescending to Fenwick and she asked the charge nurse for his name, declaring that no doctor had the right to treat her or her Nanna that way. She was critical of the decision made by the Social Services about where her grandmother was to be moved to on leaving hospital, as the social worker had only seen the family about it once. Fenwick was of course devasted when her Nanna died. 'It was a good funeral, though', she explained and Reg and Carol Ann, who had been there too, agreed.

A majority of our sample, then, were living in close proximity to large numbers of relatives of all ages who reinforced their ties to the neighbourhood.

Family occupations

Of a total of forty-five families in Shipton, Milton and Hillsborough, in nearly half (twenty-one) the parents were unemployed during the period of the study. The most acute experiences were in Milton and Hillsborough. A majority of the mothers in all three areas were employees in the traditionally female workplaces of offices, shops and factories, frequently known for poor conditions and wages. All of them worked as housewives as well. Jobs included clerk, machinist, cleaner, shop assistant and childminder. Two were made redundant while we knew them and one was disabled. In Hillsborough, the major local employer of women was a food-processing factory, a British division of an American company. Several of the mothers worked there, some on the 'twilight shift' from 5 pm to 9 pm, geared especially to women who had the care of a family all day, but who, at 4.30 pm, could hand over to husbands or other relatives. They were on three month contracts which absolved the firm from most legal obligations to their employees, although some local women had worked there on this basis for over two years.

There was more variation in the fathers' occupations, with more marked differences in employment opportunities between the three areas. Of the twenty-three fathers we knew in Shipton, most were employed for most of the time. A majority were in skilled trades, some in supervisory capacities: an electrician and a plumber with the council, a millwright, a GPO engineer, a glazier, a hospital technician, a lorry driver and several factory machine operators. Others were white collar workers: an electrical engineer, a specialist nursing officer, two sales managers and a managing director of a small local firm; or there were self-employed: a chiropodist and a taxi operator. Six fathers were or became unemployed: one went bankrupt and the rest were made redundant from different factories. Of ten fathers in Milton, only one had a full-time, permanent job, in a factory. Another worked only in the summer months, on a seasonal labouring job, and three were self-employed, as a painter and decorator, a scrap merchant and a builder. Three, a factory worker, a factory manager and a steelworker were made redundant and a fourth, a welder, took voluntary redundancy through ill health. The tenth had been forced to retire years before, disabled with angina. Of eleven fathers in Hillsborough, three were employed at the end of the study: a publican, a security guard and a delivery van driver. Three were laid off work at the shipyards while we knew them. Two who were now dead had been respectively a labourer and a policeman. Three more were long-term unemployed, of seven, eight and ten years. Their previous jobs were as a long distance lorry driver, a painter and decorator and a miner.

The same tale of unemployment close at hand expanded as we looked at sisters and brothers, extended family members and neighbourhoods as a whole. The effects of the recession were always evident. Carly reported that her dad's engineering firm had had to lay off fifteen people a month. She also described how, rather than getting paid in cash, he was getting goods: the previous year they were given six pool tables. She had to have one in her bedroom, 'I was practically sleeping on it!' Thankfully, it was around Christmas time and they were able to sell them all.

Karen related how her Auntie Christine was made redundant from the local Co-op shop, moved to a job at a cash-and-carry store, only to come under threat of redundancy there, at the same time as her husband lost his job. Reg's dad's old firm used to employ 1500 but by 1984 the workforce was down to about 50. On one visit, Charlie gave us a long list of all the Milton firms which had closed since we had last met him, a month before.

A number of sisters and brothers followed the path from school to government scheme to unemployment, a second generation following in the same, well-trodden footsteps. Older sisters were more often reported as 'married' than 'unemployed'. A lot of their time was spent looking after children, others if not their own. Those who had jobs worked as: machinist, nurse, factory worker, clerical civil servant, health service clerk, computer operator, policewoman and post office worker. Five sisters in the Milton group all worked in the local sewing and packing factories. As Pete's dad said of his fifteen-year-old daughter: 'She'll end up on the machines at Toulons like everyone else around here'.

Brothers' jobs reflected local opportunities: van driver, mechanic, factory worker, printer, welder, joiner, painter and decorator, warehouseman, electrician, engineer, and the forces. Jane's brother completed three years apprenticeship as a fitter and turner, but he had worked for less than twelve months when he was made redundant.

It was more the exception than the rule that young adults had brothers or sisters living away from the North East. Fenwick's older brother moved to London where he had one or two jobs before settling with a painting and decorating firm. A friend of his though returned to the North because 'There were too many Pakis down there'. Jimi's brother also went to London, but returned; Annie's traveller brother was in Lincolnshire and Tess and Al's brothers were in the forces, stationed in Plymouth and in Germany. Five of Shuk's nine brothers and sisters lived in Yorkshire, the Midlands and the South. With these few exceptions, the young adults had little knowledge of what it was like to live and work south of the Tees or north of the Tyne.

In contrast, they knew their home areas well and local networks could play a vital role in a young person's fortune where jobs were concerned. Morrow heard of his CP scheme through an uncle. John got his eight week Christmas job thanks to his girlfriend Barbara's dad. On another occasion he referred to a contact as 'Me lass' mother's sister's husband'! Four of Reg's relatives were all employed at the same local newsagent. After a year's unemployment, Jimi finally secured temporary contracts as a care assistant thanks to his mother still being in touch with her old place of work. Winnie said that she could get a job at the store where her mother and aunt were employed, except that she did not want to work in a shop. Theresa's mother complained at Toulons that all the other employees' daughters had got jobs except for hers and soon afterwards her younger daughter, Jeanette, started there. This factory actually included on its application form a question about whether any other family members worked for the firm. When we asked Theresa whether this was to help them choose workers who would be under their parents' eye, she did not believe so. She claimed that Jeanette acted up quite a lot, but that it did not reflect badly on her mother who was still working there after twenty-three years, despite her arthritis and bronchial trouble.

In short, the practice of securing jobs through whom you know and not what you know was alive and well and in evidence in all three areas. There were differences between families, however: if, for instance, like Stephanie, no else in the family was employed, and there was little contact with neighbours, this substantially reduced the potential number of contacts.

Family life

It was only the unusual or stressful events in family life that tended to
be reported, which makes presenting a balanced picture difficult. If,
however, no news is to be interpreted as good news, then for the greater
part of the two-and-a-half years of fieldwork, the majority of the women
and men enjoyed normal, relatively happy family lives. It was not
always easy to follow the threads of who was who:

> My dad was working on the trains or sommat, and he met my
> mam, and he told her that he didn't get on with his dad, or
> sommat . . . He went there when he was fourteen, fifteen. He was
> going to marry me aunty – it's great this one – but for some reason he
> married my ma. He's got one sister that he never sees. No brothers,
> and his father died two years ago . . . I never met any of his family . . .
> My mam's ma lived in Preston. She married seven times . . . They all
> died apart from one who she divorced, and she married him again,
> and then she died . . . It's really complicated, my family!   *Reg*

Naturally, the families varied in their basic make-up. Tess' and Marie's
families in Hillsborough were large: each had eight brothers and
sisters. Shuk was one of ten, but this was unusual for Shipton where the
next biggest family we knew was Fenwick's (five) and all the others
were four or under. In Milton, there were slightly bigger families
overall, between two and six, and when we later met Rob we learnt he
was one of fifteen. Eight of the forty-five families we knew had single
parents.

Space in the family home varied as a consequence of the number of
children. We specifically asked twenty of the young people whether
they shared a bedroom. This was in April 1983 when most of them were
eighteen or over. Seven of the twelve who had their own rooms had only
recently stopped sharing. Eight still shared with a sister or a brother.

We were only able to record details of family health when it was bad
and happened to be reported. It is worth noting at this point the general
age of the parents in the study. The oldest was Stewart's mother who
was seventy-two when he was twenty-four, and some we knew were in
their fifties and sixties, but the majority were in their forties. Despite
this, a wide range of ailments and handicaps was reported.
Stephanie's father was forty-six when he took his voluntary redundancy from the steelworks because of his heart condition. Karl's father
had died of a heart attack when he was forty-seven. Other parents,
although not necessarily the younger ones, between them suffered with
diabetes, bronchitis, arthritis, depression, cancer, angina, nervous
breakdown, stress and one mother was confined to a wheelchair after a
stroke. Illness among other family members included anorexia

nervosa, meningitis, alcoholism, epilepsy and agoraphobia. The greatest incidence of these were reported among the families in Milton.

(a) *Living at home*

Carol: Would you move out if you could?
Poppy: Definitely.
Scotch: No.
Poppy: Lads seem more settled, though, don't they?
Karl: There's a lot of things to do if you move out, like cooking and all that, cleaning up and things like that.

In the two-and-a-half years that we knew them the only young adults to leave their parents' home permanently did so because they got married. The one exception to this was Carol Ann who went to live with Reg before they were engaged. Apart from those involved with partners, some others had spells away from home: Winnie left for a nanny's job, but it only lasted two days; Joe was eventually accepted by the forces; Tony's job as a contract welder took him away from Shipton regularly; Clara, Smiler and Micky were all thrown out of their homes at different periods, Tess spent a lot of time away with the youth project, Troy's first employment in four years took him away from Marlow Dene and Pete travelled as a roadie with a band and spent six weeks in London looking for a job. The majority, however, were still based in their parents' home at the end of the fieldwork in 1984. By this time, they were aged between eighteen and twenty-six.

It was traditional for young adults to live at home until they were married or found a job elsewhere. In their communities, few went on to higher education with its opportunities for independent accommodation and none from our sample did so. Even if they wanted to move out, the restrictions of low income and the low chances of being allocated anywhere to live were binding:

You can't really afford it on social security and no job. *Heather*.

We're not independent. It's not something you really think about. *Morrow*

Poppy: That's the council. They've got a list of all the places nobody else wants.

Carly: You're only given so many choices and then if you don't take anything, you're off it.

Winnie: They go and unboard a house for you or sommat.

The average weekly contribution the women and men made towards their board and keep at home was £10, whether they were in employment or not. Families were thus supporting their young adults even before extra 'subs' were given out, as they were regularly:

> I just borrow off me mam. I borrowed fourteen quid off my dad ages ago and he just says, 'oh, pay back, you know, after so long'; so he might get it back near Christmas. Now if it was my sister, he wants it off her straightaway, but off me he never really bothers, he'll lend us anything really. *Winnie*

> Julie's Mam: You'll have to ask your dad if you can borrow some.

> Julie: Well, I asked you because I know my dad'll say no.

Families were the most ready source of financial support available to young adults. After a year-and-a-half of talking about going south to look for a job, Poppy finally said of her home with her Mam and Dad: 'I'm too comfortable there.'

When we specifically asked: 'When do you think you will move away from your family and why?', some of the answers were:

> I wouldn't like to say, if I had enough money now I would . . . it's never too early . . . It's not good being at home too long from both points of view, parents and children. *Jimi*

> Only if I get a live-in job, like a nanny's job. I won't move too far away, not till I'm a bit older. If it wasn't too far, like Southwood [five miles], I'd travel back home. I'd go abroad as a nanny as long as they spoke English. *Winnie*

> Soon. I feel the time has come to become independent. *Fenwick*

Tess' reply, however, suggested the gap in understanding between her and us, the questioners. She simply said: 'What a weird question'. In her experience, at seventeen, you did not plan to move: home was with your parents. It was not a matter that needed discussion.

Exactly how young adults felt about living at home in the years after they had left school depended to a large extent on the quality of relationships within the household. One or two commented on age-old causes for differences: Carly said there were still arguments 'over daft things, not hanging clothes up, messing up the bathroom'. But generally the conversations we had with the women and men suggested that gradually most were being accorded adults status at home.

There were always ups and downs, however. Smiler's situation belied his name. He was eighteen when we first knew him. Whenever we met, he talked of conflict with his parents, over his drinking and smoking and what they considered to be his laziness over job hunting. At one meeting, he announced, 'I've been given my marching orders' and claimed his parents had given him three weeks to get out. He went to live with a friend, but it did not work out as he had hoped and he spent the next few months living between his parents' home and various mates' flats. He returned home once to learn that his dad, a secondhand car dealer, had sold the car he had given Smiler as a birthday present.

Clara's dad locked her out of the house at one stage. She went to live with her friend Jean at her grandparents', where she had to share a bed with Jean and pay board. Clara was also expected to be in by 11 pm, although she was eighteen. She hated it. Eventually her father, who had been badly affected by the death of his wife, consented to Clara moving back home. She confided that she had cried when she was away and that she had missed her sisters and brothers, saying, 'You think you're big when you move out, but you're not'.

Other tensions in the young adults' homes were usually attributable to something specific. Asia once reported that she had had more rows when she was unemployed because her parents had gone on at her about finding a job. Jane's brother and Morrow received similar treatment for the same reason. More often than not, though, parents seemed to understand how few jobs were available for young adults and that it was not their fault they could not get one. After all, many of the parents, or relations, were experiencing the same.

Generally, relationships with parents appeared to mellow gradually over time. Jimi and Scotch were both positive about family relations. Jimi put his view in retrospect when we asked about parental authority: 'They have the right amount, mine anyway . . . I never felt that they were over the top . . . they were always right, at least I think that now, even if I didn't at the time'. Scotch thought his were 'concerned about my drinking when I was fifteen and sixteen, but not now. Mam always says before I gan out: "Don't drink too much".' He said he appreciated 'Just the way me mother's brought me up and the way we get on'. Tomma, when seventeen, said rather more phlegmatically, 'They're just me advisers'.

The men, however, seemed to come to this relaxed situation more easily than the women:

> I got a key before I was sixteen. As long as I told my mam where I was gannin, I could gan where I wanted. *Scotch*, 17.

> As you get older, some parents find you having more freedom hard to accept. My dad's beginning to. *Julie*, 18.

In every aspect to living at home, there were clear sex differences.

(b)   *Division of labour in the home*

> It's different for brothers; boys can't do the housework.   *Theresa*, 19.

Although she made this remark, Theresa was not totally sympathetic
to her older brother when he came in from his job at twenty past four
and expected his mother or one of his sisters to get his tea for him. All
the women had jobs and did not get home until after him. When
Theresa married, she admitted she did not like doing the washing or
ironing. She refused the offer from a neighbour of a free washing
machine: it would have prevented her from going round to her mam's
house to use the automatic.

We asked the young adults whether they helped at home and if there
was any difference in the help given by sisters and brothers. It emerged
clearly that the women did the most housework, and if they did not,
there were consequences:

> I don't help a lot, but I feel guilty about it.   *Fenwick*

Julie recounted at one meeting how the previous night her sixteen-
year-old brother was supposed to have looked after the younger ones,
but he disappeared after tea and Julie had had to stay in with them.
Winnie talked of her brother:

> He used to do the hoovering, but only if nobody was in. He used to do
> it smashing if no one was in, but as soon as someone came in, that
> was that. They don't like to be seen doing it.

On a visit to Mark's home, Carol was told how he never did
anything in the house. To prove it, he and his mother told the tale of
how once, when his parents were out, the power had gone off. Mark put
50 pence in the meter, but nothing happened. He had never done it
before and had put the coin in the old gas meter when they were only
connected for electricity!

There were exceptions to the rule, of course. Interestingly, they were
more evident in the parents than in the young adults. Several of the
dads did shopping and cooking. Poppy reported a few months after her
dad's business had collapsed that he was happier than he had been in a
long time, but 'he's gone a bit funny: he's started doing lots of things
around the house like cooking and cleaning which he never used to do'.
Occasionally some of the younger ones would break the stereotype:
Bernadette said she hardly did anything; Rocky did the hoovering
regularly and Reg claimed 'I like housework, I like to hoover up and do
my own ironing'.

Overall, however, whether employed or not, the men helped 'once in a
blue moon' as Joe put it, and the women, in Winnie's words, 'wash
dishes, clothes, hoover, dust – do something every day'.

(c)   *Daughters and fathers*

Relationships between daughters and their fathers were the most frequently mentioned of all the family relationships referred to by the young adults. We did not seek information specifically in this area, but it emerged as a topic as the women talked about its effects on their lives. They were used to discussing relationships in general. When we asked Tomma if he ever talked over problems with his family, he replied he did not, 'They just think you're stupid'.

One of the first to mention her relationship with her father was Annie, who at the time lived with her older sister and her father in a travellers' caravan sited just outside Thealby. In a general discussion with the Milton group at the Training Workshop, Annie, then seventeen, said that she had problems with her dad who wanted her always to be in by ten at night. What she found ridiculous was that if anybody came to the door to report that she had been fighting, he would defend her, but if he ever heard anything about her staying out or smoking or drinking, then 'he just goes mad'. In the same discussion, Clara said that she too had to be in by ten o'clock, and her brother by nine thirty, but he was thirteen, four-and-a-half years younger than her.

Later, at an individual meeting, Annie confided that she did not fight with her dad, but then they did not speak much either. She thought her sister, who was quieter than her, got on better with him. Sarah had asked Annie to help decide on a pub in which to meet some of the others from the Training Workshop the following week for a Christmas drink. Annie thought of The Farmers Arms, the middle one of three pubs situated along the main road from Thealby to Runswick. As they were outside, Sarah suggested going into the pub to discuss a venue. Annie promptly said 'Father would kill us', meaning if he found her in a pub at dinner time. The chances of him finding out were strong as she knew her dad was himself in the Market Tavern down the road and her boyfriend's dad was probably in the Farmers at that very moment.

When we first knew Asia in Shipton, she was seventeen-and-a-half. She was one of the young adults who admitted to having rows at home. One night she asked her father if she could stay at a friend's house. He said no. Asia lost her temper and swore at him furiously. Her father swore back and they had a blazing argument. It ended with Asia stomping upstairs. Not long after this, Asia told her father to 'fuck off' and he'd hit her around the ear. She said it was the only time he had ever done so. On another occasion, Asia was in an argument with both of her parents about her style of dress, but it was her father who started complaining that she never wore a skirt. In fact she wore one all day at work in the doctors' practice, and was only too pleased to change into jeans when she got home.

In August 1982, Shuk mentioned that she had not spoken to her father for two weeks. In April 1984, it was her friend Asia who told us that Shuk and her father, who lived under the same roof, had not spoken to each other for nearly a year. Shuk found it painful to talk about her situation and she never explained to us the cause of the silence.

To celebrate her eighteenth birthday, Carly went out with friends to a nightclub in Newcastle. She was very late home and the following day, her father asked her where she had been. When she told him, he said that she should not go to 'places like that, they're not suitable'. Carly pointed out that she was now old enough to go to nightclubs, but for a while her dad stopped speaking to her. Over a year later, it seemed her father had not so much changed his attitude as Carly had learnt how to avoid his censure. At one meeting, Poppy complimented Carly on her tee-shirt. Carly explained that it was actually her dad's vest and she laughed as she said she had another one which was much more low cut: her dad said she could not go out in it, so she wore a jumper on top until she was out of the house!

It was Jacki who described her father as protective towards her. His protection consisted of changing channels on the television whenever anything even vaguely sexual was shown and objecting if Jacki's mother swore in front of her. Jacki told once how she had tried to stop her dad from collecting her in central Shipton after a night out because she did not want him to know she had been to see a male stripper: her mum knew and kept teasing her that she would tell her dad where to pick her up!

Relationships between daughters and fathers arose as an issue because, while there was variation between families and ages, broadly the women were subject to much more control and for longer periods than were the men.

Neighbourhood life

Just as family circumstances and customs helped to shape the lives of the young women and men, so did the settings and traditions of the neighbourhood to which they belonged.

Weddings, of which there were five during the period of our study, illustrated the ties between individuals, families and community, and the traditions which persist over and above the individuals involved. For instance, Morrow was best man to his brother John even though normally they chose not to see each other. Similarly, Stephanie had her sister Jenny as first bridesmaid, although usually they had little time for each other and used to argue. The account in Chapter 2 of John and Barbara's wedding reception showed what an essentially local affair it was, family, friends and neighbours coming together in celebration. The purpose was to rejoice publicly in the change of status of the couple and every guest put heart and soul into the occasion. Carol Ann and Reg's engagement party, which we all attended, was the same. It seemed not to matter that towards the end of the evening neither Carol Ann nor Reg actually knew half of the people there. Someone would know these guests and the more the merrier.

The length of residence of most of the families in Shipton, Milton and Hillsborough was testament to the basic stability and unchanging nature of the communities in which the young adults lived. Many traditions, such as collecting coal from the slagheaps and securing jobs through local contacts, were long established and simply inherited by successive generations. Others, such as the service provided by the pawn shops reopening in Benditch, were thought to have died, but seemed to be returning. There were other signs that the neighbour-hoods were not as settled as they once used to be. Fenwick, for instance, remarked on the changes in her street in her lifetime. She said when she was small, there used to be a lot of activities arranged locally, like cycling and fishing trips, and street parties, but now, she said, a lot of people had moved away or grown up and 'nothing really goes on very much any more'. She thought this applied especially to New Year celebrations: once upon a time, everyone in her street had neighbours into their houses and they celebrated all night. Now this just did not happen.

On one of our visits to Sharon in Runswick, her mother described how when she had been young, the boards outside all the factories in the area had always had vacancies displayed, now there were none. She also commented on the single corner shop on the nearby estate; there used to be several, but they had gradually all closed down. Brenda in Marlow Dene had the same problem when the local grocer's shop closed. Although the newsagents then began to stock the odd tin. she found she had to travel the mile to Benditch to get all she wanted. It was in Benditch one day that we saw another sign of the times, a removal van on the back of which was written. 'Established 1847. Telephone Nos: Newcastle, Jersey, Benidorm'. At least some people had been able to widen their horizons in recent years.

These then were some aspects of neighbourhood life that arose in our observations of and conversations in the three areas. Had we been in contact with groups of mothers or middle aged men, we would have learnt of other facets of local living. As it was, in our discussions with young adults, two topics came to the fore. They were drinking and trouble with the law.

(a) *Drinking*

The strongest tradition followed by the young adults we knew was
drinking alcohol. The culture of drink was all around them and hard to
avoid even if they wanted to. Often, they had first been introduced to
alcohol by their parents or relatives. As throughout society, it was a
central feature of family celebrations, indeed of any celebration. At
Carol Ann and Reg's engagement party, we witnessed Hazel,
Fenwick's sister of fourteen, being bought halves of lager all night by
her sisters and their friends. Fenwick only sounded slightly bothered
when she commented they should stop because she had promised to
bring Hazel home sober: she probably knew that her mam would
understand. Reg described how his brothers had been the first to get
him drunk and Tony still went drinking with his dad at the working
men's club. He looked forward especially to their summer day-trips out
when they took beer to drink on the coach on the way to visit clubs in
other areas. He had joined these trips at the age of fifteen.

Nearly all the women and men participated in the custom as soon as
they could, most starting to visit pubs between the ages of twelve and
fifteen. As with most things, the young adults were involved in
drinking to various degrees. One or two, like Winnie and Mark, hardly
ever took any alcohol. Mark thought drinking and smoking were 'a
waste of money'. Sometimes they would consciously curb their intake,
like Joe and Charlie when in training, Bert and Jack who had stomach
problems or Smiler and Reg when they had been overdoing the
drinking. A large number, however, drank as often and as deeply as
they could afford to. This did not happen often because of their limited
finances but, whether in jobs or not, most of the women and men would
save what they could for enjoying themselves at the end of the week.
Morrow explained the importance of these occasions for him, 'If you're
only out once a week, you don't want to spoil it by talking about being
on the dole and getting depressed all over again'.

Drink is not only a means of escape to the young. After the death of
his wife, Clara's dad seemed to spend more and more time out at the
club in the evening. John and Morrow's dad, on being made redundant
after fifteen years at the shipyards, began by drinking morning, noon
and night, although a few weeks later, John reported he had eased off a
little.

There was a widespread, tacit acceptance of underage drinking
locally. When on the trip to the Peaks, the young un's, who were mostly
under sixteen, had to send their oldest-looking member into the pub to
bring drinks out to them, but at home, in Benditch, the publicans would
serve them all. The young women and men knew their local haunts
well. A group in Shipton reported that the pub we met them in had lost

its licence four times because of underage drinking. (Asia, a regular, was once offered a barmaid's job-when she was still only sixteen!) Fenwick, Carol Ann and Karl described how important it was not to panic if the police appeared, but just to sit calmly: 'If you don't look guilty, you don't get stopped'. None of them had ever been caught by the police. Theresa in Milton had other tactics: she kept a soft drink under the table ready for a swop should the need arise.

The men usually drank pints of Scotch bitter and the women either shorts, like whisky and orange, vodka and lime, Cinzano and lemonade, or sweet cider and blackcurrant. When they wanted to get drunk quickly, they switched to concoctions such as Snakebites (lager and cider), Black Russians (Tia maria, vodka and Coke) or a Brown Ale cocktail (a slice of orange and a cherry on a stick in a glass of ale which was drunk through a straw). Karl said that he simply moved on to gin and tonic, while Smiler's favourite was a pint of cider topped up with Pernod. The importance of drinking to the local community was reflected in the large number of words used for being drunk, including 'stottin', 'mortal', 'pissed' and 'smashed'.

Although some of the women we knew drank as heavily as the men, (if not in quantity, then in terms of net result), notions of gender and appropriate sex roles were bound up in drinking. Often, for example, the Marlow Dene lads took some persuading to accept being bought drinks by Sarah or Carol. Annie in Milton described how when she first went to pubs, she had drunk lager and lime 'because it was the only drink I knew that girls drank'. Carol Ann reported that if she and Reg were out with friends, then she would get drunk, but if they were out together, Reg would be the one: she could then take care of him. Carol Ann: 'You should have seen the time I had getting him home on Saturday night. He wanted to jump off the bridge . . . and ride on top of a car!' Reg had had twelve pints, 'I enjoyed mesel, I enjoyed it!'

Drinking was principally supported and encouraged by friends. Nearly all the women and men who drank did so in groups when they went out to pubs, clubs, discos and parties. The main exception was Karl who, on one of our weekends away, sat in a pub alone drinking his way through the money he had allocated himself.

There existed a strong pressure on men particularly to drink heavily and keep up with their mates. Simon recounted how he found that he was incapable of taking the volume of beer consumed by his friends. He switched to cider instead and drank less. 'They know its stronger and say nowt', he explained. The tradition of heavy drinking, however, permeated the local culture and the women were drawn into it as well. Asia, for instance, reported that both she and Shuk had been 'out cold' after too much alcohol. When we mentioned the health aspects of drinking, Asia said that she had recently cut down her consumption of

cider and black from about fifteen halves – 'to ten or eleven'. As she said
this, it seemed to occur to her that she had not in fact cut down as much
as she thought. She said she had no difficulty in drinking a lot: it just
slipped down.

Asia, like many of the young adults, did not accept that she drank too
much for her health. She and others gave little attention to a Health
Education Council campaign during 1982 which used David Bellamy,
a local celebrity, to encourage young people not to spoil a good thing by
drinking too much. But his advice to 'stick to two or three pints two or
three times a week' was laughed to scorn by most of the young men. We
asked Asia if she thought she might drink less in the future. At first she
said no, but on reflection considered that she might if she 'had a house
and children' when she was about thirty. Meanwhile, like so many
others, she was simply out to enjoy herself: 'I live for today'.

Simon described himself as 'mortal for a week' over Christmas and
the New Year. Asia said that during the same period she had been
'absolutely stottin'.' She laughed as she declared, 'I was saying
desperate things, like "Give us a Britvic"!' With few exceptions, most of
the young adults we knew equated celebrations with getting drunk,
and some with as getting as drunk as they possibly could; they did not
eat in order to speed up the process. At a party for the Shipton group at
Reg's house two lads, having already been to a pub, arrived with
twenty-four cans of beer and proceeded to consume these together with
some whisky in order to 'get absolutely mortal'. According to Carol
Ann, 'Their idea of a good night out is to get really pissed'. Bert arrived
saying, 'I'm going to get smashed out of my brain tonight'. The evening
ended with one lad becoming 'rubber ducked and talking to Hughie'
(being sick), and one lass having to stay with Reg and Carol Ann after
spending hours with her head in a bucket.

Asia, Jimi and Karl were among the heaviest drinkers we knew. Asia
and Jimi told us about trips across the border into Scotland, where the
attraction was the longer opening hours of the pubs and hotels. When
Jimi and his friend first discovered that the Scottish pubs 'never
closed', they installed themselves in one for the day and downed about
twenty pints each. Jimi reported that it took him two days to recover.
Asia and her boyfriend's visit to Coldstream with some friends
followed the same pattern. She claimed that the two of them in 1983
spent £160 in two days, virtually all on drink, from 11 am on the
Saturday to 11 pm on the Sunday. They only left the pub to change their
clothes. They just sat and drank, played pool, cards, dominoes, darts
and talked for the whole time, but ate very little. The weekend was
regarded as such a success that they planned to return the following
year.

(b) *Trouble*

In the neighbourhoods from which the young adults came there was a sense in which crime was as traditional a pastime as drinking or keeping pigeons. It was there, it went on and everybody knew about it, in the area if not in their personal experience. A number of those we knew were victims of crime in the locality, like Max who was beaten up by lads from Runswick and John and Barbara whose house was burgled. Several of the lads had had their motorbikes stolen, like Pidge and Phil's brother in Marlow Dene, and Bert in Shipton. Karen's boyfriend, Nick had had his taken three times and Scotch's was vandalized when he left it outside while visiting his aunt.

Identifying strongly with an area led some young people into their first brushes with the law, as when gang fights took place. At one meeting, Asia described how years before 'all of Redwood School came down' to her area and she had joined in the extensive fighting which involved 'chains and the lot'. Jimi and Smiler in Southwood talked at length about a local gang, the Wentworth Boot Boys, who were having running battles with groups from other areas. Smiler thought that the fights began when opposing gangs stood at the end of their territories and 'hoyed' bricks at each other. Jimi summed up the gang's reputation as 'canny rough'.

Drink, of course, often helped young adults get into trouble. Charlie in Milton was once in the dock, having been arrested with a friend after a fight with a group of rockers from a neighbouring village. They were both bound over to keep the peace. When Carol and Sarah asked about the court appearance, how worried he had been, whether his parents had gone with him or not (they had not), Charlie seemed unperturbed. When we asked about the fight, he simply smiled his shy smile and said that he could not remember much about it as he had been drunk at the time. It was March and in fact it was only the second time he had been out drinking since the New Year.

The Marlow Dene lads once described themselves as getting 'happy drunk' as opposed to 'violent drink', meaning that when they were together, they simply shared high spirits with trusted friends and did not look for fights when under the influence. When out individually, however, it was sometimes harder to avoid trouble. On one of the last occasions we saw Al he had drunk too much on Saturday night (eight pints and half a bottle of spirits) and had got into a fight. Al denied that it was really a fight: 'we were so drunk we were missing each other!' He obviously meant it when he said 'I showed mesel up'.

A pub was often the scene of trouble and the location of the pub could affect the young people's reaction to a fight. Rocky described how one evening in the town he had witnessed a lass 'bottle' another lass. He was shocked at what he saw, but he decided not to intervene because he did not know any of the people there. Conversely, Karen reported that her boyfriend usually knew the locals who got involved in fighting and would simply say 'leave them to it'.

Just as fights at different times and in different places were common, so were occasional misdemeanours and encounters with the police. They were part of, if not everyday life, then life as the young adults had come to expect it. The culture of their neighbourhoods included run-ins with the law as a matter of course. If the women and men were not involved themselves, they knew people who were or knew of them. The gap between our understanding of such experiences and that of the young adults was illustrated during the fieldworld on one occasion in particular.

Early one morning Sarah was woken by the telephone. It was a CID Inspector: 'Were you driving your car in Hillsborough at 11.50 am last Tuesday with three men passengers?' He explained that the investigation was being made because a security van driver had reported Sarah's car as following him and there had recently been three attacks on such vans in the area. Sarah had in fact been out that morning with Al, John and Troy to distribute sponsor forms for a fund raising event for the youth project. None of them could remember even seeing a security van. Sarah's notes from the telephone conversation ran:

> I was so taken aback that it took me some time to gain my ground and to maintain that I did not want to divulge the lads' names if possible as it could affect my research with them. The inspector's tone was courteous, the remarks like 'For all I know, you could be researching the biggest criminals in Hillsborough' made me feel that his attitude was as much one of 'guilty until proved innocent' rather than the other way round.

> Afterwards, I was so concerned to see the lads before any policeman might trace them and appear on their doorstep that I drove to Hillsborough that afternoon. As I got into the Marlow Dene estate, I saw John walking in the opposite direction and pulled over to speak to him. As soon as I explained the call I'd had, he, like me, could hardly believe it. After being surprised, John was calm, even amused and his reaction was a great relief to me. He said, 'It's great when they're out and you've done nowt. I love it'. He also said I was welcome to give his name and address and did not seem bothered by this at all. Later, when I saw them, Troy and Al had similar reactions.

> General points about the incident:
> One, the reality of potential crime in Hillsborough and, two, the police intervention that it brings about, especially no doubt because the lads were well-built and in their twenties. I wondered whether

the van driver would have reported my car if it had been full of women, for instance.

When discussing the incident afterwards, we all agreed that Sarah's reaction showed exactly the difference between middle-class women who have very little interaction with the police and working-class young men who are used to the standard methods of investigation and questioning used by the police.

Most men and a few of the women had experience of being moved on by the police: 'we used to be, always, for hanging round in a group and making a noise'. This was Jane the laboratory technician: a quiet mannered and studious woman, she did not seem a typical candidate for having the strong, negative views on the police that she held. When sitting with friends in a local park once, she had been searched by the police and her arms checked, presumably for signs of needles. She described how her brother had been stopped many times driving late at night just because he looked young. Sometimes he would get their mother to drive with him to drop his girlfriend off at her home so that she could drive back to prevent him being stopped. Jane explained that part of the reason for this was that he drove a small van and said of the police 'They associate a van and a young lad with somebody pinching something.' She added 'some policemen are "worky tickets" [who try it on] and try to provoke you into an argument. It's up to how much you can put up with'.

For some young adults, however, there was less emotional and social distance between them and the police than we supposed. Both Al's and Jackie's dads had themselves been in the police force and Tony's sister, with whom he got on well, was a policewoman. Karen and Joe had friends who were policemen. Jimi talked about the police one evening when he suspected that a man sitting in the corner with a drink of Newcastle Brown Ale was an off-duty policeman: 'I don't know, there's a feeling you get off them'. He then described one of the funniest sights he had ever seen: a woman inspector from the Drugs Squad had come into a pub dressed as a hippy. She had long hair, a patterned smock and a bandana round her forehead. When Jimi looked down, though, he saw that she had on dark blue tights and flat, sensible shoes!

Breaking the law – whether knowingly or inadvertently – was an almost exclusively male group activity. Many of the men had found themselves on the wrong side of the law while hanging around the streets or riding motorbikes with their mates. They believed that they were apprehended by the police precisely because they were young. Jack commented:

> They pick on young people on bikes and in cars. I go fishing with
> one or two coppers and they seem all right. Most of them pick on

young people in Runswick as well as here. You can be sitting in the
market place and they let cars without lights go by, but then a lad
on a bike goes by and they're after him right away.

Several reported that the police picked on young adults 'especially
bikers'.

Some of the men had broken the law, mostly committing offences
involvings car and motorbikes: speeding, underage driving, and
'driving without due care and attention' were the most common. Other
crimes included being drunk and disorderly, breach of the peace,
taking and driving away, theft, burglary (Jacki's boyfriend stole from
a butchers' and sold the meat to his mother), trespass, breaking and
entering, receiving stolen goods (Theresa's husband was fined for this:
he had unwittingly bought a stolen watch from his brother), illegal
possession of firearms (Jimi was cautioned for trying to sell World War
I bullets given to him by his grandfather) and smoking cannabis (none
were charged with this offence).

Most of those who were found guilty of these various crimes were
fined, but some of our sample had experienced 'borstal, community
service, suspended sentences, and one had served eighteen months in
prison for grevious bodily harm when he was eighteen. Only one
woman had been convicted - once for underage drinking and once for
fighting - and she received a fine on both occasions.

We learnt about these offences incidentally. They would simply come
up in conversation from time to time as when Bernadette started to
confide in Carol about the details of her boyfriend's court appearances
and her anxieties about the effects on their relationship. Usually,
however, we were most likely to hear about offences because of the
financial demands fines were making on the lads' income, or because
they would be mentioned in general conversation about friends, family
and experiences while still at school.

There was general agreement about why so many young men broke
the law: 'knocking about with lads who broke into people's houses and
shops'. Those like Jack who wanted to stop offending found new lads to
associate with: 'That was what really made me change, not the court'.
Why did they think most delinquents (even the most persistent)
stopped offending when they reached their late teens or early twenties?
'Because they learn about lasses, as long as she's not too expensive',
suggested Joe. 'They get married and settle down', thought Karl and
both Poppy and Carly agreed: 'Young people just grow out of it ... they
get involved in a steady relationship and find all those things they read
about in women's magazines'. Scotch and Pete produced different
reasons; the former thought: 'It's just like a craze when they're younger
... just like a fashion. It just becomes boring like everything else. They

do it 'cos they don't have money'. Pete argued: 'Trying to fight the police, you realize as you grow older . . . you can't win. You're fighting a losing battle'.

More generally, however, among those who had come into contact with the police, there seemed to be a sense of harrassment coupled with the need to learn to live with the police who were ever present in their neighbourhoods and so likely at some point to touch their lives. Jack summed up his feelings: 'You canna do nowt, they're always there'.

The young adults enjoyed recounting the ins and outs of any incident in their area and knew the local characters who were constantly in trouble with the police. Mark remembered a visit to the pub when a customer had ordered a round of drinks and tipped a pile of fifty pence pieces onto the bar to pay for them: everyone realised he had just 'done' the gas meter. And in a conversation one day about private videotapes, Reg informed us that he got blue movies from the local ice-cream man. Joe talked of a lad he remembered, but had not seen for years. 'He smashed a traffic warden's leg who was giving him a parking ticket. He used to shoot birds in his garden and shoot at people. He was sent to a loony bin by the courts. He set fire to his own motorbike'. Scotch talked of a lad who had 'done everything, knocking off cars, pinching anything. He was inside when he was fourteen. He's only seen three Christmases since then and now he's twenty two. Once he was taken in on Christmas Day'.

One afternoon as Sarah dropped the lads off in Marlow Dene, they pointed out 'Little Dave', a diminutive figure in the distance who was carrying what seemed to be half-empty bags of coal into a maisonnette. He was accompanied by a tall friend who stood at the end of the path, evidently on the look-out. The lads shouted across to tease the men into thinking they had been spotted. Troy explained that among other things, Little Dave was the local (unofficial) coal merchant. John had heard that Little Dave and his mate had recently sold some bags of coal and gone back the same night to steal them out of the shed.

Neighbourhood life was full of such characters and goings on, and in this context, brushes with the law could often be hard to avoid. Both Jacki and Bernadette, for instance, thought that the endless free time that unemployment created for their boyfriends had a lot to do with the trouble they got into. Some of the lads in Milton made the same connection; however, in Hillsborough, or at least in Marlow Dene and Benditch, as we understood life there, both unemployment and petty crime seemed to be so established and so part and parcel of daily life that it would have been virtually impossible to separate out the effects of each. Both, like family links and drinking, had become traditional aspects of surviving in the locality.

Commentary

The conventional wisdom among the leading commentators on working-class neighbourhoods (Young and Wilmott 1957; R. Roberts 1971; P. Cohen 1972; and Clarke *et al.* 1979) is that there has been a gradual decline in the spirit of such communities since the nineteenth century. The argument, which we have based on Philip Cohen's (1972) analysis because it is so widely known, runs very briefly like this: areas such as the east end of London, although never an undifferentiated and unchanging community, had real strengths in its social cohesion and indigenous leadership. These qualities sprang from the daily, harmonious rhythms of family life, neighbourhood and employment; they were traced by Cohen to the 'extended kinship networks', which almost became small communities in their own right, loyalty to a closely-defined area such as one street, and having a local job in a small, family concern into which son followed father.

Such self-supporting communities began to disintegrate as a result of the massive programmes of 'urban renewal', the first phase of which decanted families from closely-integrated terraced houses in the centre of cities to multistorey flats on the outskirts. Men now travelled to their jobs and women to supermarkets, thus breaking the earlier links between local firms, corner shops and home. Further fragmentation within the working-class came with the arrival of immigrants from the West Indies and Pakistan who were forced, through local housing policies and discriminations, into the multi-occupation of large, old houses (Rex and Moore, 1967). The local economy was transformed from family businesses run by skilled artisans to either automized factories or service industries. Within one generation, the extended families had been dispersed, the function of the street as a form of 'communal space' had ended, and 'the issues of the workplace were no longer experienced as directly linked to community issues' (p.45).

In the social vacuum thus created, there emerged a whole string of youth subcultures (from the Teddy boys to the Punks) whose members were trying, according to Cohen, to recapture the feelings of an integrated community which their parents' generation had lost. Cohen's full account is both complex and credible, but it contains one drawback for our purposes: however accurate its description of the Balls Pond Road, it cannot be applied as it stands to the North East. There are too many significant regional differences even if certain similarities (such as the fierce pride in skills that can no longer be transmitted from father to son) hold true. The most obvious contrast is the absence in the nothern region of new Commonwealth immigrants who, even in 1984, formed less than one per cent of the population. Also, the structure of the economy from the Tyne to the Wear has long been dominated by large concerns like shipbuilding, mining and steel-making and this type of employment has generated specific social relations, as we shall discuss presently. In addition, we would argue that the generational conflict and the various youth styles assumed a weaker and less dramatic form than in the South.

It is not being suggested that the North has remained untouched by all the social and commercial forces which have produced such tensions in other working-class areas. Rather, the argument is that more of a sense of community has survived in this area despite the economic battering which it has taken and despite all its internal divisions. We hold to that point of view although we heard from our sample of the lessened popularity of traditional New Year street celebrations and the occurrence of neighbours reporting each other to various authorities, both indications of local culture being further fragmented.

The areas we worked in were a mass of continuities and discontinuities with earlier cultural forms. Living at home until married and the importance of family and neighbourhood networks for hearing about jobs were as much features of life for the young adults as they were for their parents and grandparents, for example. On the other hand, changes in the quality of local conditions were widely discussed. On more than one occasion we heard women talk of having to travel further to do the shopping, the local shop having closed down. Clarke noted 'the changing social conditions of shopping which require more systematic large-scale expeditions' (1979, p.244), and stressed the need to see behind these 'the broad movements of capital' (in this case, the centralization of shops) which are the cause of the adaptations that women have to make at a local level. He also explored the wider issue of the commercialization of leisure addressing 'women specifically as the consumers' (p.250), a process that underlies and reinforces the sex differences in neighbourhood life.

These movements give depth to the picture we are trying to draw, although we would concede that a study of the institutions and associations in the three areas would have fleshed out our conclusions further, but that was beyond our remit. What evidence we did collect, however, has convinced us that, in the North East at least, the 'extended family' is not just an empty concept from the social sciences, but a living force for physical and psychological support, for fun and excitement. Also, the deep attachment to the locality, although it has at times a negative side which we discuss when exploring young people's 'localism', springs from a familiarity with the geography of the district, and a feeling of being a cherished part of a close network of relationships: both provide residents with 'a shared system of meaning and values [from which they] could draw upon to give a coherent account of their social life' (Williamson, 1982, p.77). The young people we met were, with few exceptions, very conscious of being Geordies or Northerners, were proud of their origins and traditions, and had a genuine affection for their place of birth: an affection that had mostly not been tested by exposure to alternatives. They were so much a part of extensive social networks and local associations (like caring for the neighbour's children or playing pool for the local pub), that the quality of their lives would have been lowered by leaving. These positive qualities, however, need to be remembered and built upon when we come to make suggestions for social policy in the final chapter.

The industrial and political history of the region helps to explain this heightened sense of solidarity. Those who have studied the dominant forms of employment in the region point, for example, to the formative influence of pit work, which 'builds up a basic attitude of helping others: it devalues competitiveness for the conditions are too dangerous. It fashions a distinctive pattern of social relationships both in families and in communities . . .' (Williamson, 1982, p.79). The clash of values between such an ethic and the cult of individualism and competition fostered by schools can be readily imagined. Schooling in the North has by and large failed to understand and capitalize on Benney's insight that 'miners make their demands on life as a community, not as individuals' (quoted by Williamson, 1982, p.68). Nowhere has that approach been more evident than in the political struggles of this century, culminating in the Miners' strike of 1984–85.

Localism

Mention of that bitter fight makes it impossible to have a romantic, rosey-tinted view of working–class life. There are likely to remain for some time deep divisions between those who supported the strike and those who did not. There are also the existing fissures between the employed and the jobless; between those who 'shop' their neighbours to the DHSS and those who do not. The provision of special programmes for unemployed sixteen and seventeen-year-olds has separated them from unemployed twenty, thirty or forty-year-olds who are officially perceived as more responsible for their own predicament; subdivisions have also been driven among school leavers, the most academically able of whom were creamed off into certain YOP schemes and others into Training Workshops. A similar typology has reappeared among Youth Training Schemes (see McKie, forthcoming). Distinctions are also made between those who can afford to buy their council houses and those who cannot. We also recorded divisions of a less serious nature between 'outsiders' from southern England and 'insiders'. All these conflicts were made more intense and hurtful by the ethos of the locality, which prides itself on mutual support, co-operation and friendliness. It remains an open question how much of the traditions of the area can withstand such fragmentations and internal dissension.

All those we knew recognized the further division between rough and respectable, which has frequently been commented on by writers such as Clarke (1979, p.246):

> one of the most fertile grounds of intra-class differentiation has been the whole repertoire of 'respectability' . . . The rough-respectable division has been firmly lodged in the visible signs of the home, street, neighbourhood and patterns of consumption.

The young adults easily identified certain housing estates and even particular streets that had been stigmatized. We began to hear of a clear hierarchy in housing with fine gradations within any one estate, which characterized the different social strata in working-class communities – for example, some stonefaced their council houses, or put in new windows or built archways to their gardens. Suttles (1968, p.7) argued that 'People who routinely occupy the same place must either develop a moral order that includes all those present or fall into conflict'. The residents of the Addams area of Chicago used the following strategies in their search for order: they withdrew into small territorial groupings, they restricted their social relations to the safest (seeing only close relatives, for instance), and they inquired closely into each other's personal character and past history. Some of these strategies were in evidence in Hillsborough, for example, where Troy was never keen to answer calls at the door and in Shipton where certain areas were avoided if possible.

The young adults' understanding of and loyalty to their home areas has been called localism, an outlook of well-defined horizons, both physical and psychological. What they considered to be their area could vary from a few streets, as for Theresa, to a council estate such as Marlow Dene, or be like Poppy's more general feeling of belonging to the whole town of Shipton. Whatever the exact size of 'their area', they knew its geography, the shops, clubs and pubs and the quickest route from one point to another. They also knew where they were in terms of their relationships with others; who, for example, were useful contacts, who not to offend and which pubs and streets to keep clear of in case of trouble.

The divisions, conflicts and self-imposed restrictions seemed to us at times to produce both negative and narrow attitudes to both people and places further afield as we discuss in Chapter 7. Their localism operated sometimes as a fortification behind which new ideas (like a multi-cultural society) could be ignored and parochialism flourish.

Localism consists, however, of two contrasting sides and its restrictive features were counterbalanced by some vital strengths. The women and men felt at one with their local setting and their attachment was real and deep. Having lived in the same areas all their lives, like their families before them, they were relaxed and uniquely at home there. The ties they felt were well founded. The interlocking strengths of emotional and financial support, security and comfort which they had there were on offer nowhere else. Above all, localism offered a ready-made system for understanding the world which infused their lives with meaning and coherence.

Family life

The families in the study lived essentially traditional lives based on a sexual division of labour and power. Young and Willmott wrote in 1955 (p.103):

> Less than a quarter of our husbands ... had the same occupation as their fathers. But all our wives had the same work as their mothers.

Change had occurred for the men, but not for the women. It is the same in our study thirty years on. There had again been discontinuity for the men – far fewer had the same jobs as their fathers – and continuity for the women who fundamentally still had no choice about women's work in the home. Daughters were expected to take it on, sons were not. The women we knew, however, were aware of restrictions placed on them because of their sex, as when they talked about their relationships with their fathers. Connell *et al.* (1982, p.176) have described subtle changes in the power relations among working-class families in Australia:

> Increasing numbers of working-class women, in their own ways, are contesting male control and insisting on independence or equality. This rarely takes the form of a conscious feminism ... But there is here a real and conscious shift from conventional modes of womanhood.

Young women like Carol Ann, Asia and Carly were not prepared to play the traditional role, were standing up to their fathers and were winning substantial gains. We did notice, however, that the traditional sexual divisions of labour and power quickly reasserted themselves after Carol Ann's marriage to Reg.

At the end of the study, the women and men we knew still lived with their parents, except for a few who had set up home with their partner. They were aged between eighteen and twenty-six. As Leonard noted (1980, p.51), 'For most people, especially in the working class, the only road to independence in housing is through marriage', and 'most local housing authorities will not accept applications from any single person under thirty' (p.68). Although some of the young women and men occasionally talked of getting their own place, only one, Phil in Hillsborough, had ever moved into a flat on his own and that only lasted four months because he missed the comforts of home. Whatever family relations were alike, the moral and practical support offered by the family home were unobtainable elsewhere and, along with the lack of alternative housing realistically available to young adults, this combined to keep them within the power of the family until well into their twenties. The question now becomes: is it impossible to become an adult without a job and while still living at home with your parents? Both they and their parents, however, accepted that home was where they should be until marriage or a partnership meant they wanted to set up a home of their own. Leaving any earlier would have meant a break with tradition. The young women and men seemed to be accorded adult status as far as was possible by their parents and increasingly so as they got older. The important exception to this rule was the case of those without jobs.

Some of those we knew came under increased parental pressure when they were unemployed, even in the short term. Arguments usually started over money, the young person finding the need to borrow more frequently from family members. In the long term, the impoverishment of unemployment in both financial and human terms appeared to lead to extended dependency on the family. It is difficult to see in working-class families how full adult status can be accorded young women and men who have never or only rarely earned a wage. For them, as Willis wrote (1984, p.476), 'the wage is still the golden key (mortgage, rent, household bills) to a separate personal household'.

Poppy described the efforts needed to set up home when unemployed:

> The dole's supposed to give you the deposit and the rent, but you've got to pay first, then get it back . . . They don't bother giving you money for ages. You've got to keep on going down . . . The first month, like, they do a check to make sure that you're definitely living there and it's just you.

Few young adults were willing or able to withstand such pressures. Effectively, therefore, they were subject to what support the family were prepared to offer.

It was interesting that the average weekly contribution they made towards their board and keep was £10, whether they were in employment or not. Although wages were low, they were always more than Unemployment Benefit or Social Security rates. Those without jobs therefore paid out a substantially higher proportion of their weekly income. And £10 was not a reflection of the real cost of bed and board, so even those who were employed were being heavily subsidized by the family. In this sense, the economic advantages to the young person of living at home were obvious. In another sense, however, it can be questioned whether they were 'advantages' at all. To refer to them as economic advantages or benefits suggests that they were preferable to some other economic option. In practice, the women and men we knew found no such alternative. Attempts to find jobs and housing in other parts of the country proved unsuccessful. They were stuck at home, growing older but hardly more in control of their lives than when they were in primary school.

Gender

One of the dangers of writing about family and neighbourhood life is the tendency to polarize the two camps, seeing women as firmly based in the family and men as out and about, away from the home. Our fieldwork did little to solve the problem as we learnt the most about families from the women because of their concern with relationships in general, and we built up pictures of neighbourhood life from the men because of their more public style of everyday living; and we also saw them less at home.

In time, however, we came to know what neighbourhood life meant for some of the women and family life for some of the men. Both sexes spent similar amounts of time in each sphere, but the time was spent differently. In some of the streets we knew, the women were always popping in and out of each other's homes. Clara said though, 'My dad won't have anything to do with the neighbours since my mam died'. He regularly went to the working men's club on the estate, however. It was Clara who knew all the gossip in her street, 'That's all you hear about around here-death and more death-or someone getting brayed or their house burgled.' At one meeting, Theresa poured out the news of local events to Carol: an attempted rape, a car crash, a deserted husband, a battered baby, young lads being molested, and Saturday night gang fighting in the town square. Theresa also commented that the chair Carol was sitting in had 'the best view out of the window'. She would sit there to watch the comings and goings of the neighbours.

In these ways, the women's neighbourhood life was as rich as the men's streetlife, but it was not as public or as visible. A comment of Jane's highlighted the difference. Although she talked of sitting with a gang of friends in the park at weekends, she also said:

> You're not safe to walk the streets at nights-not a girl.

Family life for men was equally demarcated. Particularly when they were unemployed, they could spend as much time in the house as out of it, but few helped with the running of the household, as has been seen. Of all the young men we met we came to know in some detail only about the families of Reg, Al and Joe. It took time though, especially when there were painful circumstances. We first met Joe, for instance, in January 1982 and although he had occasionally mentioned rows at home, it was not until May 1983 that he revealed that his dad had not shared a bedroom with his wife for four years, but had been sleeping in Joe's room. The news came out when Joe told us that his parents were finally considering separation. When we asked the young adults who they talked to if they had any problems, more than one lad replied like Max, 'Nobody. I keep my problems to myself'. In many ways, therefore, the men's participation in family life was as difficult to grasp and comprehend as that of the women in neighbourhood life.

What is the significance of these sex differences in family and neighbourhood life? Connell *et al.* wrote (1982, p.173):

> Relationships between the sexes are not just a matter of distinctions leading to inequalities. They are also relationships of power. When we talk about gender we are talking about ways in which social relations get organized in the interests of some groups, over-riding the interests of others.

Thus, although family life appeared to be primarily the domain of women, it was fathers who held sway over daughters' lives and young men who were allowed more freedom, including freedom from housework. Similarly, the fact that the more public domain of neighbourhood life was open to the men rather than the women meant, for instance, that the men were more likely to hear about jobs on the grapevine.

Drinking

Our sample lived in communities where heavy drinking was generally thought to be *the* way of celebrating Christmas and New Year, birthdays and anniversaries, the first Friday or the last Monday in the month. If heavy drinking was used to celebrate, it was also the most common means of dealing with problems; difficulties of all kinds were dissolved (if not solved) in alcohol. Drinking was used to pass the time, to bring life and excitement to meetings of friends, and as a pleasure in its own right. Men tested their masculinity by seeing how many pints they could drink in one evening just as they do in Glasgow and Liverpool, in university student bars and rugby clubs up and down the country.

Heavy drinking has a long history in the North East and the

traditions of drinking as a relaxation after dirty and dangerous work have been passed down from generation to generation. Before the First World War, drunkenness was 'almost six times more common than the next more serious offences' and drunken women were as numerous as drunken men on Saturday nights (Williamson, 1982, p.110). The heavy drinking done by those in our sample, then, was strongly supported by friends, relatives and adults of all ages: it was an accepted and unquestioned part of local culture, enjoyed by women as well as men.

Williamson wrote about his grandfather James' life in a North East pit village at the turn of the century and saw the need to consider his pastimes, like drinking, 'not just as an aspect of a style of life, but as reflecting the structure of the community and society in which he lived. That community was both a setting and a resource' (p.103). We tried to view the lives of the young women and men we knew in the same way, making sense of what they did with reference to regional traditions; aspects of their drinking, however, present problems for social policy which we shall tackle in the final chapter.

Trouble

Another feature of the three neighbourhoods was the above average crime rate. Whenever we introduced the topic of delinquency, the young people asked us what the term meant. They neither used the word themselves nor understood it. Our interest in pursuing it as a topic was completely at odds with their experiences. We thought that trouble with the law would be a sensitive area and consequently we at first decided to let any accounts they wanted to give us come out in their own good time. The long period it took to gain their confidence was not always because the young persons concerned were secretive, ashamed or reticent, however. As often as not, misdemeanours were not reported because they were not seen as important or anything out of the ordinary.

Juvenile delinquency is, of course, a subject close to the heart of many psychologists, sociologists and of those who concern themselves with the moral welfare of the young; but it was not a topic that the young people in our study talked about spontaneously for any length of time or with any great interest. Getting into trouble with the police was a common enough occurrence which merited neither special comment nor attention; it was simply an unremarkable part of their ordinary existence.

Once we felt that we had established strong relationships of mutual trust, we asked young adults specific questions about crime. By then, they were over eighteen years old and crime was the more appropriate term. It became clear from their answers that the issue directly affected the lives of very few of them. Those who had committed offences, and the majority of these were of a minor nature, did not see crime as a significant part of their lives. We met no one whose life was organized around crime as a career or who had adopted a criminal identity. Those without a record did not think that crime was a serious problem, even though a number of them had been the victims of either theft or personal violence. One of our sample, Karl, commented: 'They [delinquents] are not *always* getting into trouble with the police'. This remark was consistent with the views of most experts on delinquency, who are agreed that not even those young people who have been convicted of serious offences lead lives that revolve solely around criminal activities.

We collected reports of offences committed by our sample and by their close friends or relatives. We conducted group discussions on the topic and later followed up some of the answers we received to our formal questions. Whatever technique we adopted, the responses were similar: delinquency and crime were accepted aspects of life within the three neighbourhoods. Most of the offences we heard about were petty.

Although there was general acceptance among our sample of the existence of crime in their areas, very few actively approved of breaking the law. Pete was exceptional in commenting: 'If I saw the chance of breaking the law and getting away with it, I would. I've just realized since I was fifteen that you can't beat the system'. Most believed that the majority of young law breakers were well-adjusted, ordinary young people in need of money, kicks or a reputation. In Karl's words: 'It seems natural when you're eighteen 'till you're twenty-five to get into trouble with the police on a Friday or Saturday night'. Others, like Tomma, clearly differentiated between 'getting bothered by the police' and 'getting into trouble with the police' by committing an offence: 'kids sometimes work themselves [try it on] so police have got to fight back else they'll get hurt'.

Some, like Scotch, thought that relationships between the police and young people were decidedly poor: 'When on me bike, they pull you up any time they want . . . just to get you angry . . . They think we're looking for trouble all the time, think we're doing wrong all the time'. Pete's answers summed up the views of the majority: 'A lot of good coppers . . . you can talk to them okay. But the odd one or two like to pick on you and ask you questions. It's when there's two or three of them that it's bad. When they're by themselves, they're okay'. Karl realized the importance of the social context in his relationships with the police: 'Depends where you are. At a football match, you're tret like rubbish. But through the day, they're all right . . . most working people join the police 'cos it's a job like the Army'. Only two young men, Rocky and Tomma, were prepared to admit that some of the 'bother' between young lads and the police stemmed from provocation on the part of young people themselves.

We feel it important to emphasize, despite what we have recorded above, that our sample were peaceable and law-abiding: they were not anxious to change or even bend the laws of society. This can be further gauged by their attitudes to persistent offenders, who were described variously as 'nutters', 'the scum of the earth', and 'idiots looking for trouble'. Most of the young people could cite cases of local lads who had long histories of recidivism and we have already given examples of bizarre behaviour that puzzled them. Some, but not all, of this small group of persistent offenders were widely thought in their area to be 'loopy', 'crackers' or 'have a screw loose somewhere'. These few were thought to be mentally unstable and to be extreme cases. Jack described one such local lad: 'There's something missing with him . . . you can't explain him. He can't explain himself. He doesn't know what the hell he's doing . . . and that's all the time'. Psychological explanations of such unusual and disturbing behaviour are probably appropriate but the young adults rejected the notion that they could be applied to any but a tiny handful. The large majority of those who got into trouble with the police were not, in their view, maladjusted in any way. They had known them from childhood and knew that any such suggestion was nonsense.

The struggle to integrate the specific responses of our sample to questions about 'trouble' led us to reflect on wider issues, which included: the historic role of the police in controlling working-class areas and keeping the streets safe and clear of 'louts' and 'hooligans'; the stereotype held by the police of the typical young offender; and typical police practice (reported by young people as harrassment) which makes a connection 'between a dangerous place (the streets of the working-class city) and a dangerous time (youth)' (Muncie, 1984, po.147). The twin themes of crime and youth do come together in the mass media and in public consciousness as a key indicator of recurring crises in law and order, particularly if the third theme of race is added to the mix (Hall *et al.*, 1978). But our contact with young adults living in areas undergoing the severest economic pressures since the war convinced us that juvenile delinquency was an epiphenomenon, a secondary symptom which could divert us from the central issue: the threat of perhaps permanent exclusion from society of a large section of young, working-class adults. Without in any way diminishing the pain or suffering of the victims of crime who tended to live in the very same housing estates, we had to give due weight to the economic forces, outside the control of the police or the courts, which were driving more and more young people out on to the margins.

Class

We need to give brief consideration to the class position of the young adults on whose lives this book is based. The Registrar General's means of assessing social class according to occupation were particularly irrelevant to our sample on two accounts. First, we frequently had difficulty in finding out exactly what job parents held, not because the young adults were unwilling to tell us, but because often they literally did not know what their parents did for a living. Second, the standard classification of jobs is crude and misleading: for example, anyone who is unemployed falls into Category V, which therefore would have included individuals with a wide range of expertise and prospects, from Max's dad, a seasonal labourer, to Poppy's dad who ran his own small business before he went bankrupt.

If they described themselves at all in class terms, the young adults considered they were either middle or working class. We would explain their identification as middle class as a claim to belong to the top stratum of the working class. Rose (1968, p.20) refers to 'a very respectable group at the top, a "rough" group at the bottom, and the rest'. Similarly, Jenkins (1983) differentiates 'the lads, the citizens and the ordinary kids'. With one or two at either extreme, virtually all of our sample belonged to the central band. Our study, then, is concerned with that much neglected group: ordinary, middle of the road, working-class young adults.

6 Friends and Partners

Over the two-and-a-half years that we were in contact with young adults, they discussed with us their friends and relationships with partners more than any other topic. In the early stages of contact these discussions led us to question the authenticity of the North East stereotype of the working-class male as brutally sexist, violent and domineering. Though we heard jokes about and derogatory comments on females, we also saw evidence of great tenderness and mutual consideration between men and women. Gradually, however, it became clear that friendships were based upon deep-seated inequalities between males and females. Overt sexism was only one aspect of the way men and women treated each other. Far more influential and pervasive were the subtle forms of sexism practised by both men and women and, on reflection, by us in some of our daily talk, perceptions and judgements. Inequality between the sexes was a theme that influenced all aspects of young adults' friendships. This inequality, however, was so much part and parcel of our world and of theirs, that it proved difficult to perceive, acknowledge and write about.

Types of friends and activities

As one might expect, young women and men formed their early friendships with people from their school, street and local area. The opportunity to make new and often older friends was provided by YOP schemes or a job and many people widened their circle of friends through contacts made in the pubs, clubs and discos they visited at weekends. Older brothers and sisters provided some with an entrée into a social group with a wider age range. Many young people remained in contact with the same set of friends from school and added on the new friends made later. This was a pattern most often followed by young men who maintained contact with the same group of friends for many years, though Jane and Poppy also followed this pattern. Some people, like Carol Ann and Jimi, lost contact with the majority of their friends once they left school and made a completely new set. This second pattern was most often followed by women, particularly those who gradually saw less of their friends when they formed a serious relationship with a male partner.

Some of our sample had been to the same schools and, because of this, we discovered interlinking networks between young people in different areas of both Shipton and Hillsborough; and gossip travelled rapidly between the villages of Runswick, Thealby and Monkton in the Milton group. Theresa, for example, was able to keep us up to date with Annie's activities, even though they rarely saw each other, because her sister was courting the brother of Annie's boyfriend. In Shipton, a group of lasses in Hatton Moor knew all about Carly's lad who lived about four miles away, because they had been to school with him and also knew his father.

We observed five major types of friendship group. At any one time a young person was likely to belong to more than one. There was, for instance, the all-female group. Traditionally in the North East the lasses go out together on a Friday night whether they are courting or not. Groups of women can be observed moving *en masse* from pub to pub, and later in the evening to discos and clubs. Second was the all-male group, which typically went out drinking together at weekends and on some nights during the week, hung around the streets and played the occasional game of pool or football. Third, and less common, there were mixed sex groups. These consisted of a number of couples, or were a combination of couples and single people. Fourth, people spent time with their best friend of the same sex, and finally, there were relationships with partners. In a typical week some young adults would go out with the lads or the lasses, they would also spend time in a mixed-sex group accompanied by their partner, they would meet their best friend and would see their partners alone.

Our discussion concentrates on the lasses, the lads and partners. We observed these three kinds of groups during our fieldwork and they were discussed in detail with us. Asia, Pat, Pete and Charlie had groups of friends based around an interest in a specific type of music or styles of dress. Pete was actively involved in punk music as a member of a band. Pat's enthusiasm for heavy metal was so well known that she was nicknamed 'Gillan' (the name of a leading figure in a heavy metal band). Charlie and his male friends all wore skinhead clothes: they had short cropped hair, wore black, short-sleeved tee-shirts (even in winter), faded blue jeans to mid-calf length, and Doc Marten boots laced up to mid-calf. Asia and her friends were also fans of heavy metal and Asia was considered inseparable from her black leather jacket. But she suddenly changed when she was nineteen, two years after we had first met her. She arrived at a meeting wearing a smart sheepskin jacket, slacks and high heeled shoes. The other women commented:

Poppy: She's completely changed, hasn't she, her image . . . From a hippy to a smoothy!

Carly: Where's the little leather jacket?!

Asia: It's got moth holes in it now!

The most popular activities with friends included going to concerts and the cinema, playing darts and pool, watching and playing football, squash, fishing, camping, watching videos and using CB radio. For the majority of young adults the consumption of alcohol was the central focus of all their social activities as we discussed in the previous chapter.

The unpopular and the lonely

We asked about those who tended to be excluded from their group of friends. The consensus, for both women and men, was that 'snobs' (people who believed that they were socially superior to others) and 'posers' (those who tried to be something they were not) were unpopular and avoided. Additionally 'gossips', and 'cows' (women who had sex with a succession of men) were excluded by the women. The men avoided 'nutters' or 'toughs'. Al described them as, 'Yobs . . . trouble-makers who you dinna feel comfortable with'. The obvious danger for men was that associating with someone who kept spoiling for a fight could lead to trouble and violence. 'Nutters', 'posers' and 'cows' had friends who were judged to be equally undesirable.

When we asked specific questions about loneliness, women and men in the social whirl were unsure about why others felt like this. The only definite reason they gave was that some women and men had over-protective parents. Two women in our study were lonely for periods during our fieldwork. We can only speculate as to the reasons which, in the first instance, may have been partly caused by a lack of 'the skills of friendship' (Duck, 1983, p.143). Such an explanation would be quite inappropriate in the second instance where the young woman appeared to be suffering as a result of conventional notions of female attractiveness. One woman came from a family of religious funda-mentalists, had undergone a series of minor operations during her school years, was shy and awkward in company and lacked confidence. The other woman was physically large, and though talkative, friendly, confident and self assured with us, reported that she did not have any friends. She admitted to us in a written response that she was lonely. We found it impossible, however, to pursue the question further as we were sitting in a noisy pub with a group of lively, attractive and obviously popular women and men. Asking the question made us appreciate the sensitivity of this subject and the stigma attached to being solitary. Nor could we bring ourselves to return to the topic when she was on her own even though her admission about loneliness could be interpreted as a sign that she wanted to discuss it: there were some questions which we found too sensitive ever to ask.

The lasses

Between the ages of twelve and fifteen, when with the aid of make-up and clothes they looked mature enough to start drinking in pubs, the majority of young women in our study began to go out with their female friends. Carly commented: 'We used to go down the Lane every night. A resident! They used to keep our corner for us!' In the North East, Friday evening is the big night out in the week and there existed a strong feeling among the women that they ought to participate. Poppy told us repeatedly, 'I live for me Friday nights'. As they grew older and more confident, the lasses in Shipton began to gravitate towards the bright lights 'ower the toon', visiting a succession of pubs, clubs and discos during an evening, while those in the Milton group travelled into Runswick for a night out.

Friday nights out with the lasses were important to women for two major reasons. First, they went out to have a good time and 'a laff'. They enjoyed relief from the hum-drum of household chores, the monotony of their jobs or unemployment and, for some, the difficulties of coping with a boyfriend. Friday night was a social occasion which for some did not include males. Carly and Poppy expressed horror at the suggestion that they should see their partners on Fridays. Poppy commented that in the three years she had been with her lad 'I've never, ever seen Steve on a Friday and Saturday night since we started going out'. Karen and Carly reported that the purpose of going out with the lasses was *not* to meet men. This, however, seems to have applied mainly to those who already had a steady partner.

Second, women who were single went out with the lasses to meet eligible men. This could be achieved in the safety of numbers with friends to fall back on if a lad turned out to be difficult or undesirable. Typically, a group of lasses arrived *en masse* at a disco or club where they would meet groups of lads also doing the rounds. Julie informed us that as a general rule lads did not ask lasses to dance, but everyone simply converged on the dance floor. If a lad started dancing next to a woman, things could develop from there.

For some women going out with the lasses went further than Friday nights 'ower the toon'. Asia and Shuk arranged trips away for the weekend and went on holiday to Spain for a fortnight with a group of lasses. Julie and Jacki did the same. Asia still went on holiday with her closest girlfriends after she became engaged.

Friendships with the lasses provided women with different types of support – emotional, practical and financial. Even though the majority of women in Milton, Shipton and Hillsborough had a relationship with a steady partner (17 out of 22), with few exceptions they also had a best friend; women felt the need to have a confidante in addition to their male partner. A best friend was someone to trust, confide in and discuss anxieties about partners, sex and any problems. Poppy reported that she could ask her best friend to comment on her appearance and was prepared to change if her friend judged something to be wrong. Poppy also said, 'I can tell my friend something' and she'll say, "Yes, I feel like that too" '; this stopped her feeling 'strange' or 'abnormal'. Carly reported that she had long conversations with her best friend about sex, ('*Not* "this is what we did, and this is what we did then" ...'), but serious discussions about the physical side of their relationships. Bernadette said that she needed to have a friend with whom she could discuss her experiences at work and problems with her boyfriend.

Many women drifted away from their female friends in the early stages of their relationships with male partners. This happened partly at the insistence of their boyfriends. Karen, for example, reported that her boyfriend complained when she went out with the lasses. He would say, 'Well, if you prefer their company to mine ...', so she spent very few evenings away from him. Bernadette's boyfriend made more and more demands on her time so she had little opportunity to see her own friends. After a few months, however, when the new relationship was more settled, the majority of women re-established contact with the lasses, and went out on a Friday night again. Carly, Poppy and Asia all said that their boyfriends did not mind them going out on their own:

Asia: You have to come to an agreement.

Carly: Hal's trying to encourage me, pushing me out of the door ...!

They knew some women whose boyfriends would not allow them out, but Asia commented on her own situation, 'He wouldn't dare tell us that I couldn't go out'. These three women declare that they had independence from their lads, but added:

Poppy: You do feel guilty though, don't you? When you don't want to see them, you want to go out.

Carly: Hal puts it so I don't feel guilty.

Carol: Ah, but would *he* feel guilty?

Carly: No.

Over time we became acutely aware that women and men had widely differing topics of conversation. Among themselves and in the presence of Carol and Sarah, the lasses discussed their day-to-day experiences in their jobs or on the dole, relationships with families and partners (and Carol's and Sarah's partners), evenings out, the pros and cons of engagement versus living together, having children, physical appearance and clothes, and on one occasion the preferred sizes of breasts, how to get a suntan, and different styles of knickers!

In addition, at meetings where the women were close friends, or had friends in common, a considerable amount of the conversation was devoted to gossip about who was going out with whom. They used a complex internal language some of which Carol and Sarah, as outsiders, found difficult to understand. We did not consider it appropriate to halt the conversation and ask for explanations. When the women's conversations were easily understood, explained to us or we were directly included, some of the censorious and controlling features of gossip emerged that have been observed by other researchers (see McRobbie 1978; Wilson 1978). For instance, during the early stages of our contact with the group in Milton, when they were between seventeen and nineteen-years-old, we witnessed evidence of rivalries and jealousies among the young women, though they presented a united stand if provoked or threatened by the lads. The lasses gossiped about an absent member of their group, criticizing her clothes, hairstyles and boyfriends. There was an intense interest in the minutiae of day-to-day life; offence was easily taken and quarrels flared up quickly and just as quickly subsided.

Stephanie was unpopular at the Workshop and latter was described as a 'snob'. This antagonism towards her continued after she had left; the lasses complained that she ignored them if they saw her in Runswick. Annie was the most obviously concerned about her own reputation. She denied repeatedly, and loudly, that she had had any sexual experience, and on one occasion slapped Jack hard on the face when he jokingly intimated that he knew otherwise. At a later stage she was indignant at the suggestion that all the young women at the Workshop were 'on the pill'. Another young woman at the Workshop was strongly criticized for 'mucking around' with the lads and wearing a low cut tee-shirt which exposed her breasts. As an interesting contrast, Pat, who openly went out with a succession of boyfriends and admitted to having casual sex, did not appear to be censured, nor was she was called a 'cow' or 'slag'; this was so exceptional that we return to her case at the end of the chapter.

We also heard some malicious gossiping among the women in Shipton, for example:

> Both Carol Ann and Fenwick were, in their own words, 'bitchy' about lasses they knew who came into the pub. They kept laughing about the lass who worked behind the bar, describing her as a 'prat', and when we asked why they just laughed and said she just was. They also laughed at another lass who started talking to a lad and they made rude comments about him, asking 'she can't be going out with *him* can she?' and 'Isn't he ugly?'

We pursued the women's concern for reputation as a specific issue at a later session. Reflecting on her experiences when younger, Carly commented:

> These lads tried [to get me into bed], you've got to give them that; they tried, but no way. The other lads used to say, 'Wey, right little virgin her'. It didn't bother me . . .

> Asia: Well, lads don't get named, do they? If a girl screwed around she'd get called cow or slut, but a lad doesn't.

The women all agreed that reputation *was* still important to them. They openly slept with their boyfriends, but:

> Poppy: If you've got a steady boyfriend, it's okay.

> Carol: What happens if you have a steady boyfriend for six months and then another?

> Poppy: Well, I never have.

> Asia: Neither have I.

> Carly: No, I haven't. I've only done it with Hal and that's it!

> Poppy: I'd feel secondhand now if I went with anyone else. If I went with another lad, I wouldn't sleep with him straight away. And I'd feel *really* guilty. I'd have to tell him I'd slept with someone else. You know what I mean, not being for them . . .

> Asia: I'd feel ashamed.

There were some lasses whom the women in our study considered promiscuous, and as in younger female groups, these 'slags' and 'tarts' were shunned to avoid the risk of guilt by association.

The reports of rivalries and fights among women were mainly said to be caused be jealousies over lads. Annie had been involved in a fight when another lass accused her of fancying her boyfriend. Annie hit the lass over the head with an ashtray so badly that she had needed fourteen stitches. Pat, in Milton, had been involved in a fight when two lasses had 'jumped' her and punched her. They accused her of 'saying things about them'. In a nightclub in Hillsborough Nikki was challenged to a fight by a younger woman whom she did not know, but then friends restrained them so that no one was hurt. The following day the lass apologised to Nikki; she explained that she had been asked to fight by a friend who was courting Nikki's ex-boyfriend and who was jealous because he still liked Nikki. None of the other women had been involved in fights, but they had observed them taking place.

Once they acquired a steady male partner women still had to work to maintain the relationship-appearing feminine and attractive continued to be important. The majority of women with steady partners still went out with the lasses on a Friday night, or met their girlfriends, but if they wanted to be accepted by other women, they had to be seen to conform. Carly told us that her friend, Fiona, had threatened to tell Carly's boyfriend, Hal, that she had been asked out by another lad. Fiona judged that Carly had been acting improperly; flirting and going out with other lads was not allowed when a lass had a steady partner. This incident started friction in Carly's relationship with Fiona. There followed a disastrous weekend away as a foursome when Fiona wanted to spend all her time in bed with her lad; this time it was Carly who did not approve of Fiona's behaviour. The final straw came when Fiona spent an evening talking about nothing but her boyfriend, and then caught the bus home, abandoning Carly in a fish and chip shop.

The lads

We saw men together, we collected some details about the number of friends they had and what they did, but in contrast with the women they made few observations about their friends and who was important to them. It was not a topic they discussed or appeared to give much thought to. We therefore had to make inferences from the little information we obtained and some of these ideas we took back to the men for comment.

A generalized threat of violence and aggression was the context in which the men in all three areas lived, though for many this was part of their taken-for-granted world and it did not make them particularly anxious; they were careful, however, not to run risks. Some men had more reason to act cautiously, particularly those who had been involved in fights before, but as a general rule lads had less reason to worry if they stayed in their locality, where they were known and had friends. They ran risks, however, if they crossed into certain other areas which housed their traditional rivals. The need for a group of friends who were loyal and physically strong was very real for lads therefore.

During their early teens the majority of young men started hanging around with a group of lads whom they knew through school or throughout their school years, and when they looked old enough to get served, graduated with them from the street corner to the pubs. By the age of fifteen, the majority of young men could get away with drinking in pubs. At first the most mature-looking lad bought the alcohol and distributed it to the others who hung around outside the pub. By the time we met the men in our study, with few exceptions, they were going out and drinking regularly, and heavily, on a Friday and Saturday night, and, when they could afford it, on other nights during the week.

The pub also offered the lads other amusements: darts, games of pool and chatting up women. Such activities were common to most pubs, and allowed men, even strangers, to exchange a few words. For example, the Marlow Dene lads spent a pleasant evening playing pool, fitting in easily to a country pub. Very little conversation took place between the visitors and the locals, but at the end of the evening it was felt that they had all enjoyed themselves. Other lads, in particular Joe, Scotch, Rocky and Morrow, were involved in regular weekend football matches, and the majority played scratch games if they could find nothing better to do.

On the surface the structure of male groups seemed to be very casual. There did not appear to be a clear demarcation between those lads who were part of a group and those who were not. When asked, the men were vague about who were their friends which contrasted with the women's very definite answers. Males tended to join a group or to go around with the lads for a while and then disappear. Regular members would also drift away for periods of time, most often when they began courting, but other commitments such as to a job or scheme, or to family would also draw them away. Lads rejoined the group once a relationship with a partner had been firmly established or had ended, or when other commitments were fulfilled. This pattern of drifting in and out was most evident in the Hillsborough group. Al, who was for many months central to the group, gradually spent more and more of his time with his girlfriend and his family, and was later rarely seen. Morrow's government scheme and steady relationshp with his lass gradually absorbed most of his time, while conversely Phil, who had been preoccupied with his lass and had become engaged, returned to the group after an absence of many months.

Lads seemed rarely to make formal arrangments to meet–they just saw each other around. Closer investigation, however, revealed that nights out drinking followed a regular pattern of visits from one pubs to the next which were arranged in advance. Everyone knew where the evening was to start, and if some of the lads missed out on the early part of the evening, they knew approximately where the others would be and so could catch them up. Similarly, the majority of the men followed a routine so they knew where to contact each other during the day without making definite arrangements.

Most of the lads we asked specifically reported that they had a best mate, someone to confide in and talk to more intimately. Only Rocky, however, admitted that his best friend was particularly important to him. When he discussed this, Rocky had recently had a serious disagreement with his friend and the temporary loss of contact made him appreciate how 'dependent' (his word) he had been on this lad.

For the majority of men their best friend was a drinking partner, someone to go around with and, if the need arose, to help out in fights, and someone to boost confidence when chatting up women. In addition, best friends went fishing, running, riding motorbikes, shooting and on holiday together, as well as just meeting at each other's house and talking. It was very rare for a lad to introduce his lass to his male friends, but best friends did sometimes go out together with their girlfriends or wives.

We were dependent on our own observations of the behaviour of close mates because of the reluctance of men to talk about them. We did learn something through our observation of John and Phil in Hillsborough, and Jack and Ben in Milton.

When we first met John his closest friend was Gary, but because of Gary's involvement with a government scheme and his new girlfriend, the two lads drifted apart and John was openly upset when Gary did not attend his wedding reception. A few weeks before John's wedding, however, another of his friends, Phil, who had been away from the group, reappeared and the two lads spent increasing amounts of time together. During the Hillsborough trip to the Peaks they fished together, walked, talked, sat in John's car, drank rum and watched the sunrise and the rabbits. And when they returned they called round to each other's home and went fishing and shooting in the Dene. This continued after John's and then Phil's marriage, and after the birth of John and Barbara's child.

Jack and Ben in Milton also spent a lot of time fishing together, but in addition they drove around in Ben's car and went drinking with a group of lads from the area. They seemed to be well suited; Jack played the straight man to Ben's clowning. Jack and Ben had become friends while still at school after Jack had been 'a bad lad' as Ben described him. Jack had started going around with Ben and his friends in an attempt to avoid further trouble with the police.

Lack of co-operation and trust seemed to exist mainly among the groups of younger lads. When we first met the lads in the Milton group they were constantly competing with each other, trying to score minor victories and forever making sexual allusions. Similar behaviour was observed among the young un's in Hillsborough on the trip to the Peaks. They tried to impress each other with their bravery, bickered over chores, refused to do each other's washing-up, and did not trust each other with money. Simon, in Shipton, though a bit more mature, indicated that he was under constant pressure to keep up with his friends' motorbikes, drinking and girlfriends with the consequence that he got deeply into debt when unemployed.

Not surprisingly, some of the most explicit examples of sexism and male bravado occurred in Frank's conversations with the men. Joe in

Shipton had refused to complete a story in Carol's presence. When she left, he confided to Frank: 'When the womenfolk are away, we can tell you the truth'. He then launched into a story about a woman sitting in the corner who had apparently given her boyfriend a 'blowjob' in full view of a crowded pub over the 'toon' and had thus acquired such a bad reputation that she could 'only get a black boyfriend'.

On another occasion Frank noted:

> In a group with me and Karl, Joe kept making obscene remarks about girls and older women whom he neither knew nor spoke to . . . he wouldn't let me drink a half pint of beer . . . He insisted I took a pint 'like a real man.'

Men tended to avoid lads who were always spoiling for a fight and whom they called 'nutters', 'yobs', 'trouble makers'. The group in Marlow Dene stopped seeing one lad who was constantly getting involved in and talking about fights. The older lads seemed to be the most relaxed with each other. There was no evidence, while we were with them, of constant attempts to impress each other. There was quick repartee and humour between them, and some good humoured jokes at each other's expense; for example, Troy said of a friend, 'He'd give an asprin a headache!', but intense male rivalry was absent. The lads mainly discussed cars, fishing, football and women; on one occasion Al and Morrow discussed the expense of furnishing and decorating a flat, and sometimes the lads even specifically mentioned their female partners. Though they might not know the name of a mate's girlfriend, the lads did know many details of each other's lives, and sometimes the conversation lapsed into a discussion about the activities of other lads, or their various family members: the male equivalent of gossip.

There was evidence of kindness and a more relaxed style of friendship among some of the lads in Shipton too; this applied to Rocky and his group, and Jimi with his older friends. Jimi told us that he and his mates had been to see the film ET and not only had they all been close to tears, they were able to admit as much. At our second party for the Shipton group Scotch became ill, blaming it on a combination of alcohol and flu. He was sick on his clothes and then climbed into the bath fully dressed. Joe and Reg looked after him, and cleaned him up; Reg ironed his clothes dry. On our weekend away Karl became worse for drink and disappeared. His absence was noticed by Joe who immediately went out into the dark to search for him.

Getting married made no difference to Phil's and John's involvement with the lads, nor did the arrival of John's first child. Nor did marriage and a five-year-old daughter interfere with Troy's commitment to his mates. During a feedback session with some of the lads in Shipton, the consensus was that a lad might be forced to stay at home when first married because of lack of finances, but as soon as there was sufficient resources he would be out with the lads again. There were exceptions, of course. Rocky, who spent a lot of his time with a mixed-sex group, introduced his various girlfriends to these friends. Tomma shared the same friends with his girlfriend, and Reg took Carol Ann out with the lads. These instances were unusual, however, and these lads themselves were aware of this.

Relationships between women and men

We collected more information on relationships between males and females than on any other subject. This gives some indication of the importance they have in young adults' lives. No mention was made by anyone in our study of homosexual relationships. Like loneliness, it was a difficult and sensitive subject to broach, so our discussion of partners is confined to heterosexual ones.

As in the discussion of friends, conversations we had with our sample about their relationships and partners reflected the differences in male and female interests. The lads tended to discuss women in general and voice their views which were predominantly dismissive of females. They hinted at their conquests, and perpetuated an anti-female rhetoric. Rarely did men volunteer information about their partners. When Sarah once asked some of the lads directly about their girlfriends, she found that they were not forthcoming. Frank also had little success. He noted on one occasion, 'Towards the end . . . because Pete had not mentioned her, I asked him how his girlfriend was. He said that she was "okay" and dropped the subject and I found it difficult to go back to it'. Most of the men's spontaneous comments were derogatory observations about their mates' girlfriends; for example, Rick was said to be 'scared of his lass'. Pidge was described as 'hen-pecked', and Reg's friends referred to Carol Ann as 'the missus' or 'the little woman'. As a rule, however, most of the time women were conspicuous by their absence in male conversation. Joe, however, learnt early on in our fieldwork that voicing his traditional views on the place of women was good method of winding Carol and Sarah up and he seemed to enjoy trying to provoke them.

In contrast, a lot of time was spent with the women discussing men, their relationships generally and their partners in particular. Most of this conversation was with Carol and Sarah, but Frank was party to some of these discussions. Much of our information on relationships therefore was from the female perspective: women's views on men and how they treat females, and women's views on their own partner. There were a few exceptions since the sample in our study included six couples. We had detailed conversations with both partners from two of these couples and comments from members of the other four. In addition, we were able to observe some of the other men and women with their partners.

General observations

Only a few people in our study had not courted a member of the opposite sex. Men and women differed, however, in their professed interest in relationships. On one occasion Joe made it quite clear that to him football was more important than girls and on another Jimi said spontaneously that he preferred going out with the lads. Simon said that none of his mates were interested in lasses, and gave the impression that he was also fairly indifferent though at the time had two girlfriends. One reason lads such as Jimi gave for avoiding the company of women was that they were expected to modify their drinking and language in their presence; they could not relax. Scotch said he avoided going out with a girlfriend around Christmas time, 'You must be joking! They expect a Christmas present. You start looking for a girl after Christmas!' Drinking with the lads and playing football were alternative interests to having a girlfriend. But the women had no other acceptable options: if they did not have a partner they were likely to be considered a social failure. To explain her lack of a partner, Fenwick said she was not interested in having a boyfriend 'at the moment'.

The contacts and relationships with the opposite sex ranged from one-night stands, through a series of dates which soon fizzled out, to long courtships, engagements and marriage. By the end of our study, when most were aged between nineteen and twenty-one, seventeen of the women and twelve men, had a long standing partner including those who were engaged or married. Only two women, Barbara and Jane, had met their partners while at school. All the other women had started their serious relationship around the age of sixteen or seventeen after leaving school, and they and the lads had met their partners through the local network of family and friends.

The usual pattern for lasses was to leave school, start going steady, and become engaged, or feel under pressure to get engaged, after eighteen months to two years of courtship. Once the relationship was considered fairly stable, some women and men moved to a half-way stage where they slept at their partner's house, and returned home each day for clean clothes and a meal. Carol Ann moved in with Reg and his family because of friction with her parents. The majority of women seemed on their way to marrying a couple of years younger than the national average age of twenty-four. Barbara was the main exception to this having married and had her first baby at seventeen.

Many of the young adults we met had ambivalent views on marriage. In a sense it was considered inevitable, as can be seen from Charlie's comment – 'Me mam'd kill me if I didn't give her a grandchild'. As Leonard (1980, p.9) observed 'most people do not wonder *if* they should marry but rather *who* they should marry'. Some young adults resisted the expectations their parents had of them and discussed the alternatives with us.

For men this resistance mainly took the form of delaying marriage as long as possible. Joe, Scotch, Tony and Karl said that they would avoid marriage until they were in their thirties. Joe claimed that he stopped seeing a lass as soon as she started mentioning 'weddings and mortgages'. He believed that all young women were anxious to trap a man into marriage as soon as possible. This view was shared by other lads; it was one of the traditional male beliefs about women. This view of marriage as a trap was not confined to young men in our sample. For example, on one occasion John was teased by youth workers when he had told them that he would not to able to go on a trip because he was getting engaged and married.

We asked many of the young adults if there was a difference in what females and males wanted from a relationship. The initial responses from both men and women are typified by Charlie's comment 'Wey, lads want to lark about while lasses want to get serious'. When we pursued the subject further, however, many women admitted that lasses also liked to 'lark about'; they enjoyed the sexual side of a relationship, and also said that not *all* women were desperate to get married young. Some of the men said they knew of lasses who did not want to get 'serious'. Pete said, 'I've known women who are only interested in one thing too'.

Carol and Sarah had lengthy conversations with some women about alternatives to marriage. Carly, Poppy and Annie supported the idea of living together, and Sharon believed that trial marriage was a good idea, but actually preferred an officially recognized marriage for herself. Poppy was the most outspoken against marriage. At one meeting she said that she did not want to marry and have children, nor was she the least bit domesticated. Her dad wanted her to marry 'a nice boy' but her mum was not too bothered. Poppy said that she might live with someone if she met a lad she particularly liked and that she could not understand the girls at work who were all 'dead keen' to get married, and wanted to leave their job as soon as possible in order to do so. Though she continued arguing against marriage, Poppy also admitted to looking at wedding dresses and engagement rings. She would say, 'Not that I'm ever going to get married, but . . . ' Asia, who was engaged, voiced the views held by many of the other women:

> It's funny, really, but I don't think I could marry someone without
> sleeping with them first. What if you married them and slept with
> them and found you couldn't stand them? I think it would be nice to
> have a trial period before you got married. I mean, what's the point
> if you can't live with each other?

Theresa and Kirsty were both very keen to marry. It was Theresa who
suggested that she and Dave got engaged, and who later set the
wedding date. Kirsty on her own admission, devoted a lot of her
energies to coaxing Phil to the altar. Both these lasses were older-in
their early twenties-and both seemed aware of the risk of being
considered 'left on the shelf' at their age. As Leonard (1980, p.9)
commented: 'One does not *choose* not to get married, one *fails* not to get
married. Marriage is what is normal' (emphasis as in original).

Partners

Early in the study we argued among ourselves that perhaps the
dismissive attitude towards woman displayed by young men was only
a surface characteristic, and part of their male bravado. Some of the
lads on their own with us, for instance, were able to admit publically
that they liked and respected women. Scotch said that he *could*
envisage a time when a lass might be more important to him than the
lads. Some men even admitted that they cared a lot about their
partners:

> I think a lot of the lass. Well, I would do or I wouldn't have thought
> of living with her.   *Al*

While on his CP scheme Morrow said that seeing his lass was the only
thing he had to look forward to after a physically hard, boring day. We
also observed tenderness in the relationships between men and women.
Reg seemed always very attentive to Carol Ann and aware of her needs;
and though Stewart wanted to go out more, he accepted Sharon's
unwillingness and sat watching the television with her night after
night. It was not until we collected more detailed information on
relationships between women and men that we began to appreciate
fully the extent of male dominance, which could be harsh and obvious
and enforced in subtle ways.

Joe was the most outspoken in his belief that in all respects women
were inferior to men. When asked what he thought of the Women's
Movement, in common with many of the other men, and some of the
women, Joe described it as a 'bunch of lesbians'. Pete told us of an
evening out with a couple of friends. Every time the woman spoke, her
boyfriend turned and said, 'Shut up, you don't know what you are
talking about'. We also heard casually dismissive remarks about

women in general; 'They're all right in their place, but they mustn't come between you and your mates' (A1). The implicit lack of importance attributed to women was also indicated by the fact that most of the time they appeared in male conversation only as the target for sexual allusions or general ridicule. Even men like Rocky and Jimi who claimed to support women's equality were unconsciously patronizing. Jimi was horrified at the idea of a lass going to the bar and buying him drinks and, though he initially said it was equally important for a woman as well as a man to have a job, added:

> . . . the majority of women will settle down and have kids anyway; so, you know, their careers aren't going to be as long as a man's anyway. It's not as important.

Rocky said he supported women's liberation but he could still do 'the gentleman bit okay'.

Karl also claimed to support female equality. During a conversation with Carol, he asked if she approved of women with bairns sitting in the pub drinking, instead of being at home cooking the Sunday dinner. Carol said nothing, but the expression on her face provided an answer to which Karl responded, 'Don't worry, I'm not sexist'. On our second weekend away we had long conversations with Karl about many political issues, including women's rights. He was knowledgeable and articulate in these discussions, and yet did not put his beliefs into action. When the women who had helped cook the meal decided that the men should wash up, even though they all refused point blank, Karl was the only one who managed to evade the chore; he became physically and verbally aggressive when Asia tried to force him to help.

The assumed superiority of men went unquestioned by the majority of the women; for example, Jacki, Bernadette, and Kirsty stopped going out with their female friends and conformed to the demands made by their boyfriends in the interests of maintaining their relationships. Stephanie commented that men and women, 'should be equal, but there are a lot of things women can't do'. Not all women, however, accepted male dominance without questions. Karen commented, 'I don't see why women should be treated different from men'. Carly complained of the behaviour of her male friends when they became drunk and 'slobbered all over you'. She was angry and embarrassed one evening when she noticed that the zip of her jeans was undone and her male companions all leapt forward and offered to do it up. The younger lads in Marlow Dene were all taken aback when they prepared themselves to shout out of the van window at a group of lasses who got in first and shouted 'Fuck off' at them.

The attitude of the women, however, rarely went beyond raising questions about male dominance:

> Yeh, I'm going to do his hair. He's having it dyed, and he wants his trousers dyed too. I'll do them . . . I hope I don't get the dyes mixed up! *Carly*

> My dad . . . he gets £2.50 an hour, an' when you've got tax on top of that, it's not much for a *man* is it! *Poppy*

Even those who were beginning to raise questions had absorbed a view of relations between males and females which still controlled much of their thinking and their attitudes. The intellectual acceptance of the case for equal rights did not prevent either us or our sample from lapsing back into earlier forms of thinking.

Partners: the traditional style

We have called traditional those relationships that conformed to the following pattern: once they started to go steady, the couple spent as much time together as possible; the woman gave up most of her female friends, at least in the early stages, to be with her partner; and the couple conformed to the traditional division of sex roles during courtship and after marriage. Most of the couples we met appeared to be fairly traditional. We discuss Bernadette and Chas and Theresa and Dave in detail.

Bernadette's daily routine was to go home from her job, have a bath and tea and then go to Chas, her boyfriend's house, where the couple spent the evening together, and Bernadette stayed the night. Very occasionally she and Chas went out together, but more often Chas went out with his mates while Bernadette stayed in or went to see a female friend. Two major upsets occurred during our contact with Bernadette. She borrowed £200 from her grandmother to buy a car and started to take driving lessons. Chas objected to this show of independence and started to go out with the lads more. Bernadette also suspected that he began taking out other women. Despite this, she resolved to keep her car and did so until it proved too expensive for her to run. This disruption in her relationship with Chas made Bernadette aware of how dependent she was on him. At the same time, she regretted having neglected her women friends at Chas' insistence. As a result she began to enjoy occasional nights out with the lasses. This all came to a halt, however, after she bought Chas a £100 car out of her savings which he then used with a friend to move stolen goods. The two lads were soon apprehended by the police and, after an initial court appearance, Chas was put on a dusk to dawn curfew. He and Bernadette became bored with each other as they had no choice but to spend night after night in together.

There followed an anxious few months during which the couple contemplated the implications of Chas' impending court case. They believed a prison sentence to be inevitable. During this period Bernadette told us that, despite the fact that Chas never had any money, never took her out and kept getting into trouble, she loved him, and he loved her. She said that he was very keen to get married because, 'He'd have it made' and she saw their future together as her working and Chas at home. She also anticipated that he would spend much of his life going in and out of prison. In the event Chas did not go to prison, 'he got off' as Bernadette expressed it; she believed this would encourage him to commit further crimes. The couple remained together, in February 1984 they became engaged and by August were preparing to move in to their own flat.

When we met Theresa she was already engaged to Dave. They went out regularly together with other couples, played in darts matches and shared an interest in folk music. Dave lived around the corner from Theresa and was the brother of her best female friend. Once they had married, the couple went out much less together. Theresa became unemployed and spent her time receiving and making visits to neighbours and saw a lot of her mother, while Dave went out on his own. This routine continued unchanged until Theresa gave birth to a daughter a year after marrying. They then began to depart from the traditional style. Theresa and Dave shared the care of the baby, taking it in turns to get up for night feeds and to change nappies. They also spent more time together at home and going out as a couple.

Alternative styles

Some couples provided examples of people who were attempting to move towards greater equality in their relationship. The impression given was that there existed a greater freedom for both partners to do what they wanted, within negotiated limits. For example, Jane, Poppy and Carly all left their partners behind when they went away for a weekend, while women like Bernadette and Jacki who followed the traditional style did not go because their boyfriends did not approve. Poppy's and Carly's partners, however, also went away from the occasional weekend without them.

Carly's and Poppy's relationships are good examples of the alternative style. Our monthly meetings charted the ups and downs in their relationships with their steady boyfriends. Poppy and Steve were together as much as possible, except at weekends. They quarrelled, split up and were reconciled about twice a week. A typical comment from Poppy was:

> Me and Steve finished last week, but we are back together again now ... Things are great ... I mean, we'd never had it so good. An' he says to me 'I'm frightened because we're too happy . . . I'm too settled'.

During our contact with Poppy her relationship with Steve went through various phases. A couple of months after we met her, Steve went to Italy to search for a job and Poppy was far more upset about this than she had anticipated. She continued, however, spending her Fridays with the lasses and went out with other lads. Steve returned unexpectedly after three months – he had been unable to find a job – and their relationship flourished again. Both Poppy and Steve were unemployed for a while and they spent all their available time together with the consequence that they rowed, became bored with each other, split up more frequently than ever and had casual relationships with other people.

During the summer of 1983 Poppy became increasingly involved with her group of six female friends – they went to rock concerts and to London together, and saw a lot of each other during the day. This did not seem to affect her relationship with Steve. By January 1984, Poppy was employed again and thinking of getting a flat with her friends. She wrote and told us about these events in her life:

> I'm still seeing Steve – yes, it's three years now!!! Things are still the same, but we don't finish as often – I guess you could call that maturing (or just getting used to each other!).

Four weeks later everything had changed again. Steve was busy with a new venture and did not have time to see Poppy. She reported:

> I hardly see Steve any more now. Well, we haven't been talking all week.

Two weeks later she announced to the assembled company at a meeting that they were 'finished for good', but nobody believed her!

Carly and Hal seemed to go through phases of seeing each other every evening and at weekends which eventually led to tensions and boredom so they either 'finished' or agreed to see each other less often. During these periods Carly saw her female friends, in addition to their Friday nights out together. Carly also spent a lot of time with Hal at his parents' home, they went out with other couples and visited both his and her brothers and sisters who had moved away from home.

The impression given by Carly was of a very close, intimate relationship with Hal. They discussed the problems she had with her job at the kennels (such as the scratches she constantly received from the dogs), getting a suntan, suitable styles of clothes and Carly's difficulties with her closest female friend. More important, perhaps, they were able to talk to each other about their own relationship and the difficulties they encountered. Hal was taking a correspondence course which included occasional residential weekends. His absence did not seem to worry Carly at all. In September 1983, when asked how they were getting on, she replied with a smile, 'Fine, it's dead boring!'

At the beginning of 1984, Hal moved south to a temporary job, making only the occasional trip home. Carly seemed quite happy at the separation and the freedom it allowed. She reported that when Hal finally returned they planned to start living together:

> We're getting a flat on the strict understanding that we'll not be sitting over each other. I mean, I says, 'There's no way I'll be sitting in there every night'. I mean, he's not like that, he just goes out when he wants. We've never talked about getting engaged. I suppose we will sometime if the flat turns out and that.

Commentary

Many of the themes in the previous pages will be familiar to those who know the literature on adolescent friends and partners. The overriding interest in attracting a partner, for instance, reminds us of the girl in Veness' (1962, p.xx) study whose three ambitions were that what she 'wanted to *have* was a wedding ring, what she wanted to *do* was to get married, what she wanted to *be* was a wife and mother'. For most young women in our study, marriage and parenthood would soon be entered into: they would decide 'not *whether* they would marry, but *when* they would marry' (Leonard, 1980). The young men, on the other hand, were trying to postpone these responsibilities as long as possible.

We have, however, observed some features of young adults' relationships that differ from observations made by researchers such as Griffin (1982) and Leonard (1980). These differences have emerged partly because we were working with an older age-range, partly because the North East has some cultural variations and also because the quality of the relationships we developed over an extended period enabled us to collect detailed information about friends and partners.

Friendships between women

The friendship patterns we observed among women differed in two major respects from those reported by other researchers. First, even after they had acquired a steady boyfriend and even after engagement, most women maintained contact with their closest female friend; and second, many women also continued to go out regularly with an all-female group. The trend observed by researchers such as Sharpe (1976), who worked with schoolgirls, was for contact with female friends to cease gradually. This pattern has also been observed among women of a similar age to those in our study. Leonard (1980, p.81) remarked of women in Cardiff, 'As they grow up girls go out less with groups of girls or one girlfriend, whereas boys go out more . . . ' Griffin (1982, p.4) wrote of the Birmingham-based women in her study:

> Once a young woman starts to go out with boys, and particularly after she has left school, feminine culture based on supportive friendships begins a gradual process of breaking up.

We observed this drift away from female friends happening to some of the women in our study during the early stages of their relationship with a lad, but others rejoined their female friends when the relationship was felt to be fairly secure. It seems that the north east tradition of the female Friday night out was sufficiently strong to encourage some women to remain in contact with their female friends and best friends for longer than in other areas of Britain.

The traditional style of relationships between men and women in the North East may also have encouraged women to remain in contact with the female group. Williamson (1982, p.131) commented, 'The final force shaping domestic work was the prevailing social attitude about the place of women. There was no work for women in a mining community, outside the house . . . There was, too, a clear sexual division of labour in the family'. These traditional conventions still play a part in shaping both women's and men's expectations of marriage, making the women aware of the need for a group of female friends for future companionship and practical support. Such reliance on self-help groups among women also has a long tradition in the area. Jack Common (1954, p.116) wrote about life in the North East in the 1920s: 'Those [mothers] who were sociable, as mine was, supported each other. She had to have friends . . . The second great virtue of the ma gang, as they saw it, was that they were always ready to help each other'. The assistance provided by the modern version of the 'Ma gang' could be vital after young women marry and have children.

Griffin (1982, p.2) also commented:

> In one sense, strong feminine cultures and space for women to be together at whatever level pose a potential threat to male power . . .

We certainly came across examples of men who were pressurizing their girlfriends to withdraw from the female group, a common occurrence among the women in Leonard's study (1980, p.85) who had 'virtually no leisure activities which were not courtship orientated'. Some of the women we knew argued with their partners about restrictions, but eventually compiled, while others insisted on the freedom to go out with their own friends if they wanted. The customs associated with going steady that Leonard observed in Cardiff were actively encouraged by the women's families: the tradition in South Wales demanded that the women restricted their activities, staying at home in the evening or visiting their future in-laws. In contrast, the tradition in the North East of women having one night a week free to go out with female friends was used by the women we knew to justify their demands for some measure of independence from their men. They could usually rely on their mothers, sister and aunts to support these demands, and even to give active encouragement.

Controlling female sexuality

Among adolescent girls who are still at school, concerns for and speculation about sexual reputation predominate (see McRobbie 1978; Kitwood 1980). In contrast, the women in our study did not discuss their reputation during the normal course of conversation. Once a woman acquired a steady partner, she could openly embark on a sexual relationship with him without risking her reputation. This may be a function of age as much as anything else.

The double standard in matters of sex among adolescents described by researchers such as McRobbie (1978) and Wilson (1978) still applied to young adults. There were two different sets of rules governing female and male sexuality. The men *and* the women in our study believed that a man could have a series of sexual partners, which far from tarnishing his reputation, enhanced it; but it was only acceptable for a woman to have sex with a man within a permanent relationship and having committed herself, she had to remain faithful. Women's sexuality in early adulthood, therefore, was still controlled directly by males: promiscuous men were virile, but sexually experienced females were 'slags', 'whores' and nymphomaniacs. These male standards were also enforced directly through the female group who used the same derogatory terms as men to censure women who slept around, and such women were usually ostracized. As McRobbie (1978) argued, 'the girls' own culture is itself the most effective agent of social control'.

There were the exceptions, however, of women such as Pat in our study who cheerfully admitted to having a succession of sexual partners, but did not appear to be stigmatized as a result. It is possible that other women did not censure her behaviour because she was so obviously *using* men to enjoy herself rather than being *used by* men:

she was in control. We can only speculate because Pat specifically wrote and asked to be omitted from our study at an early stage. It is also possible that women like her were members of friendship groups which conformed to a different set of rules and moral standards for sexual conduct, and thus their actions were judged by them to be perfectly acceptable. Or perhaps Pat, who firmly believed that she never wanted to get married, was consequently not inhibited by the necessity of conforming to the approved code of sexual conduct which ensured that other women found a suitable marriage partner and, as Wilson (1978, p.72) put it thereby 'safeguard their entry into the mainstream of adult social life – namely marriage . . . '.

Once women were in a steady relationship and their reputation was more secure, they had to conform to a different set of pressures to continue to be accepted by the female group; that is, they were expected to conduct their relationship correctly by moving it towards engagement and marriage. The demands and standards set by the female group began to overlap with the concerns and interests of their mothers and they gradually became part of a 'Ma gang'.

Some of the women were immersed in their own new families by the end of our research, while others were at a half-way stage – staying at their boyfriends' houses most nights. These women slept with their male partners away from their own home which enabled their parents, particularly fathers who tended to be very protective, to turn a blind eye to sexual relationships outside marriage. We were interested in this compromise, whereby the couples were almost, but not quite living together. The formal rhetoric of British society still condemns pre-marital sex. In practice, however, in working-class communities babies conceived or born out of marriage have usually been accepted into the family and the community with little comment. The half-way house arrangement seems, therefore, to be a continuity of this implicit acceptance of pre-marital sex, although its expression has been slightly changed. For at least two decades university students and middle-class women generally have had a freedom to experience sex before marriage. Living together and trial marriages have become commonplace among these groups and such practices are now becoming part of working-class life, although an element of social defiance was still attached to the women involved. On the whole, however, among the women in our study the codes of behaviour governing female sexuality were still the same as those followed by large sections of the working class for generations: strict and prudish rather than permissive.

In stark contrast, the codes of conduct governing male sexuality were more relaxed and parents were far less concerned about their sons' sexual behaviour. They allowed them to sleep with their girlfriends at home, and as long as lads did not 'bring trouble home', their exploits were tolerated, and were even something to be proud of: parents consequently helped the double standard in sexual behaviour to continue.

Friendships between men

The stereotype of working-class males as strong, aggressive and domineering is well documented, and evidence from writers such as Willis (1977), Parker (1947), and Jenkins (1983) shows that this macho style is reflected in friendships between men. It influences their conversations and interests and how they interact; they tend to compete rather than co-operate with each other. We certainly found evidence of the harsher features of male friendships, but our fieldwork brought to light a side to the friendships between men that is rarely found in the literature: evidence of kindness, trust, loyalty, gentleness and warmth between men.

How did this aspect of male friendships come to light in our work? There seem to be two interrelated explanations. First, the friendships between the men changed as they grew older and more mature. Once they had established a steady relationship with a partner, though they might still be interested in casual sexual encounters, the men were no longer under the same pressure to pursue women as a way of proving their masculinity to each other; they were therefore no longer rivals to the same extent.

The second reason was methodological. Sarah and Carol did much of the fieldwork with the men, whereas the classic studies on males from Thrasher (1927) and Whyte (1955) to Willis (1977) and Jenkins (1983) were all written by men. Possibly these studies overlooked or dismissed the gentler side of male friendships because of what Jackson (1984) described as the 'masculine taboo against tenderness'. The general climate in society is currently changing, moving women towards greater independence and enabling men to talk about emotions, but still, Jackson argued, men 'had so many ways of expressing the "tough" side of their nature', but 'rarely ... have the opportunity to utter their tender feelings'. Sarah and Carol, however, gave more attention to the expression of tenderness because discussion and interest in relationships and emotions are among topics central to the female agenda. They saw and heard what a male researcher may not have noticed: comments about female partners that hinted at deep emotion and conversations between friends, which suggested that they confided in each other about their partners.

Another major variation from the conventional wisdom on male friendships emerged from our work. There was little evidence that the male group began to break up and disperse as men became involved in marriage and fatherhood. Researchers such as Willmott (1969), Downes (1966), Knight, Osborn and West (1977), Osborn and West (1979) have all speculated that men drift away from their male friends once they have established a steady relationship with a woman; and this gradual dissolution of male groups has been used to explain the fall in delinquency in late adolescence. We found that men initially saw less of their friends, but once their relationships with girlfriends were established, they returned to the male group after a period of a few weeks to a few months.

Various factors may explain this difference. The tradition of Friday nights out with the lads may make it easier for the men to remain in contact with their male friends: like the women (if questioned by their partners) they could use local traditions to justify their actions. Also, in the traditional style of relationship between partners in the North East, men and women tended to pursue separate social lives soon after marriage, so it was usual and expected for men to see their mates regularly. In addition, the men did not become involved in domestic commitments when unemployed, and so had plenty of opportunity to maintain their friendships, which helped to fill in their days. A combination of local traditions and the economic slump may therefore explain the durability of male groups.

We did not find evidence of a dissolution of boys' groups in late adolescence and would suggest that this does not appear to happen, at least, not in the North East. Most researchers who mention such a dissolution have ended their work at the point when the lads moved away from the groups to concentrate on a serious partner, and therefore have not witnessed, as we did, the men's return to the group once they were going steady. In the friendship between Jack and Ben, we did, however, have an example of a young man moving from one group of friends to another in an attempt to give up delinquency.

Patriarchy

The women and men in our study had views about each other based upon stereotypes: they responded to each other in accordance to set beliefs about the supposed biological characteristics of males and females, and not as individuals. We also interpreted many of the men's and women's actions and beliefs to be sexist, all to the detriment of females.

The importance of this issue is that the system of patriarchy, like class, is best seen as a means of distributing power among people rather than a category such as blue eyes or red hair. Patriarchy, as it has been practised, has been handed down from generation to generation in the north east of England. This has meant that working-class women are paid less, are much more likely to be in part-time jobs, have access to lower level jobs and have fewer chances of promotion; are virtually in sole charge of running homes and bringing up children, have their sexuality controlled first by their fathers and then their boyfriends, and are frequently discounted by their menfolk as scatterbrained, emotional and frivolous; at best, they are thought to be a pleasant and ornamental distraction after the 'real work' of society has been completed.

In the days around the turn of the century when there were few jobs available for women besides domestic labour in their own homes, housework was, and still is, essential to the local economy. As Williamson (1982, p.118) described a collier's family in the north east: 'Without women mining communities would not exist: they would be labour camps . . . Housework was as central to the winning of coal as the graft of the miner underground. It was through housework that the miner could be prepared day in and day out to return to his work'. And yet the men failed to see how much they depended on the labour of their wives.

More recently, the call has been for employed mothers to return to their homes to look after their husbands and children and thus solve the unemployment problem: as though men would line up in sufficient numbers to become typists, nurses or cleaners and accept the low wages and status traditionally accorded such female jobs.

The characteristic ways in which men and women interact with each other are, in the work of Connell *et al.* (1982), called 'gender relations'. These writers make the valuable points that class and gender relations are not independent of each other but always interact vigorously, and that both class and gender are 'historical systems, riddled with tensions and contradiction, and always subject to change' (p.180). The life of a young, working-class woman in the north east of England is in vital ways different from that of her male counterpart; and an analysis in terms of class alone would be like playing bridge with half the cards missing. For example, some of the women in our sample were struggling against fathers and fiances to achieve the sexual freedoms that their brothers have always taken for granted, and which their middle class sisters have recently won for themselves.

Stereotyping according to gender and sexism were not, however, issues that young adults discussed spontaneously in conversation. These were themes that we pursued with them with varying degrees of success. Yet it was difficult to discuss such a topic, which was and is so pervasive and deeply embedded in young adults' day-to-day experiences that they appeared unaware of it. During one attempt a group of women were asked if they thought men controlled their lives in any way. 'Oh yes', they replied and quickly moved on to discuss another more tangible subject.

Statements like Winnie's, 'Some women get married so as not to work . . . I'm sure they do', brought home to us how deeply embedded sexist views were. Even a thoughtful and articulate woman like Winnie did not judge the tasks she performed at home to have value equal to that of paid labour and in this she was accepting the dominant view. Men who were seen to enjoy domestic chores were derided. 'You'll make someone a good wife one day', Joe commented to Sarah's husband who had just cooked Sunday dinner at the same time as minding the children. A man who was prepared to do 'women's work' posed a real threat to male power and solidarity.

We were disagreeably surprised by the extent to which our own views and behaviour were sexist. When we came to write reports on our fieldwork, we were made uncomfortably aware that we tended to concentrate on the men. We were taken aback by the number of times we unconsciously considered the situation of men in our study before that of women, by the fact that we had few explanations to offer about women's action but plenty to account for men's, and by the fact that we readily came up with examples from the men to illustrate a point but were at a loss to think of one instance from the women. In our early analyses of our data, women tended to be peripheral to our thinking and it took a conscious decision on our part to begin every discussion with references to the women rather than automatically considering the men first.

We subscribe to the view that, on the whole, the system of patriarchy seriously constricts the lives of young women. Consequently they lack of control over their own lives: 'they stand outside the world of power, contest and conflict' (Powell and Clark, 1975); they are unable to utilize many available resources, lack choice, rarely participate in decision making, and many do not have the language or the concepts with which to assess and change their circumstances. Working-class men have little interest in changing the status quo, as they have nothing to gain and everything to lose. And what hope is there of more rapid change when many women not only accept the status quo but also actively maintain and perpetuate it? We did, in fact, find evidence of some movement towards greater equality. Some men were sharing domestic responsibilities with their partners – looking after children, shopping, cleaning and cooking. More important, a few were examining their own assumptions about women: 'She's as equal as I am', Reg said of Carol Ann. Changes in the structure of employment, with many of the low level jobs in industry being offered to women and with the collapse of apprenticeships in the traditional heavy industries for men, were already affecting the power structure within families. Some women had begun to question the inevitability of patriarchy, but the social pressures in favour were often too great and they submitted to them. The most we can say is that the seeds of doubt had been shown in the minds of some of the women and a few of the men.

Section IV
The Wider Perspective

---

7   Physical and Mental Horizons

Nightmare of glue village

Glue sniffers and teenage motorists are making life a misery in—.

Shopkeepers and families in the main street say they have to watch at night as crazed glue sniffers play 'chicken', leapfrog in front of passing cars and smash up telephone kiosks and public toilets.

The owners of the Central Stores in Main Street, claimed they saw youths, 'bombed out of their minds,' running wild. 'They smash up anything they can put their hands on and jump in front of cars. We also have to put up with youths in cars speeding through the village at over 60, ignoring all the traffic rules.

'The worst thing is the way the glue sniffers often pull the telephone out of the kiosk and push the wires into their ears and make a mess in the toilets. These youths are very frightening. Our customers are wary of leaving the shop when they are around.'

Last week, two residents saw a car driven at high speed, racing another, which hit their garden wall. 'The youths knocked all the bark off a tree, skidded sideways into our wall and then continued along the pavement for a short distance before going back onto the road and speeding off at over 60. We were very lucky they did not hit the house, but we will have a big bill to face for the garden wall,' said one.

Coun. Mrs— said she had seen youths high on glue playing chicken in front of speeding cars. 'We have a lot of trouble with these glue sniffers.' At night they just wander around the area without knowing where they are going. 'I have had them leapfrog in front of my car without taking any notice of the speed. I worry that someone could get killed,' she said.

181

A complaint about the toilets had gone to the District Council.
Coun. Mrs.— said there were plans for them to be cleaned up. The
police have promised to investigate.

Protest over report

Teenagers representing the youth of— handed a petition to the
editor of this paper on Tuesday complaining about a Page One story
in the June 21 issue headlined 'Nightmare of glue village.'

The petition, signed by 110 residents, read: 'We strongly protest
against the article 'Nightmare of glue village' which gave the
general impression that the youth of our village are hooligans,
vandals, and constant glue sniffers. We also deplore the reference
that—is a glue village.'

Before handing the petition to the editor, one of the delegation read
a statement saying: 'We, the youth of—are sick and tired of being
labelled as no-good vandals and glue-sniffers by inaccurate
newspaper reporting.

'Many incidents in the report were over-exaggerated.

'Not every teenager in—is bombed out of their mind or going around
smashing things up,' said one girl.

'There are some glue sniffers like any other village, but not everyone
like the article emphasizes.

'It is a shame the newspaper reports anything bad where teenagers
are concerned. Most teenagers have nothing to do and nowhere to
go, which is not printed.'

This is a more reflective chapter. We draw together a number of themes
and ideas into a discussion of how young adults saw themselves and
the world around them, and how they viewed the reactions of others
such as the media to them. We also consider the extent to which women
and men were prepared to explore the world both physically and
intellectually. Essentially we are trying to give some insight into how
young adults viewed the world, and to provide some understanding of
how these views differed and changed over time.

'Not quite a gadgy': The transition to adulthood

When we first met the young people the majority were aged sixteen or
seventeen and had recently left school. At eighteen they became adults
in the eyes of the law but responses to our questions on the feelings
women and men had when they reached this age revealed some of their

anxieties. They readily outlined what they felt were the major steps on the way to becoming an adult. Asia said, 'Most probably when I left school, and when I got a job and when I started coming out and when I started telling my mum and dad what to do!'; while Stephanie observed, 'It helps being among older people – in the factory there's all ages', and Reg volunteered, 'When they leave school they've got to be treated like adults. When they start working'. Thus, leaving school, starting a job, associating with older people and most important, being treated as an equal by parents and other adults, were judged to be crucial developments. Simply imitating adults was not sufficient, however. Reg commented, 'Some people think that to become a man all you need to do is drink, smoke and have sex. . .'

Paradoxically, although the majority of those we asked were able to identify the critical steps towards adulthood, very few felt themselves to be adults. Rocky observed, 'I see myself gradually being drawn into adulthood, but I don't see myself as an adult', and Jimi said, 'I suppose I never will [feel like an adult]. I imagined that when I was sixteen I'd feel it. Now I'm eighteen, I *am* an adult and I still feel exactly the same as when I was seventeen and a half. . .' Many were ambivalent: they did not yet feel adult, but they wanted to be treated as such. Though in the eyes of the law they were adults, many still did not feel ready for the associated responsibilities. Indeed, remaining young could have its advantages:

> That's another good thing. It's a good excuse for doing things. You can do really evil things and people think, 'Ah, he's just a young un'! *Jimi*

Incidents reported to us and our own observations suggested that older adults rarely showed the tolerance of young un's that Jimi hoped for. In fact, in our experience, the young people were often more tolerant than their elders. The high-handed and dismissive attitudes of officials such as the Training Workshop manager (in Chapter 4) who made snap judgements about trainees based on rumour and gossip or the workers at the community centre in Marlow Dene (see Chapter 2) who quickly banned the lads for an isolated misdemeanour, despite all the help they had previously given, seemed more typical. Many young people reported that they were treated in ways that they judged to be unfair by those in authority, such as their employers, officials at Jobcentres or the DHSS and the police. It was common for them to encounter hostility and lack of understanding from older adults.

> . . . I mean, older people don't exactly go for young people who keep beating them up and that, but young people do other things that are all right. *Asia*

> They go on about knowing everything about life, but life's changed
> so much that they haven't experienced what you have. Like they go
> on about getting a good job. Wey, you canna–you're stuck with
> whatever you can get.   *Jane*

> Some are okay. A lot of them aren't. They don't know where they're
> at. They don't know nothing.   *Jimi*

Many like Asia, had few enjoyable experiences with older adults. She
reported that involvement with us was 'the first time I've been out with
old people. . .Old people! [Laughter]. I suppose I realized I could talk,
you know, to older people.' Another bone of contention was the mis-
representation of young adults in the media, particularly newspapers.
Without exception, those we asked felt that people of their age were
portrayed negatively, as the local newspaper cuttings at the beginning
of the chapter illustrate. Joe commented that the unfavourable stories
were always on the front page while the stories that reflected well on
young adults were tucked away inside. Rocky's view was that their
good deeds were soon forgotten, but never the bad. He complained that
young adults were all 'lumped together as youth'. Carly and Poppy
both felt that the image of, for example, skinheads presented in the
media did not tally with their personal experiences of skinheads, and
Max commented,

> If [young people] dress scruffily or punk they think they're
> hooligans. TV and newspapers all think we're hooligans and
> vandals.

There were clear differences in the way the young people perceived
themselves and how they were treated by older adults and portrayed by
the media. This could cause them minor irritations and incon-
veniences, but did not have much impact on their lives or their image of
themselves: they simply dismissed the unfavourable treatment.
Misunderstanding and unfairness from older adults were only of
significance when they came from those who had direct power and
authority over them.

Physical horizons

All of the women and men in our study felt a strong sense of loyalty to
the North East in general and a deep commitment to the particular
areas where they lived. Their feelings about their areas could be gauged
from the observations they made about other places and from the
feelings of unease some of them experienced when they moved even
half a mile from their own locality.
   Many voiced opinions about nearby estates and about other towns

and cities which were based on a hierarchy of reputations. Regardless of how bad they considered their own area, they all knew of somewhere else that was worse. Winnie, for example, lived on a large council estate, parts of which had a bad reputation. She commented of other estates:

> Hedge Croft's got a bad reputation and Framling definitely. Whatever they try to do, you know, modernize...anything...they've still got that bad reputation and people don't want to be put in.

Tomma also talked about Hedge Croft and how rough it was. He claimed he had been beaten up there by some lads while waiting at a bus stop. At one stage, Troy had been waiting to get a council house for months, but he would not contemplate moving to one he was offered half a mile away, in Sandhills. Phil remarked of this estate, 'The sun's scared to come out down that way in case it gets pinched!' After a pool match in an estate on the other side of town, one of the Marlow Dene lads commented, 'We were like fish out of water there'.

Joe and Scotch took much persuading to accompany Frank to a notorious area of the 'toon' and, when they arrived, were nervous and tense, alert for the first signs of trouble. Scotch said of the area, 'You'll only get a bat in the mouth here' and Joe added, 'I wouldn't come here at night if you paid me'. At this point, five lads in leather jackets and boots appproached. Scotch whispered that if he was recognized from previous fights they should split up and run for it. The lads on either side eyed each other up as the distance closed. When the gap was reduced to about twenty yards, Scotch recognized one of the lads as a friend from college and the silence was broken by shouts of greeting and genial horseplay.

Some young adults had views on other towns which convinced them of the superiority of their own. Al said that Middlesborough was 'full of prostitutes', Reg called London a 'dirty little place' and Troy said of it, 'everywhere's a rip-off'. Joe, who was from Shipton, said that he did not like people who lived in Hillsborough, which was eight miles away, though he had never been there nor did he know anyone from the town. His views reflected the traditional rivalry between Shipton and Hillsborough. Women and men often felt hostile towards other nearby towns and believed that people in these areas felt the same towards them. Kirsty from Hillsborough reported that during a trip into rural Milton she found people's reactions to them were so unfriendly, she had felt that their group might as well have had 'things sticking out of our heads'. One evening while sitting in the pub a lad stared so much at John that he felt he had to go over to ask why.

For the men, especially, their unease had some basis. Al and others of the lads from Marlow Dene did not like going into the centre of

Hillsborough because 'You don't know who you're going to see'. Away from their own territory they felt open to physical attack. Smiler and Jimi from Shipton reported that they did not think it was safe to go alone to certain areas of Newcastle at night as this was asking for trouble. Simon, who lived a few miles from Shipton, was visibly ill at ease when we had a drink with him there one evening. 'They don't like lads from Horton Grange', he explained. When he went to Hillsborough he was only safe drinking there because he had the protection of friends from the locality. Charlie dared not to go the four miles into Runswick in the evening, and Max was beaten up there one night because the local lads conducted a running battle with lads from his home town on Monkton, ten miles away. There was a long-established rivalry between Monkton and Thealby, which were two-and-a-half miles apart and there were frequent fights between lads from the opposing villages.

When we asked the women and men specific questions about their areas and where their families lived, it became clear that their understanding of 'near' and 'far' and their perception of distance differed from our own. In response to the question, 'Which of your relatives live near you?', Theresa for example, said her mother whose home was in the next street was her only relation who lived *near*; her aunts and uncles all lived in Highley and Monkton, which were two and two-and-a-half miles away. Charlie said most of his relations lived 'miles away'. When Carol asked where, precisely, he named an area which was half a mile away on the outskirts of Hambridge, the town where he lived. In contrast, the possession of a car allowed us to visit relatives whom we would call 'living nearby' if they could be reached within an hour's drive.

The difference between our own and young adults' perceptions of distance was also brought home to us when Karl and Bert asked us if we were staying overnight in Shipton after our meeting with them. They were amazed when we told them we drove to Shipton and back to Durham in one evening. Asia was equally astonished when Carol told her that she was driving to West Yorkshire at nine in the evening and would get there before closing time. Some of the young women and men also had rather vague notions of the geography of the North East. For example, when the Hillsborough lads were planning a trip to Middlesborough they judged it to be twice the actual distance.

Most of our sample, like the majority of northerners, believed that people in the South were less friendly than those in the North, Jane, however, the only one who had ever lived in the South, told us:

> Everyone who comes up here says it's really hospitable and all that, and you're really made to feel welcome. That's like, if you're visiting. But if you're a stranger moving in, especially the kids, it's a bit different. . .as soon as your accent is changed, you're accepted.

Some believed that people in the South had a general disregard for the North. Winnie commented, 'Some people from the South don't even know this place exists. They think that it's up in Scotland somewhere. "Oh you're Scottish', they say'. Karl observed, 'What they're trying to do is just make London like a banking centre and keep only very profitable industries going. . .The lower half of the country prospers and the upper half dies.'

Given their set views on other areas, the hostilities-whether anticipated or experienced with strangers-and the very real benefits derived from their own communities, it is perhaps not surprising that the majority of women and men did not contemplate leaving the North East permanently or even venturing out of their own neighbourhoods to find jobs. About three-quarters of our main sample, however, had been on holiday; half of them to places in Britain, the others to resorts abroad. During our contact with them it was only those with a job who could afford a foreign holiday and by no means all of them. Not all had enjoyed their trips away from home. For example, when Morrow went to the small market town of Wolsingham in Co. Durham, he commented:

> What would you do in a place like this? There's nowt. . .no
> nightclubs. . .no nothing. . .

On one of their visits to the nearby Fells, Gary sat in his car with the radio on full blast. John commented, 'He's not the sort for the country, you can tell!' Nikki from Hillsborough described a local beauty spot as 'trees, trees, more trees and water'.

Some of the young adults' horizons were further restricted by lack of opportunities. Sharon's ambition was to travel on a high speed 125 train and she bemoaned the fact that she had never had the chance to go to London. When Winnie, at nineteen, travelled to London for a job interview as a nanny she had her first ride on a train. Stephanie had always hankered after a trip to Norway, but saw little chance of this ever happening, or of going anywhere while she was unemployed.

Above we have described the typical outlook of the majority of our sample. There was, however, a group of about a third of our main sample who were eager to broaden their horizons through travel. They were knowledgeable about their own areas and had travelled a lot on holiday or with their job. They talked with enthusiasm and interest about the places they had visited. Jane and Tomma, both of whom were employed, went to Greece two years running and Spain during the third summer that we knew them. Jimi and his friends had travelled around Europe. Asia and Julie went to Spain on holiday with a group of young women. Simon had been to Spain, Italy, France and Germany. Pete travelled all round Britain as a roadie with a band, and Tony also travelled in his job. Ben and Jack drove all over the North East on fishing trips. Jack was very enthusiastic about Scotland and hoped to move their one day; the contrast between the West Coast of Scotland and Thealby made him appreciate how 'awful' his home town really was. On their trips out with Sarah, Phil and John showed a genuine interest in and appreciation of the countryside. And Sharon, given a choice between a trip to Blackpool or a caravan site near Redcar, chose the latter because she said that she enjoyed the tranquillity of the countryside.

Poppy travelled to Hastings, London and Milton Keynes to stay with friends and attend rock concerts. She was one of the few who seriously considered moving away to find employment. She did not go, however, and freely acknowledged that her ties at home were too strong. Winnie also planned to find a job away from home. But after her interview in London she reported that she no longer wanted a job there as she knew neither the place nor the people; she preferred Shipton where she was known and where she knew her way around. Rocky felt he ought to move away, but knew that he would really miss the street, and the people where he lived, 'I don't know why, I just know I would', he remarked.

Gordon was more typical in that he had lived in the same flat for all his eighteen years, he had never been anywhere on holiday, and he had a love/hate relationship with his locality. His favourite phrase was, as he pointed out the empty berths in the shipyards, 'It'd be a great place for a graveyard'. Yet he claimed to know between three and four hundred people in the neighbourhood. This was no idle boast; he had had a paper round for years and, as he and Frank walked round, he named everyone he met, and knew which school they had been to, how many brothers and sisters they had and the kind of job they used to have.

Mental horizons

Throughout our period of contact with young adults we were struck by the wide variations in their understanding of officialdom. Like many older adults, they were defeatd by the complexities of the education, employment and welfare systems. For instance, shortly after we first met Joe he became very angry about his younger brother's treatment at school. The boy had been accused of breaking windows, although at the time of the incident he had been out shopping with his mother. Joe believed, however, that his mother would not be able to give evidence on her son's behalf. Again, when Scotch became unemployed he had to ask Joe how to claim benefit, how much money he would receive and how often.

Karl seemed generally knowledgeable and politically aware, but even he admitted that he did not know the difference between a university and a technical college. On another occasion Bert informed us that his friend was a student at Durham University. More discussion revealed that the friend had just started an evening class at the Further Education College. Neither Karl or Bert saw any difference between these two institutions; to them all educational establishments after school were colleges, which were so remote from their own experiences that they were unaware of any distinctions.

This lack of understanding of the eucational system concerned us as it made us realize that some of the women and men did not fully understand our involvement with them. At the very onset, we gave each young person a written introduction to our study, invited them to participate and stressed that what they said would be treated in confidence. Despite this, after a year of meetings with Reg, he asked us why we saw him every month.

On the other hand, some young adults were well informed about some aspects of society. It was important for those struggling to survive on Social Security to understand this system so that they could apply for the benefits to which they were entitled. John and Barbara and Theresa and Dave, for instance, were only too aware that they had little chance of getting an income from paid employment and so had to ensure that they received their full benefits from the DHSS. John and Barbara waited until their baby was born before applying for their own council accommodation as they knew that this would increase their chance of getting a house rather than a flat. Kirsty and Phil knew that they would receive some basic furnishing which they could never have afforded out of their weekly social security payments.

We also came across a range of attitudes towards officialdom. The majority of young adults were compliant and claimed that they only became antagonistic if directly abused by people in authority such as teachers, bosses or the police. Some, like Al, who described himself in his earlier days as having been 'a rebel' had, as he put it, 'learnt to compromise'. Joe and Theresa seemed the most actively resistant. Joe said he felt oppressed by 'the system' which left him feeling helpless and powerless. He admitted being aggressive and obstructive in his encounters with the officials of the DHSS and Employment Office. Theresa's resistance was more passive. She complained about how useless, ignorant and inefficient 'They' were (referring to doctors or to the staff on her TOPs course). Her attitude was that, as 'They' did not know anything, so she was not going to take any notice of 'Them', but she never actually complained to 'Them'.

Social issues

During our discussions with young adults we covered a wide range of issues from politics and women's liberation to nuclear weapons, the Falklands war, homosexuality, sex education, mental illness and handicap, and racism. The contrasts between individuals were very marked. Some had rather rigid views, which they held to, despite counter arguments from us and their friends. Others were thoughtful, open minded and prepared to consider alternative ideas: discussions indicated that they read and reflected. Most showed both open and narrow mindedness depending on the topic under discussion. They also held what we considered to be racist views which were derived from local stereotypes since they had little or no direct experience of ethnic minorities. On other issues, however, the same people could be far more tolerant. Many of them in the course of conversation also expressed views that were contradictory and both sets of views were held to without difficulty. More understandably, over two-and-a-half years we recorded views that had changed with time. Reg, for example, in February 1982, said that he would *never* live with a girlfriend before marriage. By August of the same year he was asking Carol Ann to move in with him and she had done so by December. Some individuals knew they were ambivalent and uncertain about their views. As Tomma remarked:

> Every time I think about something it always changes. I don't know what to say.

Others simply refused to discuss certain issues, they seemed to lack confidence in their own ideas and their ability to articulate them. If asked about a particular subject, they responded with 'I don't know anything about that' which was a determined attempt to end the conversation.

Some of the discussions were initiated by us when we asked questions on pre-selected topics, but most issues arose spontaneously in conversation. For reasons of space, we have concentrated on only a few of the many issues discussed.

Politics

When invited to give his views of the different political parties, Joe wrote:

Communist	:	bastards
Conservative	:	The sensible ones
Labour	:	Nearly comi (*sic*)

Liberal	:	Yellow
National Front	:	Racist Thugs
SDP	:	All actors

Rocky responded as follows:

Communist	:	Russians and Reds
Conservative	:	for the rich
Labour	:	for the workers
Liberal		for poofs
National Front	:	for idiots
SDP	:	not worth bothering about because they'll never get into power.

These two lists illustrate the variations in young adults' views about politics. On the whole, however, women and men slumped deeper in their chairs, rolled their eyes to convey utter boredom, groaned, and muttered at the very mention of the word politics. That was the standard reaction which we witnessed, for example, during a 'Life and Social Skills' course being attended by the group in Shipton. Individual conversations and group discussions which we held later helped to increase our understanding of their views, but there tended to be an immediate and typical response which was exemplified by the way Annie shrugged off a question from us about her view on the causes of unemployment: 'I've no idea at all. I don't know anything about these things. I just don't know and I don't care'. Or Bert, on being asked about his interest in politics, replied, 'Not bothered. I've better things to do. . .more interested in enjoying myself'. Even in the middle of the Falklands War, Jimi said, 'Bored to tears with it. . . it's always on the news. Not bothered either way [about who would win]'. At the same time, Smiler commented that the invasion bored him too, as did every other political topic: 'couldn't care less. . .even if I was called up. . .let them get on with it'. We asked Jane about her interest in politics and she replied with a question of her own: 'What's that got to do with me?' These young adults reacted in much the same way to our questions as the majority of people respond to a party political broadcast on television by reaching as quickly as possible for the off switch.

For instance, we recorded their views of politicians in general as being 'a load of crap' (Asia and Ben), 'a load of balls' (Karen), 'prats, stupid prats' (Fenwick), 'a bunch o' bairns' (Tomma), 'dishonest' (Jimi), 'boring' (Max), 'self-centred' (Carly) and more, much more in the same vein. Their answers to our questionnaire revealed that in the main they, in common with many older adults, did not know the names of their Member of Parliament, of their political constituency, or of their local councillors. For some, like Smiler, the experience of voting in a

General Election for the first time in 1983 had been a joke. He and a group of mates had arrived at the polling station together, had given each other three seconds to decide whom to vote for, and 'by chance' had all plumped for the Conservatives. When Stephanie was asked whom she intended to vote for in the General Election she replied that she thought that she had already voted. She had confused the Local Elections with the General Election. When she did eventually vote she told us she had just put her cross anywhere and 'it turned out to be Conservative', but it could have been any party. About a third of our sample, like Ben, did not cast their vote at all, 'There's no point. It does nowt for us'. (In abstaining, they were joining eleven million other adults who behaved similarly in 1983).

Our final questions about trade unions produced the shortest replies of all. Most were not members ('Not so far as I know', replied Karen), they had no knowledge of their functions or history, and so had no views of any kind to express. When pushed by us to say something, a few replied that they thought unions had too much power and Ben added: 'They make people go on strike when they don't want to'.

Long-term fieldwork, however, revealed an interesting paradox in the attitude of many towards politics. The women and men claimed in no uncertain terms to be turned off completely by the topic and yet simultaneously held strong views about some issues which were intensely political. Sharon, for instance, made clear her general distaste for the subject, describing how one afternoon at the Training Workshop in Milton there had been a talk on trade unions. She had been 'bored to tears...I had to strain my lugs and I didn't hear owt'. She had never joined a union and yet, as the General Election of 1983 drew near, Sharon volunteered her views, 'Thatcher wants shot'. Her boyfiend, Stewart, another self-confessed apolitical person, agreed that Thatcher was partly to blame for unemployment as were 'the foreigners coming in and getting all the jobs'. Sharon added that in her opinion no woman should have been allowed to become Prime Minister.

A variant on the tactic of not voting because 'I don't know anything about it' was used by Carol Ann and Fenwick. They were both bright, articulate women who had definite views on all manner of topics with, apparently, the one exception of politics. Whenever the subject was brought up by us, they attempted to sweep it away immediately by an open and honest confession of total ignorance. The aim, it seemed to us, was to kill the topic stone dead at the outset. This interpretation received some confirmation when we were dicussing friends and relations one evening and the term 'nuclear family' was used. Fenwick broke in to say, 'Oh, I don't agree with that at all', and went on to describe the fears of a neighbour's six-year-old boy who had been found crying in his bedroom because he was scared by the prospect of a nuclear war. Carol Ann added quietly, 'I think it's better just to live your own life until something actually happens', and, when Frank pointed out that they had both begun to talk politics for once, the usual confessions of ignorance were made, the theme of the conversation was changed, and no amount of gentle encouragement could elicit any further information.

The nuclear issue was discussed more fully on other occasions, however, and the young adults confessed that this was one of their major concerns. First, there was the anxiety that a mistake might lead to nuclear war:

> We've had that many alerts, haven't we? It's getting to the stage where we're taking off and then someone realizes it's not a proper attack. *Karl*

There was also concern about the resources wasted on nuclear arms:

> They're spending money on trying to kill people rather than saving people's lives . . . What's the point in defending the country if there's no one left in it? *Winnie*

There was an overriding feeling that a nuclear exchange, at some point, was inevitable, 'I think we'll all die in a nuclear war' was Jane's summary. Consequently, feelings about the future were gloomy:

> Even out here you wouldn't stand a chance, you'd just be wiped out. And after they blow us up, there's no way of reaching each other . . . so they'll forget about us when they've blown little old England out of the water. *Poppy*

Joining CND or taking political action to effect change was considered to be pointless. 'Well, you can join CND, but they're not taking much notice of them, are they?' Carly observed. This observation reflected the typical attitude which was to feign ignorance, to vote, if at all, in General Elections but not Local Elections, to vote 'blind' or for the party supported by their parents, and to be unsure of what they themselves stood for but to have a growing awareness of what they were against.

On social questions such as crime and punishment, they either espoused uncompromisingly hard attitudes or they again pleaded ignorance of the whole subject. Reg, for example, wished to bring back

> hanging and flogging because people have no respect for the police or authority at all. They spit at the police at football matches. If they fetched back hanging, it would make them realize they'd be punished rather than two months in jail for killing or stealing from an old woman.

Karl, an active Labour supporter, wanted to reintroduce the death penalty but restrict it for use against those who interfered with children or those who deliberately planned murder.

Having discussed the attitudes of the majority, we wish to convey something of the total range of political views by mentioning those of a few individuals. Joe was on his own at one extreme end of the political spectrum, with a collection of rigid, uncomplicated and mutually reinforcing opinions, which included a solution to the problems of Northern Ireland. He reasoned that the British government knew the leaders of the IRA and so they should simply be rounded up and shot. He was prepared to shoot them himself, given the chance; he spoke with admiration about the Russian Communists (whom in all other matters he saw as an implacable enemy), because they executed their opponents without fuss. The women at Greenham Common, he insisted, should also be taken out and shot, the perimeter fences of all nuclear bases in this country should be mined, and any protester who still managed to penetrate the defences should be 'blasted'. In general, he believed it was of no consequence if a few innocent people were killed as long as the underlying problems were solved. Such views were vigorously backed up by specific and up-to-date knowledge of the state of readiness of Nato's defences and their comparative lack of conventional forces; he culled all this information from extensive reading of military text books while unemployed. Wives, he argued, should give up their jobs, stay at home to look after their kids and so solve the unemployment problem, local coloured people were 'rich swines' and so on. After one unsuccessful attempt, Joe finally secured a place in the Navy.

At the other end of the political spectrum were Rocky, Karl and Pete, who were all actively involved in politics. Rocky's political education began when he – at the age of twenty and a friend of twenty-one – tried to book a local council room for a meeting of young adults who had registered themselves as a formal group. This application was rejected by councillors on the grounds that the group had no adults on its Committee. Rocky was angry about this incident, pointing out to us that the majority of the group were over eighteen and therefore legally adults. This experience encouraged Rocky to press for young adults to be represented on the MSC's area boards. He met with yet another refusal and he began arguing (like Stephanie) for as much time to be spent in schools on political education as on religious education.

Karl's involvement in politics began when he joined a CND demonstration while still at school. His interest in the topic was not shared by any members of his family; we watched his political awareness grow until by the end of our project he was selling copies of *The Socialist Worker*, attending ward meetings of the local Labour party, reading Marx and Trotsky, and working for his party in both local and national elections. Unlike so many of his contemporaries, he could and did argue his views at length. The Falklands war, for example, was in his opinion a means of diverting the peoples of both Argentina and Britain from more pressing economic problems. He went on to question how genuine was the new found British concern for civil rights in Argentina when Britain actively supported so many countries that were controlled by military dictatorships.

Pete was another political activist but his causes were anarchism, CND and animal rights. He worked hard against animal vivisection and experimentation, distributing leaflets, organizing boycotts against certain hairsprays, collecting money and, on one occasion, hitch-hiked to Edinburgh to take part in a rally.

These three were, however, the exceptions that proved the rule. The clear majority of our sample were racist, they were tough rather than tender-minded about the treatment of offenders, they held politicians in contempt, they failed to see a connection between national politics and their own lives, they were unable to sustain a political argument, and they saw little to choose between the main political parties. In Asia's words, 'All the parties are crap...Labour makes things bad and the Conservatives make them worse'.

Race

Few people from ethnic minorities live in the North East. The 1981 census records the immigrant level in the North East was just under one per cent. Despite these low numbers, the view was still expressed that 'the place is riddled with golliwogs', as a local postman put it when he interrupted a conversation between Frank and Hal. Karl, commenting on the small population of coloureds, said:

> You don't see many blacks up here, it's nearly all Pakis. A lot of the
> shops that are doing well are the Pakis, but their windows have
> been broken and there's paint squirted all over.

The only clearly identifiable group was the large Polish community in Shipton. The only contact the women and men had with individuals who were non-white were the local Pakistani and Indian shopkeepers and business men, Chinese restaurant owners, foreign students (mainly Iranian) at the Local Colleges of Further Education and a few West Indians. It was difficult for us to discover the ethnicity of non-whites mentioned in conversation since the majority of women and men were unsure about differences between various ethnic groups. One conversation with Poppy was typical. She told Carol of a friend who had been thrown out of home because she had a black boyfriend. Carol

asked the lad's ethnic origin, to which Poppy replied that she thought
he was Indian, but that he was very black. Carol deduced from this that
the lad was probably of West Indian origin.

Despite their minimal contact with black people, and despite their
limited knowledge about them, many had explicitly racist views, while
others who claimed not to be racist, frequently made racist statements.

Reg, who was otherwise warm and friendly, was the most overtly
racist. He first expressed such views when we met him on the 'Life and
Social Skills' course, but it was not until we were well into our monthly
meetings that he stated, point blank, 'I hate blacks', even though he
had a Pakistani friend. He said that he could not help it, but he believed
that 'they shouldn't have come into this country to take up jobs'. He
repeatedly stated his views, which he knew were prejudiced, but said,
'I'm, not going to change or be changed.' Nor did he, no matter who
tackled him on the issue. To Frank he admitted, 'I hate the black
bastards'. When he was asked why, he replied:

> I just don't like 'em. Never liked 'em since I was a small
> kid...when I was eight. Family like 'em, it's just me. I'm just a
> pig...a prejudiced person. At me engagement party, I was
> telling me mates I'd be proud there would be no niggers. An'
> what did me Mam do? She invited two niggers. I wouldn't
> speak to her. I tried to fight with 'em...told 'em to piss off. But
> me Mam told me she'd invited 'em so I left it.

Reg made sure that his mother did not invite them to his wedding.

Joe and Scotch also admitted to feeling hostile towards black people.
Joe recounted an incident during a football game when he had fouled a
Pakistani member of the opposition who had made him look foolish.
The Pakistani player had outmaneouvred Joe so he had tackled him
and brought him down. Later in the game Joe had kicked this lad
deliberately and been sent off by the referee. Joe also reported that he
and his friends had threatened to 'kill' an Iranian man who had offered
one of the women at college £50 to go to a party with him. He reported
that the English lads gave all the foreign students a hard time, always
threatening them. During one meeting with Asia and Shuk, Carol
mentioned that she had lived in Bradford. Asia made a sound of
disgust because 'a lot of blackies live there'. She said that she did not
like black people, though she had never met any. Shuk responded by
saying that she had met a very nice black woman recently on her
hospital ward, so some black people were all right.

The lads in Marlow Dene also had some strong views on race. After
one too many beers, Al once reported that he 'hated' black
people–mainly Indians and Pakistanis, though Chinese and Malays
were all right. The other lads present indicated that they found the

topic uncomfortable and wanted to get away from it. They all
disapproved, however, of the extreme behaviour of a man they knew
who had approached black people in the street and threatened them
with, 'What the fuck are you looking at?' On another occasion Al told us
that he had been upset when his application for a council house was
turned down, but enraged to learn later that houses were being
allocated to Vietnamese boat people.

On a weekend away with the lads, Sarah heard Phil comment that a
lad who had asked if sausages had to be peeled must 'have been a black'
because of his ignorance; the lads also made jokes about not getting a
suntan which made them too dark. Phil said that he had a conscience
and he always owned up about things. Sarah replied that this was why
he was such a nice person. He then looked her straight in the eye and
said, 'But I still don't like blacks', although he admitted he knew about
'three black people who were all right'. On the way back from the trip
the lads wanted to offer a hitch-hiker a lift until he turned round and
they saw that he was a 'darkie'.

Many women and men seemed aware that their racist views were
unacceptable, certainly to us, but they did not change them; rather,
they held on to them all the more firmly. Some of their views seemed
contradictory. One evening, John made a derogatory remark about a
black person in the pub and minutes later was complimenting the
record playing on the juke box by 'that new black group, they're topper,
great'. Others, such as Karen, thought 'black people were all right...it's
Pakis I hate'.

Some of the women and men expressed tolerant, liberal views about,
for instance, individual coloured people or families whose take-away
restaurants they made use of, while at the same time objecting strongly
to blacks 'taking over the country and all the street corner-shops'
(Tomma). This is precisely what Cochrane and Billig (1984) have called
'the Leroy syndrome' of liking an individual but hating the race she or
he comes from. Poppy, for example, knew 'a Paki at our shop and he's
dead canny', but 'John Travolta Asian types are all smarmy and a bit
of a pain'. Other women objected to 'smarmy Pakis' or lecherous
Iranians' who they singled out from all the men they met at discos and
clubs, judging their attentions to be unpleasant and unwelcome.

Homosexuality

This topic was one of the few that was not spontaneously mentioned in
conversation so we decided to ask specific questions about it. Their
answers reflected the general status of homosexuals in British society.
The typical reponse to our question, 'What do you think of

homosexuals?' was 'They're a bunch of poofs' ('they' usually referred to male rather than female homosexuals). When we pursued this answer, the replies were that 'they're all right as long as they stick to their own kind' (Carly) and 'as long as they keep themselves to themselves' (Joe), or 'I haven't got anything against them if that's what they want to do' (Bernadette). Poppy, one of the few who admitted to knowing homosexuals commented, 'We've got gay friends...they're easily hurt, the boys especially...'

Three of the men had much harsher attitudes. Tomma's reponse was, 'shoot all of them...there's something wrong with them'. He though that they had 'warped minds'. Reg said, 'I don't want to think of them...it makes me sick...they make me feel bad'. Joe told us that he had once gone to a student party and had become violent towards a couple of gay men who were holding hands. While at college Joe had also taken exception to the activities of a young man who was openly gay, and who sold *Gay News* and distributed leaflets and information about facilities and social events for homosexuals. Sharon added, 'It's filthy...two lasses poking at each other'.

Some women and men claimed to have tolerant views of homosexuality, but these contrasted with the views they expressed when they talked of their experiences. Carol Ann and Fenwick claimed to have 'nothing against' lesbians but then proceeded to recount an incident in a pub 'over the toon'. Unwittingly, they had gone into a 'gay' bar where they had been approached by two women and this had made them feel 'awful . . . sick . . . and ill'.

Our Influence

At the end of our final questionnaire we asked the majority of the young adults whether they thought that their meetings with us had influenced them in any way. A few simply said 'No', but the answers given by some of the others suggested that they had come more aware of alternative ideas and ways of viewing the world. Carol Ann reported that she had 'opened up more' as a result of our discussions. Fenwick commented that she had 'come out of herself more and could talk better about things'. Reg's answer was similar, 'Brought me out more. I can speak to people easier now. I was very, very shy before'. We did not, however, do anything that counteracted his racist views. Rocky said that he had gained 'knowledge about things that I hadn't got before'. Jane replied 'It makes you realize there's a whole lot of other people the same', a view shared by Jimi. Carly answered that we had made her feel that she could do something to change her working conditions, and Bernadette remarked that the meetings had made her realize that her life was 'boring and unexciting' and she was determined to make some changes.

Commentary

Becoming an adult

During the course of our fieldwork, most of the young women and men in our sample changed from enthusiastic, optimistic school leavers into more level-headed and realistic young adults. We watched with interest as each one developed and matured but we also saw disillusionment and pessimism set in.

However, the discussion on becoming an adult revealed that, though legally adults, many of them felt they were not treated as equals by older adults and were not accorded adult status. This is not a new state of affairs: the unwillingness of one generation to accept the next is a recurring theme in all writing about young people from Homer's *Iliad* onwards. What is new during the 1980s is the impact that unemployment is having on the transition of young people into adulthood. Leaving school and getting a job were mentioned by our sample as the first major steps in becoming adults. They had all left school, but those unable to find a job could not win from family, friends and older adults the status and respect given automatically to a wage earner, and so could not even start to move along the path to adulthood.

Our evidence suggested, however, that alternatives were being explored, particularly by young women. Getting married, setting up home with a partner or having a child were ways of acquiring status and being treated more as an equal by parents and relations, if not DHSS officials. In areas of persistent unemployment and in families where successive generations join the dole queue, it is likely that more and more alternatives will develop to replace the traditional steps to adulthood.

There are important new elements, then, in the transition of working-class young people into adulthood: the period of the transition has been lengthened, is likely to be lengthened still further, and has become much more fluid and uncertain. The long-term effects of such changes on the family and the peer group have still to be calculated.

Physical Horizons

In chapter 5, we considered the 'localism' of the women and men we knew, referring to their deep understanding of and fierce and loyalty to their home areas. We noted some negative points, but also acknowledge the positive strengths such an outlook provided of well-founded ties and support. In this chapter, where we have recorded our sample's views and experience of places further afield than their doorsteps, it is the more negative aspects which have come to the fore.

We are all too aware of how easy it is for commentators who have had the privileges of travel to decry the often localized outlooks of those who have not. It is hard to imagine what it is to know for the first twenty or more years of life only the pubs in the nearest town centre, the same corner shop and to travel beyond these boundaries, if at all, perhaps once a year on holiday. But what do we mean when we refer to the negative aspects of this localism? The primary notion seems to us to be the restriction of opportunity. This operates on at least two fronts. First, there is the very real restriction of lack of money, which comes into play at all levels, but most obviously when the young consider going abroad; the further you travel, the more it costs. Second, there is the restriction of the mind and consequently of the desire to travel. When the security of what is known is so strong, what leads anyone to seek insecurity in new horizons, even if those horizons are so physically close as to be in the same town? Whether warranted or not, the reputations of particular estates, for instance, were enough to restrict the movements of women and men at a local level and in this sense were a real force in circumscribing their horizons.

It is perhaps too neat to separate the physical and mental horizons of any group of people. The one informs the other in a continuing cycle.

Mental Horizons

The physical and mental horizons of the young people we studied were being simultaneously expanded and limited. They were being pulled in opposite directions at the same time by, for example, their strong ties to the locality conflicting with the positive pull of jobs in the south; and their personal experience began to expose the weaknesses in local myths and stereotypes.

On two major issues, race and politics, the majority of young adults' views were clearly defined. Despite living in the region which had the lowest percentage of immigrants in Britain, white racism was endemic. Extremist views, however, did not seem as pervasive and dominant as they were among the Midlands school pupils studies by Cochrane and Billig (1984). We heard no one advocating the repatriation of non-whites, there was no chanting of racist slogans and the crude bigot was exceptional; though we did see National Front slogans painted on the occasional motorway bridge, a few school walls and pedestrian underpasses. Most young adults could be best described by Cochrane and Billig's notion of 'genteel fascism' by which some young Midlanders rejected the violence and extremism of the National Front, but claimed that it had some 'good ideas'. Racist beliefs were firmly embedded in the minds of both young and older adults in the North East, and because they were so much part of everyday thinking, they were difficult to confront and discuss and are likely to be highly resistant to change.

Educational programmes to counteract white racism need to be introduced, not only in areas with a high percentage of non-whites in the population, such as Brixton and Toxteth, but also in areas like the North East where immigrants form less then one per cent of the population. However, such innovations should not simply provide knowledge about members of different ethnic groups, but need to tackle values, attitudes, and local myths with the aim of promoting tolerance and understanding.

The majority of young adults also had fixed ideas on politics: they were not interested. In this way they were strikingly similar to people of similar age in large, nationally representative samples. The survey conducted, for instance, by the Youth Service Review Group of 635 young people showed that 'Around three-quarters of the 14 to 19-year-olds acknowledged being politically apathetic, and political involvement at this stage was minimnal, only two per cent attending any political meeting/parties' (HMSO, 1983, p.25). Again, 'a considerable proportion of the 14 to 19-year-olds expressed conservative, and in a legal sense reactionary, attitudes to punishment of offenders, in that around 6 in 10 favoured reinstatement of hanging for murder and the use of corporal punishment' (Ibid, p.24).

The women and men in our study shared with many older adults their lack of factual information about the democratic system (they did not know the names of local MPs and councillors), but knowing the name of the local MP is not the stuff of politics. What is a far more important requirement is that they should have not only some understanding of their relative position in society (and that of their families and communities), but also a range of political skills to enable them to participate in improving or defending or transforming those positions. They also lacked an historical or economic framework to help them make sense of national events and their own private circumstances. And we felt that they (as much as we) needed a sociological imagination to help them decide when a personal trouble had become a public issue (Mills, 1970).

Western democracies are currently pouring money into increasing computer literacy rather than political literacy. In Ian Lister's (1976) words, we live in 'don't know democracies' where most of the electorate are politically uneducated; and yet according to a survey by Stradling and Noctor (1983) more than 85 per cent of the secondary schools in England and Wales *claim* to be teaching political education. Only four of our sample could remember any such classes at school; Karen remembered that it was confined to one lesson and Stephanie claimed to have completed a project in political education . . . on the topic of horses. We did not understand her remark either.

Certainly, we do not wish to underestimate the difficulties of introducing political education into the curriculum when it is resisted not only by Local Education Authorities, parents and teachers but also by young adults; Reg, for example, had been 'bored silly' by attempts to introduce the topic during a 'Life and Social Skills' course and thought such attempts were a waste of everyone's time. Our own experiences suggested that a curriculum based on the differences between the main political parties or on the functions of political institutions was unlikely to succeed; but a programme that started with the immediate concerns of young adults, such as their finances or their job prospects, may be more appealing. There remain large questions, however, over the future of political education while so many of our schools are themselves so undemocratic.

But the difficulties are not confined to the steep hierarchies within the schools or to the rejecting attitudes of young adults. Some politicians also regard political education as a hot potato. Witness the directive on the content of the Youth Training Scheme from Mr Peter Morrison, then Minister of State at the Department of Employment, which laid down that 'matters related to the organization and functioning of society should be excluded unless they are relevant to trainees' work experience'. The furore that followed in late 1983 forced the Minister to retract, although 'political or publicly controversial material' was still prohibited. The distinction between balanced political education and indoctrination into the politics of any one party had temporarily been forgotten. For surely no democratic politician of whatever persuasion can accept with equanimity the deep cynicism and ignorance about democracy that we have described in this chapter?

The attitudes of young adults that we have conveyed have been predominantly negative: we have shown them to be inward looking, resistant to change, racist and politically apathetic. There were exceptions, however, and we saw new ideas breathing life into women and men: some of their horizons were broadening. For example, Tess and Rocky became involved with youth projects, which gave them the opportunity to travel and exposed them to new ideas, and Pete became politically active through his interest in Punk music.

But these young adults were exceptional. For most, their marginality both in terms of their age group and their region severely limited the options open to them, and restricted the opportunities for change. For the majority, their chances in life seemed to have been unaffected by eleven years of formal schooling: it remains to be seen how many will break the powerful bonds of class but, on our evidence, it is likely to be a handful.

8 A New Social Contract for Young Adults

'Forgive me, but on the rare occasions when I peep into the world of the young I find it about as recognizable as, as medieval Patagonia.' So says Alfred Nash, a psychiatrist in Kingsley Amis's novel *Stanley and the Women* (1984, p.55). Physically, medieval Patagonia is to be found in the bedroom of the nearest young person; and psychologically, do the young adults we have described in earlier chapters really inhabit another country and another century? Is it not rather that the unemployment of Stephanie, the low wages paid to Max, the friction between Carol Ann and her dad, the powerlessness of the group of young adults on the Marlow Dene estate, and all the problems with which we began are all *too* familiar and close at hand? If only we *were* dealing with medieval Patagonia, our consciences would be still and that may be the defence mechanism used by the Alfred Nashes of this world. In the minds of certain adults, then, the gulf between the generations is apparently unbridgeable and that attitude is perhaps the greatest single obstacle to improving the lot of young adults.

It is our view that the unofficial, unwritten contract between young people and society has finally broken down in most Western countries. Its limitations have been obvious for a very long time; for example, the status and position of young adults in society has been a problem ever since the adolescent was invented by Rosseau in 1762; even in the prosperous 1960s, when social scientists could write books with such titles as *The Transition from School to Work*, there were periodic moral panics about the behaviour of young people, as Musgrove (1964), Stan Cohen (1972) and others argued at the time. (By young adults we are referring in this chapter to the large majority who leave school with few or any qualifications rather than the group selected for higher education, for whom a far superior form of social contract exists.) The final end of the social contract, however, came rather suddenly with the alarming increases in youth unemployment in all West European countries in the late 1970s and early 1980s.

But the social contract, as we use the phrase, should be concerned with more than the question of unemployment, as can be seen from the descriptions in Chapter 4 of the exploitation of young people in some government schemes and in shit jobs. The treatment of young people by official agencies such as the police, DHSS officers and MSC officials, by the media and by older adults generally shows how the present contract is acted out. By using the term 'social contract', we also want to include the means whereby society seeks to integrate each new generation of young people into all its essential activities, which include the formation of new families and the raising of children as well as employment and the creation of wealth. The political nature of the current agreement is clear from the rhetoric of all the main parties which holds out promises to young people of equality of opportunity and individual, merited rewards for hard work, ambition, honesty and 'toeing the line'. By the contract we also mean the structure of opportunities, the range of choices and the quality of life available to young people; the contract is a shorthand way of referring to the official means whereby young people attempt the transition to adulthood, and the ways whereby they can achieve a sense of personal dignity and worth in the modern world. The need for some such contract is self-evident: it is part of the social cement which holds the generations and society together. At present, in efforts to cope with the downfall of the old contract, new structures are being built with sand and water but no cement.

For their part, young people are invited to honour the contract by becoming productive and law-abiding members of society, who are supposed to transmit in turn to their own children the values of industry, democracy and commitment to the state. In this way, it is hoped that harmonious (or at least workmanlike) relationships will be preserved – in a deeply unequal and divided society – and that the job of reproducing the present political order will be accomplished. This over-simplified account of the ways in which society reproduces itself from generation to generation has already referred to the failings of the system which existed even in times of plenty; these failures are now being fully exposed by the major discontinuity we are now experiencing.

Not only young adults but many parents, who were themselves young in the boom years of the 1950s or 1960s, simply do not know what is in the best interests of their offspring. The labour market for young people has been transformed in the last twenty years and is radically different from the one most parents *think* their daughters and sons are growing up in. Parents in the North East, for example, are still talking the language of apprenticeships and are unaware of the widespread collapse of that system. The main type of apprenticeship that is still available in the North East is an apprenticeship in unemployment. Over the last three years we have watched young people learning to do nothing on estates where unemployment, now raised to the status of a social institution, has become as familiar as the local church or school and is often of longer standing. Many of the jobs that young adults used to do have disappeared permanently. Most economic commentators agree that we are not in the middle of another cycle of 'stop-go', with which the parents of our sample became familiar in their own early days of employment. It is no longer a question of waiting a few

years on the dole until the economy recovers but of whether large
sections of the population, and especially young adults, will ever be
employed again. The discontinuity is concerned with the very real
prospect of jobless growth, of an economic revival, which creates a
restricted number of jobs that demand higher qualifications. Previous
technological revolutions have tended to increase the levels of
employment although there have always been Luddites who claimed
the opposite would happen. Perhaps Ned Ludd was simply two
hundred years too early. The upshot is that young people, who have
always been marginal to modern industrial economies, have been
driven even further to the margins and those who happen to live at the
geographical periphery of the country (as in the North East, North
West, Scotland, Wales or Northern Ireland) have been and are likely to
be doubly disadvantaged.

A further difference between the experiences of the two generations
is that the parents of the young people we studied moved with
comparative ease from school to employment, picking and choosing as
they went, and so were able to establish adult status and independence
as wage earners with homes and families of their own. Getting married
and/or raising a family on Social Security is a very different matter,
both psychologically and financially. Our evidence suggests that the
customary roles of young women as domestic labourers have become
intensified, while the traditional means of progressing from childhood
to adulthood have been broken for hundreds of thousands of working-
class young men. The social consequences of an ever-extending period
of dependence on parents and the state have still to be calculated
because the phenomenon is so new. The almost endless adolescence,
which for decades has become the lot of middle-class youth, is now the
daily experience of their working-class contemporaries with one
critical distinction: for the latter there will be no elite jobs to
compensate for the long denial of status.

Because the nature of this major discontinuity was misread as a
temporary problem, with unparalleled numbers of sixteen-year-olds
flooding a depressed job market, the official response of both Labour
and Conservative governments was predictable: they introduced
under central control a bargain-basement counterpart, MSC schemes,
to 'the adventure playgrounds' used by the daughters and sons of the
middle classes, as Ian Lister has called the institutions of Higher
Education. The school-leaving age could have been raised to seventeen
or eighteen, but that option was not open to the present government,
some of whose leading members had laid the blame for the country's
economic decline at the door of the schools. (Since the 1880s, in both
Britain and in the United States, schools have been held responsible
for periods of economic decline in efforts to distract public attention

from the failure of the economy to generate enough jobs. See Grubb and Lazerson, 1981.) But in the late 1970s, a new structure (YOP) had to be found, the content and style of which could be controlled by the MSC, and which could later be expanded from six months to the present one year of YTS and soon to two or perhaps even four years, as Charles Handy (1984, p.99) has argued.

Attempts to solve deep-seated economic problems by means of vocational training have always failed and, in the words of Grubb and Lazerson (forthcoming), programmes such as YTS are best seen as 'ageing vats' for working-class school-leavers. The central purpose of YTS is clearly social control–to keep young people out of the job market, out of the unemployment figures and off the streets. A secondary purpose is the provision of free (not cheap, but free) labour to industry, which has a year to select the recruits it wants; another form of social control. Is it possible that the initials of the MSC stand for More Social Control? Although the total sum of around £1 billion spent on YTS in any one year at first sounds impressive, the average cost per person on the scheme on £1800 has to be contrasted with the money invested in the higher education of a doctor, which has been calculated to be £100,000 (Drake, 1984, p.66). Compare also the training times involved: six to seven years as against thirteen weeks off-the-job training, a time 'so short as to mock the very term "training" (Braverman, 1974, p.433). YTS is a scheme designed for other people's children.

What has brought about this major discontinuity in our affairs? There is no simple, agreed explanation. A number of factors coming together have transformed the job market facing those young people leaving school at sixteen or seventeen. The chief factors that have been implicated include:

- the world recession, which has affected employment more seriously in Britain than in the rest of Europe;
- technical advances, which have destroyed some traditional teenage jobs;
- a marked decline in jobs in the manufacturing sector, which has amounted to almost 30 per cent in the North East since 1979;
- 'the internationalization of production and distribution, which allows multinationals to export unskilled jobs to less-developed lands where labour is even cheaper, more abundant and non-unionized' (Roberts, 1985, p.41);
- the increase in the demand for jobs from the extra numbers of young people;

- the allegedly high cost to employers of the wages paid to young workers;
- and official policy, which has invested money in training rather than in job creation.

It would be foolish to hold the present government solely responsible for a crisis with so many contributory causes, some of which are international in origin and most of which are not under their control: the argument here is that their actions have exacerbated an alredy deteriorating situation. But the scale of the crisis, its permanent and structural nature, and the depth of the suffering it has already caused have all been seriously misjudged.

However, Peter Kelvin has sounded a note of caution:

> . . . historians have become somewhat wary of the notion of 'industrial revolutions': the fact is that if we add them all up, there have been industrial revolutions – *major technological develop-ments accompanied by socioeconomic dislocation* – in six out of the last seven-and-a-half centuries. (1984, p.410)

Kelvin is also right in emphasizing that not even the *rapidity* of current changes is historically new:

> The social psychological question is therefore *not* 'How do we cope with the unique problems of our time?', but 'Why do we still have almost exactly the same problems in coping with industrial change as earlier centuries?' (1984, p.411)

There are also economists such as Leontief and Duchin who argued that by the year 2000 technological changes are more likely to increase the demand for labour rather than reduce it, provided people are retrained fast enough to make use of the new opportunities (see Huhne, 1985). Even in their most optimistic scenario, however, the main job losses will be suffered by female clerical workers.

To this, we want to add a few questions of our own: what is the morality and what are the likely results of visiting most of the negative consequences of an industrial revolution on one particular section of the community? Surely any Government needs to do much more than offer training schemes which, in the North, return the majority to the dole queues? Has the intense public debate over YTS distracted attention from the plight of 18–24-year-olds? (In the North in 1984, the Community Programme offered places to only 10 per cent of unemployed adults; NECCA, 1984, p.25.) Is it possible that the suffering of the young unemployed has been largely ignored because they are considered to be political pygmies without the knowledge, skill or organization to turn their frustrations into effective protest? It took the inner-city riots of 1981 to galvanize Government into some forms of

limited action, but the effect was short-lived, as the recurrence of
rioting in the late summer of 1985 has made clear. The social climate
currently devalues compassion and empathy, perhaps therefore only
appeals to self-interest will bring political action; a society divided
against itself is unsafe even for elite groups.

It has become fashionable in recent years to refer to the divisions in
British society that we have already discussed, but there are others:
between those in comfortable, secure jobs and the long-term unemployed, between the prosperous South and the 'giro cities' of the North,
between those in favour of more authoritarian 'solutions' imposed from
the centre and those arguing for a more participant democracy which
could revitalize the regions. There are two other splits which need to be
added: the social fissures between and within the generations.

To use a phrase of Burke's, 'the partnership between the generations'
has been unilaterally ended. There is even a split between school
leavers without jobs and the older long-term unemployed. It is the
young who have taken the brunt of the economic recession in Europe
out of all proportion to their numbers in society, and rightly there has
been much political and media concentration on the plight of school
leavers. Unfortunately, however there has been a corresponding
neglect of the long-term unemployed over the age of thirty or forty.
Although the same causes underlie the unemployment of both groups,
government acted to train school leavers, who are widely seen as
blameless, but attributed the joblessness of forty-year-olds to their lack
of skills.

We have the second split developing within our own sample and
within their contemporaries: the division between those who have
ended up in paid employment and those in long-term unemployment.
Those who obtained jobs have clung to them despite many dissatisfac-
tions, mainly because the high levels of unemployment have created a
climate of fear which has reduced their expectations. Couples such as
Reg and Carol Ann, and Jane and Tomma have continued the
traditional pattern of moving away from dependence on their parents
by getting engaged, having the money to go on holiday together, and
planning to set up home together – all made possible through their low
but steady wages. Lasses like Sharon and Winnie and lads like Scotch
and Charlie, after periods of moving on and off govvies and in and out
of shit jobs, have settled down to increasing periods of unemployment.

Official statistics show that a disproportionate number of the young
have been jobless since the 1970s. When the national total for those
registered as unemployed stood at just over three million in the middle
of 1984, over one and a quarter million of them were under 25 years of
age. What is even more serious is the age distribution of the long-term
unemployed, which indicated that almost 350,000 (or 29 per cent)

young people under 25 had been jobless for more than 52 weeks in April 1984: that figure represented an increase of more than 600 per cent on the total of 57,000 in October 1979. The immediate prospects for this age group are grim indeed: in December 1984 the OECD predicted that about one quarter of all people under 25 in Western Europe would be unemployed by the middle of 1986. Can Western governments take the risk of producing a new underclass of state pensioners aged 18 and 20 and 22 and 24? The latest government proposal to end supplementary benefit for those school leavers who refuse a place on YTS shows how much freedom of choice will be left to those who are dependent on the state; some may be driven by such a measure to withdraw completely from society and join alternative, black economies, if they can.

Some relief will be afforded governments by the fall in the birthrate, which will mean fewer young people seeking jobs in the late 1980s and early 1990s. In the meantime, the age group that we studied will grow into early middle age in an increasingly technological world: to a large extent unqualified and untrained, too old at eighteen to be considered for YTS, most will only be thirty-four-years-old in the year 2000. As we asked at the end of Chapter 3: are we knowingly going to allow large numbers of them to look back in that year over sixteen years of unemployment and to look forward to a further twenty-five or thirty years of unemployment before 'retiring' at the ages of sixty or sixty-five?

Another indication of the sorry state of the social contract between the generations is the current status of young adults in Western society. At various points in our project we examined the attitudes of our sample towards older adults: were they becoming increasingly criticial of their treatment by older adults? Were they filled with anger against adult society? Were they on the point of rioting? Had they abandoned the will to work? Were they withdrawing into alternative lifestyles? What we found were non-political, pragmatic young adults who were all still eager for employment even on modest wages, who were conservative on most social issues, and who had turned their frstrations not against their elders but against themselves. As our study progressed, what became worthy of notice was not hostility to or a retreat from the world of older adults by our sample, but the abuse of power and position by many adults who belittled, humiliated and derided young people. Exactly twenty years ago, after questioning groups of younger adolescents and members of the local adult population, Musgrove (1964, p. 2) came to the same conclusion: 'What emerged with the greatest clarity was the rejection of the young by adults'.

The young women and men were still learning the hard lesson that many older adults, who did not know them well, treated them not as equals who were worthy of respect, but either as representatives of the media stereotype of The Rampant Teenager, or as Wrong Uns or Troublemakers or Shysters. From their schooldays they had become accustomed to the fact that older adults often tended to judge them not on their ideas or interests but on their appearance; what genuinely surprised them was that their elders could not see the vast range of differences within the *same* group of young people whether dressed 'straight' or as Punks or New Romantics or Skinheads. They were also taken aback by the realization that often they themselves behaved better than the elders they had been brought up to respect.

The sensational treatment of young people by the media was also deeply resented by the women and men we knew; the stigmatization of earlier generations of the young has been well documented by Cohen (1972). We discussed together, for example, the series in the *Daily Mirror* at the end of April 1983. The front page headline and lead story ran as follows:

> **BLOODY KIDS!**
> Bloody kids-they're everywhere. There are 15 million of them crawling, toddling, running, jumping, lolling, leaning, lounging, lying, boogeying, sitting, slouching, skating around the face of the British Isles.
>
> They're frightening, aren't they? They used to look as if they were from a different world but now they look as if they are from a different universe.

For four days, the front and centre pages were covered with headlines such as 'Who Do They Think They Are?', and the topics chosen were, predictably, sex and marriage, violence, the police and drugs. What annoyed the young adults who read the articles was the contrast between, on one hand, the screaming headlines and the photographs of exoticly dressed Punks and Skinheads and, on the other, the mature and thoughtful responses of most of the young people interviewed. The daily drip of exaggerated reporting is likely to have unintended consequences by presenting all young adults as a social problem.

What is even less acceptable and more worrying is that some professional groups discuss young people as though they were *all* deviant. Conferences, particularly those run by psychologists, are entitled 'Teenage Problems' or 'Stress and Adolescence' (two examples of national conferences in 1984), and the individual sessions concentrate on unrepresentative groups involved in either drug addiction or underage sex and abortions, or serious delinquency. We want to repeat the argument, mentioned in the Introduction, that most young people progress through their late teens and early adulthood without anguish or torment. A quotation from the Thompson Report (1982, p.33) on the youth service in England sums up the same finding succinctly:

> ... youth is *not* a time of continuous crisis - a sort of developmental disaster area ... the majority of young people are not in a state of crisis.

In this regard, some of the dominant psychological theories about adolescence, Erik Erikson's identity crisis for example, may be partly responsible for the widespread acceptance of adolescence as a deviant category. The intelligent layman and the overburdened practitioner who works with young people are unlikely to have read Erikson's sophisticated and detailed argument in the original. However, what has become part of everyday thinking and conversation is an association between the two ideas 'youth' and 'crisis', which happen to be the subtitle of Erikson's (1971) book on identity. The emotional crises in late adolescence that have been experienced by exceptional individuals - Martin Luther's fit in the choir and Jean Piaget's philosophical novel written at the age of nineteen - may well have had curative as well as creative aspects, but has it been sensible to generalize from these intellectual giants to all young people? Certainly, none of our sample nor for that matter any of the three authors, had experienced a life crisis in adolescence; nor did any of us know of anyone who had had such an emotional disturbance in their late teens or was likely to.

We are not suggesting that Erik Erikson's work on identity confusion in adolescence is without value; far from it. One has only to recall his remark to the effect that, 'In general it is the inability to settle on an occupational identity which most disturbs young people' (1971, p.132), to appreciate the enduring significance of his insights. If only the same could be said of more recent psychological studies such as John C. Coleman's *The Nature of Adolescence* (1980); it ends by presenting a new focal theory which shows how far academic psychology is at times removed from the real world of young adults. The theory, which is depicted in the accompanying diagram (Figure 3), suggests that adolescents cope with one issue or relationship at a time as they grow up; it also contains the reasonable deduction that problems are most likely to occur when young people have more than one issue to deal with at the same time. But why is this thought to be particularly true of adolescents? Could the same not be said of younger children, middle-aged parents or old-aged pensioners? Not even the subsequent modifications and improvements of Leo Hendry (1983) can save the theory from the charge of triviality. For instance, the topics of unemployment, shit jobs and finances are not mentioned by Coleman:

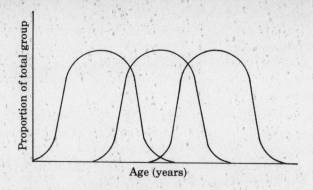

Figure 3   Coleman's focal theory of adolescence

the nature of adolescence in contemporary Britain is explored in two hundred pages that contain no reference to class, culture, community, power, poverty or inequality. Excluding both employed and un-employed young people, the sample consisted solely of those still at school: 'those who took part were simply a random group, selected by teachers as being articulate, willing to participate, and between the ages of fifteen and seventeen ... While I actually interviewed a large number of adolescents, in the final analysis I have only used material from about a dozen individuals' (Coleman, 1980, p.viii).

Let us return, then, to the prospects facing the vast majority of ordinary, working-class young adults. Before emerging government schemes become well established, young people are likely to be subjected to even more uncertainties than have been usual at their time of life. Until new structures become familiar to them and their parents, certain key questions need to be asked: how are young adults, eager for jobs but at the very margins of the economy, to be integrated into society? How is the transition to full adult status to be achieved on state handouts of £17 or £18 per week? What are the future prospects for those who had the misfortune to be 18 or 20 when the juvenile labour market collapsed? Our answers, where we have any, are sketchy because of our own limitations. A project such as our involves researchers in many aspects of young people's lives where, frankly, we have no expertise; and nowhere is this more true than the field of social policy about which psychologists tend to be particularly ignorant.

An integrating model

However, before, discussing the outlines of a new social contract we wish to draw together the findings of previous chapters into one descriptive account and to assess the prospects for young people in the North East. We have constructed an integrating model which attempts to bring together what we consider to be the central factors in the lives of the young adults we knew. Out of all the factors we recorded as influential in the lives of those we met, we have chosen what occurred to us as the most significant to incorporate in the diagram (see Figure 4).

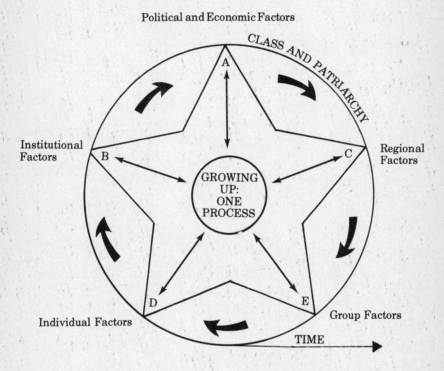

Figure 4   An attempt at an integrating model

Class and patriarchy are means whereby some gain advantages over others; they are best thought of as relationships between people which accord power, wealth and status to some and deny it to others. Connell *et al.* (1982, p.180) have argued effectively that in Australian schools the process of class and gender interact vigorously:

> The situation of a working-class schoolboy is always different from the situation of a working-class schoolgirl; they cannot (except for very summary purposes and at the cost of sloppiness) be lumped together as if there were just *a* working-class situation.

Our argument is that *all* of the main factors in our model tend to interact vigorously, creating different patterns of problems and opportunities for individuals.

The arrows and circles used in the diagram should not be interpreted as indicating a deterministic or closed system in which people are pushed around like so many billiard balls or space invaders. Although political and economic factors are portrayed as dominant, we do not wish to suggest that they *directly* control the lives of individuals; rather, national and international economic forces impose constraints on the choices available to young people. We *do* wish to argue that the range of choice is becoming increasingly limited for young adults in the North East. Being able to choose between shit jobs, govvy schemes and the dole, as our sample expressed the options open to them, is not exactly the equivalent of having the world at your feet; and, as we argued in Chapter 3, for too many of them and their contemporaries there has been a sudden constriction of opportunities. As the sample became older, those who were still unemployed could not find even a shit job or a six month government scheme. Giving up all hope of a job, lowering one's expectations of life and retreating into oneself to avoid more psychological damage is not what has traditionally been understood by the terms 'occupational choice'.

We chose to represent as a circle the all-pervading influences of both class and patriarchy because they had an impact on all aspects of the lives of our sample. Let us illustrate with reference to patriarchy. At the level of individual factos (D), young women were, of course, aware that the conventional standards of physical attractiveness were used in the selection of receptionists and office staff. At other points in their lives (C and E), they encountered the sexism of the region, of teenage magazines designed for girls, and the presures to get a man among their own age group (see Griffin, 1985). In the institution of the family (B), they experienced greater control by their fathers over their personal lives than their brothers did. When they did manage to secure a typically low-paid female job such as shop assistant, or temporary, part-time typist (B), they faced the sex stereotypes of employers and sexual harrassment from male colleagues. At the level of national policy (A), all women are at the receiving end of an institutionalized sexism, which is still largely unselfconscious and so self-perpetuating. Witness the MSC, which tends to lump together 'women, disabled people and members of ethnic minorities' (1981a, p.4). In contrast to Coleman, who argues that young adults cope with one issue at a time, we would claim that most of them are struggling to cope with all these different aspects of life, which impinge upon them simultaneously.

There are, however, limits to the explanatory power of any model. We are not attempting to capture the essential features in the lives of *all* young people, but only of our own sample. Inevitably, a one dimensional, static diagram does injustice to the complexity and dynamism of real lives. The model also attempts to set all the factors into one single, developing historical process in which upheavals or initiatives and successes or failures in one area affect all the other areas. The task of growing up could then be described as steering a successful course through the interplay of all those factors that affect the lives of young people at one and the same time.

The model has other unavoidable defects. It separates out phenomena which are interlinked and interdependent. For instance, individual and structural factors are neither so independent nor so opposed, as our model suggests. Let us give two illustrations. First, Norris (1978) has argued convincingly that human qualities (such as occupational skills), which appear at first glance to be individual characteristics, are better viewed as the results of an interaction between personal and institutional factors. Skill levels, as well as reflecting individual ability, are also constantly being negotiated with management and are a function of the hiring practices of local managers in particular labour markets. Nowhere is this clearer than in the position of a young unemployed person who may be forced to accept whatever job is available, irrespective of the level of skill she or he possesses. Second, the young adults we knew made decisions about their lives partly by drawing on their own perceptions and interpretations of national and regional treds; in other words, young people and social structure are not independent but they interact with each other. Our sample had views of how society is or should be organized inside their heads. Such interactions, however, are difficult to capture in a simple diagram.

Despite these difficulties, we have persevered with the model because too often one isolated aspect of young people's lives tends to be studied (e.g. delinquency or homelessness) and the totality of the forces impinging on them is apt to be forgotten. For all its simplifications and imperfections, the model has at least the merit of attempting to bring together psychological and sociological factors and different levels of explanation into one account. It also serves as a reminder that the education of most psychologists is still confined to a study of individual and group factors or only the lower section of the diagram; this does not appear to prevent psychologists from making professional judgments about the 'whole' person. Similarly, too many sociologists seem to think predominantly in political and institutional terms and important characteristics such as physical and emotional maturity tend to be underemphasized.

The North East

We also used the model in discussions with our sample to counter their
strong belief in individualism, which we defined in Chapter 3 as 'a
general principle whereby young adults explain social mobility,
financial success and failure, employment and unemployment by
exclusive reference to the characteristics of the individuals concerned'.
But the future is not theirs to make alone: it is intimately tied up with
the economic prospects of the North East. There are deep-seated
regional differences built into the particular economic structure which
sets the broad parameters within which all young people in the north
have to live out their lives.

This is not the place for a detailed statistical breakdown of the
region's economy but some measure of its entrenched deprivation
needs to be given. The area now seems to be lost to public consciousness
somewhere between north Yorkshire and Scotland, but it was not
always so. In the nineteenth century, the North, far from being at the
periphery, was at the very heart of industrial Britain; her engineers nd
craftsmen kept the region at the forefront of technological advance
with inventions such as the first passenger railway, the first tanker
and the first turbine. The concentration, however, on a few heavy
industries such as coal, steel and shipbuilding made the area
particularly vulnerable to economic depressions as in the 1930s. The
Second World War brought a temporary boom, particularly to the
armaments industry, but later the vulnerability of the region was
increased by attempts to diversify the industrial base, which brought
in branches of multinational companies without centres of research
and development. Control over the local economy was now in the
hands of either nationalized industries or firms with headquarters in
Rotterdam, Detroit or Tokyo. The historical domination of the job
market by a small number of very large firms means that there is no
tradition of self-employment in the area; it also means that the closure
of any major works has far-reaching effects.

The results of a long period of persistent decline were to be seen all
around: the main streets of local towns and villages were becoming
dirtier, shabbier and showing all the marks of a prolonged economic
slump: boarded-up shops, secondhand furniture stores displaying
posters which read 'DHSS estimates given free' and amusement
arcades full of women and men playing one-armed bandits and bingo.
The area has had for years the highest unemployment rates in
mainland Britain and 'poverty is once again a real problem in the
North ... (with) ... the lowest average household income in the whole of
the country – indeed one household in every six has an average weekly
income of less than £50!' (NECCA, 1984, p.1). The dirty and dangerous

conditions of local industry are reflected in the health statistics, which show that the North East has four out of the ten districts in England and Wales with a marked concentration of health problems–higher mortality rates, more than average sickness and invalidity benefits, and lower standards of primary health care (Black Report, 1980). The percentage of pupils staying on at school or entering full-time Further Education remains the lowest of all the English regions. In this case, the economic history of the area and the experience of unemployment in the 1930s is still thought to be influential:

> That experience established the tradition that . . . for the majority–and it was a larger majority here than in many parts of the country–the best, indeed often enough the only possible, course was to leave school as soon as the law allowed, and to take a job, any job, which would contribute to the family income and offer some possibility of security. (Christopherson, quoted by A. Townsend, 1985, pp.106–7).

Our sample, then, have inherited a bleak legacy from the North's industrial past. A combination of interlocking disadvantages in employment, health and education has produced a set of opportunities that are markedly inferior to those of their contemporaries in other more prosperous parts of Britain and Europe. Their immediate prospects are worsened by the fact that in 1987 the 20–24 age group will peak in numbers, with 20,000 more in the region at that time (NECCA, 1983, p.20). The loss of manual jobs is also expected to accelerate over the same period, and the North's stake in the new technologies is not an impressive one (see Thwaites, 1983). The outlook, therefore, is that greater numbers of unskilled young people than ever before will be competing throughout the rest of the 1980s for a declining number of dead-end jobs.

Faced with this crisis, we have felt obliged to outline our own ideas for a new social contract for young people. We are not specialists in social policy and realize that the following suggestions will need to be improved by public criticism and debate. None of the proposals is totally original so it is not only debate that is needed but also the political will and the resources to implement them or something like them. We have also restricted ourselves to issues that have emerged directly from our fieldwork and do not range across the whole field of youth policy. But a start has to be made somewhere or the young adults of this country will have to be content with a two-year YTS and an extension of the Community Programme–that was the consensus arrived at by all the main political parties at the time of the Budget in 1985. Our alternative programme would include:

1   A strong regional dimension in all aspects of government policy

As we have argued above, the North has in recent decades been
transformed into a 'global outpost' (Williamson and Quayle, 1983, p.29)
It has neither the economic resources nor the political clout to solve its
own problems. There is also no one to speak for the region in Whitehall,
Brussells or beyond in the way that the Secretaries of State for
Scotland and Wales represent their areas. Is it significant, for example,
that the Consett steel works were closed but Ravenscraig in Scotland
and Llanwern and Port Talbot in Wales have so far avoided closure
because such a move is considered politically unacceptable? This
suggests that the assisted regions in England require a minister of
Cabinet rank to protect their interests.

A campaign has been mounting steadily to obtain a fairer deal for
the North ever since the first strategic plan for the area was drawn up
in 1977 and the first annual state of the region report was published in
1979 (see NECCA Reports). Others have since entered the debate (see
Holliday 1982; Robinson 1982; and Chapman 1985) and have presented
more detailed criticisms and proposals than is possible here. So far the
present Government's response has been to announce, in November
1984, cuts in regional aid of £300 million. The decision was made after
the EEC had calculated that Britain already had ten out of the
Community's fifteen most disadvantaged regions. The EEC analysis,
based on unemployment and productivity, showed that, in the words of
the latest NECCA report (1984, p.1): 'Northumberland, Tyne and Wear,
Durham and Cleveland are in the bottom 12 out of 131 regions in
Europe. They are accompanied by the recognized "poor men of
Europe", such as Calabria, Sardinia, Sicily and Northern Ireland'.

To this needs to be added Hudson's (1985, p.77) telling point: not only
are state policies for the region uncoordinated and chaotic, but they
themselves are 'the major proximate cause of employment decline'
because of the policies adopted by such nationalized industries as the
National Coal Board and the British Steel Corporation.

Whatever new structures are introduced, they need to play to the
strengths of the region. The guiding principle, suggested by reading
Papert (1980), would be that the regeneration of communities is most
likely to succeed if it springs from the roots of local culture and is most
likely to fail if the plans are imposed by distant bureaucrats.
What then, are the strengths of the North? As we argued in Chapter 5,
there is still a strong sense of community, a rich network of supportive
families, a long history of skilled work and pride in craft, and a deeply
felt loyalty to the area. Its distinct geographical boundaries have
helped to give northerners an historical, regional and cultural identity

and this collective self-respect could help to launch an economic revival. But for how long can any region survive the increasing emigration of the most talented of its young people in the search for jobs?

2 Link training to jobs and jobs to training, wherever possible

At present, we are being asked to believe that the supply of skilled workers *by itself* creates jobs: a new economic law is being promulgated to the effect that it is mainly skill shortages that cause unemployment. Who believes that more than 180 collieries in the North East have been closed since 1947 because of skill shortages? Are there silent and empty shipyards on the Tyne and Wear because of a lack of skilled manpower? Was the Consett steel works closed for lack of skilled workmen? The skill shortages which *do* exist are serious but strictly limited even according to the MSC's evidence to the House of Lords Select Committee on Science and Technology (MSC, 1984a).

The young adults we met were remarkably consistent and unswervingly realistic in judging all training schemes by their chances of landing a job as a result. Is that any wonder when in 1983 in Country Durham only 26 per cent of 'trainees' secured employment in the final year of YOP (Careers Officer's Report, 1985)? In the first year of YTS in the same county the percentage obtaining jobs increased to 40 per cent, but the corresponding figure for Great Britain was 70 per cent, according to Ministers. A careful MSC postal survey of a 15 per cent sample, which was nationally representative, put the figure at no more than 59 per cent (MSC, 1985); the same survey also showed that by far the most significant reason for leaving YTS was to take up a job. If we do not listen to what young people are saying and if we do not draw the appropriate conclusions from their actions, then vast sums of taxpayers' money may be wasted.

Before extending YTS and the Community Programme, would it not make more sense to ensure that all those who completed an MSC scheme obtained a job and used their newly acquired skills rather than returned to the unemployment register? The following table (adapted from MSC 1985, Table 3.1) describes the destinations of those leaving YTS in 1984.

The present proposal would create jobs for those 28 per cent who became unemployed and would ensure that there were opportunities for day release and further education for them and for all those who went straight into employment. Such a proposal is more likely to provide the bridge from school to work which the MSC are anxious to build and it would also check on the quality of the jobs and training in industry and commerce. It is acknowledged that there may be a small

Activity	*Percentage*
In full-time work	59
Unemployed	28
On another YTS	5
Back at School	1
Full-time FE	4
Doing something else	3
	100

percentage who, for a variety of reasons, may be difficult to place in paid employment, but the fact that the vast majority of each age group would be obtaining jobs is likely to have a powerful impact on the motivation of young people. The time to start extending YTS to two years would be when young people, after successfully completing a one year YTS, were flowing regularly into jobs and *not* when almost one-third of them leave only to become unemployed. If this suggestion were implemented, young people would become employees (rather than 'trainees'), they would be paid a wage (rather than a 'training allowance'), and they would be given legal rights to further education and training (as happens in France).

The magnitude of the task has been underlined by Charles Handy who reminds us that 'over the next twenty years there will be an extra 1.5 million people of working age, most of them wanting jobs' (1984, p.17). He also feels it would be 'dangerously naive to think that the Government, any Government, could buy enough jobs to solve unemployment' (Ibid., p.35). We are aware that our proposal has little chance of success unless it is combined with a radical review of the concept of 'work', as suggested by Watts (1983) and Handy himself. Such a review has already begun in other countries with shorter working weeks, longer holidays, job sharing, earlier retirement, partial retirement, paid educational leave, and bans on overtime.

A more optimistic view has been taken by the Greater London Enterprise Board, which claims to have created several thousand jobs at an average cost of less than £4000 per job. Their question points the way to a major revival of the construction industry:

> Are we as a people so well housed, so well served with hospitals, schools, transport networks and basic social infrastructure that there is nothing constructive for half a million building workers to do?   (Palmer and Cooley, 1985, p.20).

Because of 'the disproportionate sensitivity of youth unemployment to both the ups and downs of the employment cycle', David Raffe (1983, p.23) has asked whether a youth unemployment policy 'can be effective without a similar attack on unemployment among all age groups'. An assessment of alternative strategies makes one conclusion clear: youth unemployment is not inevitable, it is a political option.

3 A comprehensive system of 16+ education, training and employment

Present provision deserves to be called the most confusing, inadequate and hierarchical sector in the world of education and training. The MSC are attempting to unravel the confusions by setting up a review of vocational qualifications under George Tolley, but introducing greater equality and flexibility will prove more difficult. A start could be made by accepting Edwards' (forthcoming) suggestion of providing common status and common benefits for all those aged 16 to 18. The Labour Party's *Charter for Young People* (1985) is, however, in favour of a clear differential between a minimum allowance of £36 per week for trainees on YTS and an educational award of £27 per week to encourage young people to stay on in full-time education: the argument to justify the difference is that someone with a job or on a scheme should be paid more than someone on a full-time course. A unified, comprehensive system post-16 is only likely to offer a wide range of options to young adults if they are able to move easily round that system without incurring financial penalties. The provision of all forms of education and training in the one building, called the tertiary college, may also help to break down the deep divisions between academic and vocational streams.

4 The closer involvement of employers in the training of young people

For almost a decade employers have been lambasting the educational system and young people for failing to meet the unspecified 'needs of industry'. The idea that young people have legitimate requests (about training and the quality of jobs) to make of their employers is not seriously entertained. With some honourable exceptions, the training record of most employers in this country has been poor, to say the least. Chapter 4 showed how some companies operate with crude stereotypes of young workers and exploit them by employing a series of MSC 'trainees' and offering real jobs to only a small percentage. Some local companies also admitted in interview that, in an economic recession, the first budget to suffer is always training; hence, the collapse of the apprenticeship system. Nationally, only one-third of young people who enter employment directly from school receive any form of part-time further education (FEU, 1985). But, if Britain is to catch up on its industrial competitors in this field, it needs a new partnership between employers and teachers and not a slanging match.

It is, however, doubtful whether British employers are likely to match their German counterparts who voluntarily contribute 80 per cent of all expenditure on vocational education (NEDC MSC, 1984, p.16). That suggests the need for a legal requirement on employers in this country to contribute substantially to the costs of training and educating all their young workers. That still leaves the wider question, asked by Ken Roberts, of 'how firms can be made to generate types and levels of unemployment and to distribute the prosperity from economic growth so that all young people can benefit' (1985, p.42). A start could be made by adopting the suggestion of Tucker (1985, p.35) that 'the Government should adjust corporation tax to enable employers to spend one per cent of their profits' on job creation and investment in their local communities.

5 Change the model of learning at the heart of the new initiatives by the MSC and DES

A series of comparisons have recently been made between education and economic performance in such countries as Germany, France, the United States and Japan (NEDC MSC, 1984, and Worswick, 1985); these comparisons have all tended to be highly unfavourable to this country.

Visits by Frank Coffield to the Federal Republic's *Barufsschulen* and dual system of training made a deep impression, partly because the Germans have a long established *system* of vocational training and partly because the level of up-to-date equipment was so lavish. But cracks are beginning to appear in the solid structure of their much praised 'dual system'. Reardon, for example, has described how no more than 6 per cent of the Ford Motor company's apprentices in West Germany will obtain the skilled job for which the company has trained them at a cost of £7000 each because of the introduction of robots (1983, p.7).

Interestingly, the international comparisons referred to above have much to say about 'inputs' and 'outputs' of vocational education, but are silent about the processes at the heart of all learning: the quality of relationships between teacher and taught, and the model of learning adopted. Allowing for some predictable variation in the German system with almost 2,500,000 pupils in vocational schools in 1982, the general ethos of such institutions may be characterized as formal, teacher-centred, rule-governed, traditional, highly systematized and, at times, even authoritarian. As a consequence, the social distance between teacher and taught tends to be considerable, thus reducing the prospects of producing creative, flexible and self-motivating learners. In addition, a 'behavioural objectives' model of learning has been enthroned at the heart of the German system and pupils (who do not have the status of students) work their way through hundreds of small, specific behavioural objectives every year.

There may well be parts of our own educational system that could be described in similarly unflattering terms. Indeed, some of our Further Education Colleges appear to have become temples to the same behavioural objectives approach to learning, which prevents students seeing connections, learning generic ideas and going beyond the information given (Bruner, 1974). Devastating critiques have also been produced in this country of the manpower service model of education (Jonathan, 1983), of the 'core skills' in YTS (Philip Cohen 1984, and Jonathan, forthcoming), and of the 'education for capability' movement (Thompson, 1984). On the whole, however, staff–student ratios enable teachers in Britain to be closer to their students and to take a more personal interest in them than happens in France or Germany.

Our more open and relaxed teaching relationships could be married advantageously to a more powerful model of learning, based on the work of Piaget, Bruner, Donaldson and Papert, whose influential book *Mindstorms* (1980) is based on the dictum: 'The best learning takes place when the learner takes charge' (p.214).

A third ingredient could be added to improve the quality of learning. Throughout Great Britain, universities and local industry are developing closer links through the creation of 'science parks'. Local variations in the North include Cleveland's CADCAM centre, Durham University's Centre for Materials Science and Technology and Newcastle's Technology Centre. What is missing from all of these initiatives is an educational dimension. If local schools and Colleges of Further Education are left out of the plans, the cultural gap that already exists between the latest research and the curriculum of schools may widen still further. It is not enough to produce new knowledge and processes: each new generation (and not just an elite sub-group) needs to be challenged by that new knowledge and their initiation can no longer be left to chance: it needs to be planned.

Elsewhere (Coffield, 1983), a proposal has been outlined to bring together universities, local industry and schools to form a new body from which all the partners would benefit. The Technical and Vocational Education Initiative (TVEI) needs to be built into some such system if it is to survive and remain up to date when MSC support comes to an end. TVEI, financed by the MSC, 'aims to stimulate the provision of technical and vocational education for 14–18 years old ... in close liaison with the DES and Her Majesty's Inspectorate of Skills' (*sic*), (MSC, 1984b, p.19).

6   Community education to combat racism and to promote social awareness and health education

It is a formidable list. Eleven years of formal schooling have not managed to dent, never mind change, some of the prevailing values of the young adults who have been introduced on these pages. The North East as a community will have to face and deal with the uncomfortable fact that large sections of ordinary, decent young people in the region hold firmly to their racist opinions. Among the many useful recommendations of the Swann Report (1985) concerning 'all-white' areas, there is one of particular significance: exchange teachers from all-white schools with those in multi-racial institutions in other parts of the country. One encouraging note is the spread of community education in an area where the soil has long been ripe for such a development. Some sectors of the youth service now provide community-based programmes; and, slowly, some comprehensive schools in the North have begun working with various interpretations of the term 'community school': from involving teachers and pupils in the running of the organization, to greater participation in the life of the school by the surrounding community, and on to turning the school building into a community centre. The final stage would be to base the curriculum in the community with the aim of developing in all children 'a critical and constructive understanding of the environment in which they live' (Hargreaves, 1982, p.120). All pupils growing up in the North East should be aware of the economic prospects for the region. The objectives would be to widen the horizons of the young and release them from the limitations of what we have termed 'localism': a strong sense of regionalism should act as an antidote to parochialism. We need to record, however, that no such developments were taking place in any of the schools attended by the young adults in our sample.

The crisis in the economy has produced a crisis of confidence in secondary schools and the changes in future manpower needs are already being reflected in different streams catering for different types of fourth former. One scenario for the future (Beynon, 1983) suggests that modern industry will produce high-level 'scientific work' and low-level 'donkey work', to which we would add the need for a restricted number of technicians at an intermediate level. The introduction of TVEI into 8 per cent of the country's secondary schools is likely to encourage the re-emergence of the discredited tripartite division within education. As before, a small academic group will prepare for higher education and membership of a well-qualified elite; a second stratum will opt for TVEI in the hope of improving their chances in the scramble for the declining number of skilled and semi-skilled jobs; and the rest will be contained until age sixteen when they will be moved on into YTS, 'donkey jobs' or unemployment. The Swedish experience since 1973 shows that the provision of vocational training for as many as 49 per cent of pupils in upper secondary schools has had only marginal effects on the enrolment of students from privileged families in any other courses apart from traditional academic subjects (Hartmann, 1985, p.7).

David Hargreaves (1982, p.113) has posed the fundamental questions in this area: 'What kind of society do we want to create and how can the education system help us to realize such a society?' The answers he and a small committee produced for the Inner London Education Authority in the publication, *Improving Secondary Schools* (1984), could, with appropriate changes, be more widely implemented. There is space here to emphasize only one aspect of their detailed proposals: the desperate need for all pupils to understand the changes that have already taken place and to discuss the most likely scenarios for the future. Increased leisure is the only scenario that tends to be seriously entertained at conferences on the likely shape of society. And yet since 1983 Tony Watts has explored four possible futures and the leisure scenario appears to be the *least* likely. How, after all, could we run either schools or society with two diametrically opposed philosophies: would a small elite, imbued with the protestant work ethic, carry out what tasks were necessary, while at the same time watching large numbers of helots swilling beer, snorting cocaine and watching porno videos?

In Chapter 5 we described the heavy drinking of both sexes as an accepted and unquestioned part of local culture. Our own subjective impressions about the serious health consequences of such drinking are supported by comparative statistics. Various surveys have repeatedly found 'higher expenditure in the Northern Region on alcoholic drink and tobacco than for any other region of England . . . the proportion of male heavy drinkers . . . in the North was at least half as great again as the average for England, and well over twice as much as in the South East' (Kaim-Caudle, 1985, p.154). It would appear that the heavier consumption of alcohol and tobacco has remained after many of the dirty jobs which gave rise to it have disappeared. Research with schoolchildren shows that throughout the country alcohol is now part of daily life; at the age of eleven, over half the boys and a third of the girls claimed to be drinking alcohol once a week (*Health Education News,* May 1985, p.8). The evidence we presented makes clear that the licensing laws on underage drinking are being widely flouted and it may well be that it is those laws and the puritanical streak in British society from which they came which need to change. The promotion of sensible drinking in schools and society has been an initiative pioneered by the Health Education Council in the north east of

England (See Brandes, 1985). It remains to be seen whether such initiatives can counter the strong historical and cultural patterns of heavy drinking in the area by changing the behaviour and attitudes of young people.

This chapter has so far made much of fundamental discontinuities in the job market, radical economic changes and rapid technological advances. Such newsworthy events tended to grab the local headlines and our immediate attention, but our fieldwork kep reminding us of deep continuities in the region, namely, cultural traditions and values that continued to influence the behaviour of young people. For example, neither the unemployment statistics nor the talk of alternative life styles nor arguments in favour of a move to a 'life ethic' (Clemitson and Rodgers, 1981) in any way shook the attachment of young adults to the protestant work ethic. Methods of coping with unemployment in the 1930s, namely leaving school at the earliest possible moment and taking *any* job, were still influencing behaviour in the 1980s, as we discussed earlier. Similarly, sexism, racism and the negative aspects of localism were still virulent in the three areas we studied. These cultural beliefs and practices have been passed on and continue to be passed on from generation to generation and are not likely to be dissipated by thirteen-week training courses run by the MSC or anyone else. All the more reason for young people to receive a broad general education before more specialized training in order to tackle such issues directly and repeatedly over the years of formal schooling. Citizens of a democratic, multi-cultural and technologically sophisticated society need much more than vocational skills, which may never be employed. The crucial question, as McKenzie (1985) has argued, is *not* whether the educational system has contributed sufficiently to economic growth but whether it is fulfilling its historical role in holding together the social fabric and thereby sustaining the democratic traditions of British society.

7   Programmes of positive discrimination in favour of young women

Our fieldwork furnished examples of a few young women who were fighting to escape the restricted roles envisaged for them by fathers, partners and employers, but the majority of young women (as well as men, needless to say) accepted the status quo in respect of traditional sex roles, both in the home and the workplace.

A new social contract would need to take account of the existing distribution of power between the sexes. Men have so much to lose that they will not devolve power easily. The broadening of horizons and seizing of opportunities therefore has primarily to be done by women for those women who often need first to discover the reasons behind their oppression. This is easier said than done. Our attempts to explore with young women why and how their choices were limited met with a large amount of resistance (passive rather than active) and the few examples of liberated thought which emerged were often contradicted by actions, such as Carol Ann assuming the main responsibility of running the home as soon as she was married, despite earlier plans to share such tasks.

Just as on the home front where the young women's lives were largely reactive, shadowing and responding to the lives of men (fathers as well as boyfriends), in the labour market, they were subject to male expectations of them (see Griffin, 1985). The adoption of new technology also represents a structural change which will affect the young female worker disproportionately. The Equal Opportunities Commission, for instance, has calculated that the introduction of the word processor will lead to a national loss of 170,000 jobs by 1990. Those most affected will be female copy typists.

Positive discrimination in favour of young women needs to be introduced at all levels to combat their unequal position. An example of how this can and is being done is to be found in some youth work practice where, gradually over recent years, groups of women have organized to work specifically with girls, leading in a (very) few areas in the country to the creation of posts geared to this purpose. Other examples are courses for women organized by the Workers' Educational Association and run during the day with creche facilities. Forums are thus created in which young women can explore the choices available to them and why. More than the opportunity for discussion needs to be provided, however, and occasionally this is acknowledged in schemes, in industry and in training. These are not always successful: the MSC, despite a range of special programmes to encourage women to enter training for the new technologies, are running into severe difficulties as the very low number of women attending Information Technology Centres testifies. Griffin (1985, p.191), when describing young women's preference for traditionally female jobs, has suggested a reason for the poor take-up of equal opportunities policies: 'This was not a mark of their conservative views, but a pragmatic decision made in a situation of limited available options'.

The young women in our study were nothing if not pragmatic and they were full of enough concerns about employment without the effort required to break new ground. It is in the context of their whole lives, therefore, that any programmes to promote their views, their status, their expectations and, ultimately, their parity, must be set. This context includes men and while women's initiatives on behalf of their own sex remain the first strategy, there is the corresponding need for men to engage in an exploration of traditional sex roles. We have written elsewhere (Marshall and Borrill, 1984) of the specific difficulties in working with both sexes and of how, even more than single-sex studies, a mixed sample highlights the oppression of young women.

A new social contract for young women can only be new if it musters enough strength to challenge the relentless continuity of their lives as carers of children and men.

8   Involve young adults in the formation of social policy about young adults and give them the freedom to develop alternatives

If we are to take seriously one of our own main findings, namely, that the young adults we met, irrespective of a general lack of formal qualifications, displayed a whole range of intellectual, emotional and social abilities, then they should not only participate but play a leading role in any decisions made about their future. The greatest injustices that could be paid them would be to write them off as unskilled, unqualified and untrained. Their considerable abilities and qualities had, in the main, been left untapped and unrecognized by their schools, their MSC schemes and their employers (if any). We saw them on both formal and informal occasions; during the latter, the seemingly inarticulate and hesitant became fluent and knowledgeable as they began to challenge and defeat us in argument. Discussions with them about our conclusions revealed a maturity and a complexity in their thinking; their concerns were the main issues facing us all – jobless growth and nuclear warfare. Indeed, some of the key ideas mentioned earlier, such as linking training to jobs and jobs to training, came first from meetings with Poppy, Gordon and Karl.

Such a proposal would find mandatory places for young adults on, for example, the Youth Training Board of the MSC where the consumers' view would add a much needed corrective to official thinking. The official world is full of the rhetoric of participation – it was one of the three themes of the United Nations International Youth Year in 1985 and was used in the title of the Thompson Report (1982) on the Youth Service in England – but the voices of the young are not heard where it matters.

Young adults generally are also asking for the freedom to try out different lifestyles appropriate to the changed economic climate. Such alternatives need space in which to develop and various municipal authorities, such as Munich for instance, have provided autonomous, less controlled places for young people where they began by repairing each other's motorbikes and are now experimenting with co-operatives and alternative lifestyles. The meeting places are under political and police protection at the highest level and guidance and advice is available from trained youth workers. Society has nothing to fear and much to gain from the active participation of the young.

Concluding comment

The standard riposte to any set of alternative proposals is that the expense alone would prevent implementation. Sinfield and Fraser (1985) calculated for the BBC North East what they called 'the real cost of unemployment': not just the direct exchequer costs, but the lost taxes (both income and indirect), the lost national insurance contributions and local authority costs (e.g. initiatives to help the unemployed like Durham County Council's Youth Employment Premium to employers). They concluded that it would be reasonable to work with an estimate of £7000 as the annual cost to the Exchequer of an unemployed person. NECCA (1984, p.18) has particularized the argument for the northern region, using the House of Lords lower estimate of £5000, which was calculated in 1982: 'If this figure is applied to unemployed claimants in the North, the total cost becomes a staggering £1125 million per year'. Seen in this light, the financial implications of alternative programmes including job creation seem less forbidding. Moreover, these calculations have omitted any wider social or individual costs such as the effects of unemployment on health, family tensions or personal suffering.

Our study has concerned itself, however, with wider issues than youth unemployment. We began by examining the lives of particular individuals such as Stephanie, Max, Reg and Carol Ann and the group from Marlow Dene, but we soon found that we could not understand them without reference to the ways in which power and wealth are distributed in Britain; namely, by means of class, patriarchy, racism, and the marginal status of both young people in general and of the North East in particular. We have at all points noted the marked differences in growing up as a working-class female or as a working-class male in the North East: young women have been drawn back even further into their traditional role of domestic labourers, while the time-honoured transition of working-class males from school to low-paid jobs has largely broken down. We have considered the effects of these economic changes on the friendships among young people, although we admit that the relationships with their families remained a largely uncharted area in our study. But the main conclusion can be stated simply: the problems of young people should not be confined to a discussion of spectacular incidents like mohican hair cuts, glue sniffing or football hooliganism; the increasingly marginal status of young adults in countries as diverse as Sweden and the United States is intricately bound up with the political crisis created by the inability of modern industrial economies to generate sufficient jobs.

All such countries, including Britain, are faced with a stark choice and both the alternatives will be unpalatable to someone: they can either decide to incorporate young people into society or they can seek further powers to control a large, apathetic underclass. Both options will involve costs and sacrifices and so are likely to be strongly resisted. The first calls for a quiet revolution in our thinking and in our values and would involve major changes to present constitutional, industrial and educational structures, as we detailed earlier; more immediately, we need to reassess what forms of creative work society needs and is prepared to pay for and what jobs we would all be glad to be rid of; we also need to cut the connections between paid employment and status, wealth and power; and increase taxation to link training schemes to worthwhile jobs and vice-versa.

For such a policy to work, the comfortable middle class, who are wedded to a constantly improving standard of living and the successful middle-aged who have effectively closed down posts for the next twenty years, would have to make room for young adults by, for example, sharing power and paid employment, retiring earlier, and paying for more education and training. But the very people who would have to make such sacrifices are exactly those who have most to gain from a continuation of the status quo. What evidence is there that those in positions of power are prepared to make way for those who currently stand like passive spectators on the touch-lines of society? At the time of writing, in August 1985, the evidence is all in the opposite direction as the status of young people is eroded still further: the differences between adult workers and 'trainees' are being deliberately widened, chief education officers have been instructed to report young people who refuse places on YTS to the DHSS, who in turn are having to force young adults to move on from their board and lodgings while hunting for jobs, and the protection of Wage Councils is to be removed from the 500,000 low-paid workers under the age of twenty-one. Altruism is currently as popular as Aids.

For these reasons, western societies are more likely to follow the second option even though it contains even more risks for all our futures. It is understandable that at a time of such uncertainty and anxiety, Western democracies tend to vote for more control and an intensification of the economic patterns of the past. However understandable such a craving for security may be, we are currently learning that even the toughest of police states, such as South Africa, can dampen down legitimate expectations for just so long before the excluded and the rejected decide to take matters into their own hands.

Britain has already entered a transitional period which may last for as long as twenty years and which will take us into a post-industrial society. Of central importance will be the quality of life and the civil liberties enjoyed by all citizens. There is a real danger that successive governments, of whatever political colour, will take increasingly authoritarian powers to ease Britain's transition into that new age; the Police and Criminal Evidence Act, 1984 is one of a number of steps taken in this direction already. To paraphase Ivan Illich (1978, p.84), the quality of society and of its culture will henceforth depend on the status of its young adults. Vast numbers of people under twenty-five suffering from long-term and perhaps even permanent unemployment are a new factor in Britain and we have to turn for a parallel to the black ghettoes of the United States where three and sometimes four generations have lived off state benefits. To avoid getting down that road, we have called for nothing less than a new social contract to give all young adults a stake in the ordinary life of their communities. They have a right not just to eke out an existence in poverty, frustration and boredom but to live lives worth living.

Abbreviations

In alphabetical order

CB:	Citizen's Band radio
CEP:	Community Enterprise Programme
CP:	Community Programme
CSE:	Certificate of Secondary Education
DHSS:	Department of Health and Social Security
ESRC:	Economic and Social Research Council
MSC:	Manpower Services Commission
PHAB:	Physically Handicapped and Able Bodied
TOPs:	Training Opportunities Scheme
WEEP:	Work Experience on Employers' Premises
WOC:	Wider Opportunities Course
YOP:	Youth Opportunities Programme
YTS:	Youth Training Scheme

Glossary

The list is in alphabetical order and includes phonetic spellings as well as dialect.

a bit carry on: joking about
bairn: child
bait: food/meal
battlin: fighting
bevvies: beverages
to bottle (another lass): to hit with a bottle
bottling out: backing down
brayed: beaten
can lad: yougest worker/apprentice
canna: cannot
chippy: fish and chip shop
coble: local fishing boat
comes wrong: goes wrong
crack: conversation/gossip
dinna/divvent: do not
dole wallah: unemployed person (pejorative)
doon: down
dunno: don't know
to fair up: to improve (of the weather)
gadgy: adult male
gan/gannin: gone/going
geet canny: a superlative, like 'really wonderful'
to get shot of: to get rid of
to get wrong from: to be criticized by, ticked off
have a dodge round: come and visit
to hoy away/hoyed: to throw away/threw
laff: laugh
lugs: ears
mesel: myself
m'n: phonetic spelling of colloquial expression 'man' which can be applied to
    either sex
mortal: drunk with alcohol
na/nee: no
nowt: nothing
nutters: people deemed to be mentally abnormal
ower the toon: in town
owt: anything
playing the nick: playing truant
posers: people who tried to be something they were not, who were not genuine
provvy cheques/the club: Provident cheques/tickets are a means of credit,
    repaid with a minimum of 10 per cent interest to an agent who calls at
    borrower's house for the agreed weekly payment
to pump iron: to bodybuild

rubber ducked: colloquial rhyming slang
running messages: doing errands, going shopping
scrapings: end pieces of batter
sommat: something
started on: began employment
stottin/smashed: drunk with alcohol
topper: a superlative, like 'excellent'
tret: treated
wey: colloquial opening expression, like 'well . . . '
to work themselves: to create trouble/a nuisance
worky tickets: troublemakers

Bibliography

ABRAMS, P. (1982) *Historical Sociology*, Open Books, London.

AMIS, K. (1984) *Stanley and the Women*, Hutchinson, London.

BEYNON, H. (1983) 'British Workers and the New Technology', in WILLIAMSON, B. and QUAYLE, B. (eds) *Technology and Change in the North East*, University of Durham: North East Local Studies, **3**, 48–62.

BLACK, D. (1980) *Inequalities in Health*, DHSS, London (Black Report).

BLACKIE, J. (1983) 'Survey of Young People Unemployed', Youth and Leisure Services Working Group, City of Newcastle upon Tyne.

BRANDES, D. (1985) *An Illuminative Evaluation of an Alcohol Education Project*, unpublished Ph.D. Thesis. Durham University.

BRAVERMAN, H. (1974) *Labor and Monopoly Capital*, Monthly Review Press, New York.

BREAKWELL, G. (1984) 'Knowing Your Place; Finding Your Place', *ESRC Newsletter*, **52**, 29–30.

BREAKWELL, G., HARRISON, B. and PROPPER, C. (1982) 'The Psychological Benefits of YOPs', *New Society*, 494–95.

BRUNER, J.S. (1974) *Beyond The Information Given*, Allen and Unwin, London.

CAREERS OFFICER'S REPORT (1985) *Annual Report 1984*, Durham County Council, Education Department.

CASHMORE, E.E. (1984) *No Future–Youth and Society*, Heinemann, London.

CHAPMAN, R.A. (ed.) (1985) *Public Policy Studies: The North East of England*, Edinburgh University Press for the University of Durham.

CLARKE, J. (1979) 'Capital and culture: the post-war working class revisited', in Clarke, J., Critcher, C. and Johnston, K. (eds) *Working-Class Culture*, Hutchinson, London.

CLARKE, J., CRITCHER, C. and JOHNSON, R. (1979) *Working-Class Culture: studies in history and theory*, Hutchinson, London.

CLEMITSON, I. and RODGERS, G. (1981) *A Life to Live: beyond full employment*, Junction Books, London.

COCHRANE, R. and BILLIG, M. (1984) 'I'm Not National Front Myself, But . . .' *New Society*, **68**, 1121, 255–58.

COFFIELD, F. (1983) 'Learning to Live with Unemployment: what future for education in a world without jobs?', in Coffield, F. and Goodings, R., (eds) *Sacred Cows in Education*, Edinburgh University Press for the University of Durham.

COHEN, P. (1972) 'Subcultural conflict and working-class community', *Working Paper in Cultural Studies, No. 2*, University of Birmingham, Centre for Contemporary Studies, 9–27.

COHEN, P. (1984) 'Against the New Vocationalism', in Bates, I. *et al.* (eds) *Schooling for the Dole? The New Vocationalism*, MacMillan, Basingstoke.

COHEN, S. (1972) *Folk Devils and Moral Panics: the creation of the Mods and Rockers*, MacGibbon and Kee, London.

COLEMAN, J.C. (1980) *The Nature of Adolescence*, Methuen, London.

CONNELL, R.W., ASHENDEN, D.J., KESSLER, S. and DOWSETT, G.W. (1982) *Making the Difference schools, families and social division*, Allen and Unwin, Sydney.

COMMON, J. (1954) *Kiddar's Luck and the Ampersand*. Frank Graham, Newcastle-upon-Tyne.

DAVIES, B. (1981) *The State We're In: restructuring youth policies in Britain*, National Youth Bureau, Leicester.

DAVIES, B. (1984) 'Thatcherite visions and the role of the MSC', *Youth and Policy*, 2, 4, 1–8.

DAVIES, L. (1979) 'Deadlier than the male? Girls' conformity and deviance in school', in

BARTON, L. and MEIGHAN, R. (eds) *Schools, Pupils and Deviance,* Nafferton Books, London.

DOWNES, D.M. (1966) *The Delinquent Solution,* Routledge and Kegan Paul, London.

DRAKE, K. (1984) '16–19 Year Olds: education, employment and income support', *Public Money,* September, 62–6.

DUCK, S. (1983) *Friends for Life: the psychology of close relationships,* Harvester Press, Brighton.

EDWARDS, A.D. (Forthcoming) 'Education and Training 16–19: rhetoric, policy and practice' in HARTNETT, A. and NAISH, M. (eds), *Education and Society Today,* Falmer Press, Lewes.

ERIKSON, E.H. (1971) *Identity: Youth and Crisis,* Faber and Faber, London.

FIDDY, R. (ed.) (1983) *In Place of Work: policy and provision for the young unemployed,* Falmer Press, Lewes.

FINN, D. (1983) 'The Youth Training Scheme–a New Deal?', *Youth and Policy,* 1, 4, 16–24.

FINN, D. (1984) 'Britain's Misspent Youth', *Marxism Today,* 20–24.

FRASER, C. (1980) 'The Social Psychology of Unemployment' in Jeeves, M.A., (ed.) *Psychological Survey, No. 3,* Allen and Unwin, London.

Further Education Unit (FEU) (1985) 'Further Education and YTS', *FEU Bulletin,* February, DES, Elizabeth House, London.

GLEESON, D. (ed.) (1983) *Youth Training and the Search for Work,* Routledge and Kegan Paul, London.

GOFTON, L. and GOFTON, C. (1984) 'Making Out in Giro City, *New Society,* 280–82.

GRIFFIN, C. (1982) 'Cultures of Femininity: Romance Revisited', Centre for Contemporary Cultural Studies, Birmingham University.

GRIFFIN, C. (1985) *Typical Girls?,* Routledge and Kegan Paul, London.

GRUBB, W.N. and LAZERSON, M. (1981) 'Vocational Solutions to Youth Problems: the persistent frustrations of the American experience', *Schools, Youth and Work,* in Watts, A.G. (ed.), *Educational Analysis,* 3, 2, 91–103.

GRUBB, W.N. and LAZERSON, M. (forthcoming) *Vocationalism in American Education.*

HALL, S., CRITCHER, C., JEFFERSON, T., CLARKE, J. and ROBERTS, B. (1978) *Policing The Crisis,* MacMillan, London.

HANDY, C. (1984) *The Future of Work,* Basil Blackwell, Oxford.

HARGREAVES, D.H. (1982) *The Challenge for the Comprehensive School,* Routledge and Kegan Paul, London.

HARRÉ, R. (1980) Preface to Kitwood, T. *Disclosures to a Stranger,* Routledge and Kegan Paul, London.

HARRISON, R. (1976) 'The demoralising experience of prolonged unemployment, *Department of Employment Gazette,* 84, 339–48.

HARTLEY, J. (1980) 'Psychological approaches to unemployment', *Bulletin of the British Psychological Society,* 33, 412–14.

HARTMANN, J. (1985) *New Forms of Youth Participation and Youth Work in Sweden* UNESCO, Paris.

HEALTH EDUCATION NEWS (1985) 'The once-a-week drinkers aged 11', 52, 8.

HENDRY, L.B. (1983) *Growing Up and Going Out: adolescents and leisure,* The University Press, Aberdeen.

HILL, J. (1978) 'The psychological impact of unemployment', *New Society,* 118–20.

HIRSCH, D. (1983) *Youth Unemployment: a background paper,* Youthaid, London.

HOLLIDAY, F.G.T. (1982) 'The Lands Between: some thoughts on regions, resources and representation', Durham City Sword Address by Vice-Chancellor of Durham University.

HORNE, J. (1983) 'Youth Unemployment Programmes: a historical account of the development of dole colleges', in GLEESON, D. (ed.), *Youth Training and the Search for*

Work, Routledge and Kegan Paul, London.

HUDSON, R. (1985) 'The paradoxes of state intervention', in Chapman, R.A. (ed.) *Public Policy Studies: the North East of England,* Edinburgh University Press for the University of Durham.

HUHNE, C. (1985) 'If we adapt fast enough the jobs will still be there', *The Guardian,* 7 February.

ILEA (1984) *Improving Secondary Schools,* Swindon Press.

ILLICH, I. (1978) *The Right to Useful Unemployment and its Professional Enemies,* Marion Boyars, London.

JACKSON, B. (1984) *Fatherhood,* Allen and Unwin, London.

JACKSON, P.R. and BANKS, M.H. (1982) 'Unemployment and risk of minor psychiatric disorder in young people: cross sectional and longitudinal evidence', *Psychological Medicine,* **12**, 789–98.

JACKSON, P.R. and STAFFORD, E.M. (1980) 'Work involvement and employment status as influences on mental health', Paper presented to British Psychological Society, Canterbury.

JACKSON, P.K., STAFFORD, E.M., BANKS, M.H., and WARR, P.B. (1983) 'Unemployment and Psychological Distress in Young People', *Journal of Applied Psychology,* **3**, 525–35.

JAHODA, M. (1979) 'The impact of unemployment in the 1930s and the 1970s' *Bulletin of the British Psychological Society,* **32**, 309–14.

JAHODA, M. (1981) 'Work, employment, and unemployment: values, theories and approaches in social research', *American Psychologist,* **36**, 184–91.

JAHODA, M. (1982) *Employment and Unemployment: A social-psychological analysis,* Cambridge University Press.

JEFFERSON, T. (ed.) (1975) *Resistance Through Rituals,* Centre for Cultural Studies, University of Birmingham.

JENKINS, R. (1983) *Lads, Citizens and Ordinary Kids: Working-class Youth Life-styles in Belfast,* Routledge and Kegan Paul, London.

JEWKES, J. and WINTERBOTTOM, A. (1933) *Juvenile Unemployment,* Allen and Unwin, London.

JONATHAN, R. (1983) 'The Manpower Service Model of Education', *Cambridge Journal of Education,* **13**, 3–10.

JONATHAN, R. (Forthcoming) 'The Youth Training Scheme and Core Skills: an educational analysis'.

JONES, P. (1984) *What Opportunities for Youth? Deteriorating Employment Prospects for School Leavers and the Role of Government Schemes,* Youthaid Occasional Paper No. 4, London.

KAIM-CAUDLE, P.R. (1985) 'Health Issues', in Chapman, R.A. (ed.) *Public Policy Studies,* Edinburgh University Press for the University of Durham, 149–81.

KELVIN, P. (1981) 'Social Psychology 2001: the social psychological bases and implications of structural employment', in Gilmour, R. and Duck, S. (eds) *The Development of Social Psychology,* Academic Press, London.

KELVIN, P. (1984) 'The Historical dimensions of social psychology, the case of Unemployment', in Tajfel, H. (ed.), *The Social Dimension,* Vol. 2, Cambridge University Press, 405–24.

KING, S. (1984) 'Entering the Labour Market: the experiences of school leavers in Gateshead', *Northern Economic Review,* **9**, 13–19.

KIRTON, D. (1983) 'The Impact of Mass Unemployment on Careers Guidance in the Durham Coalfield', in Fiddy, R. (ed.) *In Place of Work,* Falmer Press, Lewes.

KITWOOD, T.M. (1980) *Disclosures to a Stranger,* Routledge and Kegan Paul, London.

KNIGHT, B.J., OSBORN, S.G. and WEST, D.J. (1977) 'Early Marriage and Criminal Tendency in Males', *British Journal of Criminology,* **17**, 4, 348–60.

LABOUR PARTY (1985), *Charter for Young People*, Walworth Road, London.

LEONARD, D. (1980) *Sex and Generation*, Tavistock Publications, London.

LISTER, I. (1976) *Aims and Methods of Political Education in Schools,* Council of Europe, Strasbourg.

McKEE, L. and BELL, C. (1984) 'His Unemployment: Her Problem. The Domestic Consequences of Male Unemployment', Paper given at British Sociological Association Annual Conference.

McKENZIE, M.L. (1985) 'Education as social control', *Times Educational Supplement in Scotland,* 15 November.

McKIE, A. (Forthcoming) Ph.D thesis, Sociology Department, University of Durham.

McROBBIE, A. (1978) 'Working-class girls and the culture of femininity' in *Women take Issue: aspects of women's subordination,* Women's Studies Group, Centre for Contemporary Cultural Studies, University of Birmingham.

McROBBIE, A. and GARBER, J. (1975) 'Girls and subcultures: an exploration', in Jefferson T. (ed.) *Resistance Through Rituals*, Centre for Contemporary Cultural Studies, University of Birmingham.

McROBBIE, A. and McCABE, T. (eds) (1981) *Feminism for Girls: An Adventure Story,* Routledge and Kegan Paul, London.

MADGE, N. (1983) 'Unemployment and its effect on children', *Journal of Child Psychology and Psychiatry,* **24**, 2, 311-19.

Manpower Services Commission (MSC) (1981a) *A New Training Initiative,* Moorfoot, Sheffield.

Manpower Services Commission (MSC) (1981b) *Guide to Training Workshops,* Moorfoot, Sheffield.

Manpower Services Commission (MSC) (1983) *Corporate Plan 1983-1987,* Moorfoot, Sheffield.

Manpower Services Commission (MSC) (1984a) *New Technologies*, Written Evidence to House of Lords Select Committee on Science and Technology, Moorfoot, Sheffield.

Manpower Services Commission (1984b) *Annual Report* 1983-84, Moorfoot, Sheffield.

Manpower Services Commission (1985) *Leavers in July-September 1984: 15% Follow-Up,* Youth Training Board, Moorfoot, Sheffield.

MARSDEN, D. and DUFF, E. (1975) *Workless,* Penguin, Harmondsworth.

MARSHALL, S. and BORRILL, C. (1984) 'Understanding the Invisibility of Young Women', *Youth and Policy,* **9**, 36-39.

MILLS, C.W. (1970), *The Sociological Imagination,* Penguin, Harmondsworth.

MUNCIE, J. (1984), *The Trouble with Kids Today: youth and crime in post-war Britain,* Hutchinson, London.

MUSGROVE, F. (1964) *Youth and the Social Order,* Routledge and Kegan Paul, London.

National Economic Development Council/Manpower Services Commission (1984) *Competence and Competition: Training and education in the Federal Republic of Germany, the United States and Japan,* National Economic Development Office, London.

NECCA (1982) *The State of the Region Report,* North of England County Councils Association.

NECCA (1983) *The State of the Region Report,* North of England County Councils Association.

NECCA (1984) *The State of the Region Report,* North of England County Councils Association.

Network Training Group (1983) *Training and the State-Responses to the Manpower Services Commission,* Network Training Group, Manchester.

NORRIS, G.M. (1978) 'Unemployment, subemployment and personal characteristics', (A) 'The inadequacies of traditional approaches to unemployment', *Sociological Review,*

26, 1, 89-108. (B) 'Job separation from work histories: the alternative approach', *Sociological Review*, **26**, 2, 327-47.

ORWELL, G. (1962) *The Road to Wigan Pier*, Penguin, Harmondsworth.

OSBORN, S.G. and WEST, D.J. (1979) 'Conviction Records of Fathers and Sons Compared', *British Journal of Criminology*, **19**, 2, 254-56.

PALMER, J. and COOLEY, M. (1985) 'Mobilising on an economic war footing', *Guardian*, 30 July, 20.

PAPERT, S. (1980) *Mindstorms: Children, Computers and Powerful Ideas,* Harvester Press, Brighton.

PARKER, H.J. (1974) *View from the Boys,* David and Charles, London.

POWELL, P.H. and DRISCOLL, P.F. (1973) 'Middle-class professionals face unemployment' *New Society*, **10**, 2, 18-26.

POWELL, R. and CLARKE, J. (1975) 'A note on marginality', in JEFFERSON, T. (ed.) *Resistance Through Rituals*, Centre for Contemporary Cultural Studies, University of Birmingham.

RAFFE, D. (1983) 'Can There Be an Effective Youth Unemployment Policy?' in Fiddy, R. (ed.) *In Place of Work*, The Falmer Press, Lewes.

REARDON, S. (1983) 'Supply and Demand put pressure on West Germany's youth training', *Employment Gazette*, 7-10.

REES, T.L. and ATKINSON, P. (eds) (1982) *Youth Unemployment and State Intervention*, Routledge and Kegan Paul, London.

REES, G. and REES, T.L. (1982) 'Juvenile Unemployment and the State Between the Wars', in Rees, T.L. and Atkinson, P. (eds) *Youth Unemployment and State Intervention*, Routledge and Kegan Paul, London.

REX, J. and MOORE, R. (1967) *Race, Community and Conflict*, Oxford University Press, London.

RIDLEY, F.F. (1981) 'View from a disaster area; unemployed youth in Merseyside', *Political Quarterly*, **52**, 16-27.

ROBERTS, K. (1982) 'Contemporary Youth Unemployment: A Sociological Interpretation', Paper delivered to the *British Association for the Advancement of Science*, 9 September, Liverpool.

ROBERTS, K. (1984) *School Leavers and their Prospects*, Open University Press, Milton Keynes.

ROBERTS, K. 1985) 'Work: is there a future for young people?', *Youth and Policy*, **13**, 40-42.

ROBERTS, K., DUGGAN, J. and OBLE, M. (1982) 'Out-of-School Youth in High Unemployment Areas: an Empirical Investigation', *British Journal of Guidance and Counselling*, **10**, 1, 1-33.

ROBERTS, K., NOBLE, M. and UGGAN, J. (1982) 'Youth Unemployment: An old problem or a new life-style?', *Leisure Studies*, **1**, 171-82.

ROBERTS, R. (1971) *The Classic Slum*, Penguin, Harmondsworth.

ROBINSON, F. (1982) *Economic Prospects for the North*, Centre for Urban and Regional Development Studies, University of Newcastle-upon-Tyne.

ROSE, G. (1968) *The Working Class*, Longmans, London.

SHARPE, S. (1976) *Just Like a Girl*, Penguin, Harmondsworth.

SIMMONS, C. and WADE, W. (1984) *I like to say what I think*, Kogan Page, London.

SINFIELD, A. and FRASER, N. (1985) *The Real Cost of Unemployment*, BBC North East.

SMITH, D.M. (1970) 'Adolescence: A Study of Stereotyping', *The Sociological Review*, **18**, 2, 197-211.

SMITH, D.M. (1981) 'New movements in the sociology of youth: a critique', *British Journal of Sociology*, **32**, 2.

STIRLING, A. (1982) 'Preparing school leavers for unemployment', *Bulletin of the British Psychological Society*, **35**, 421-22.

STRADLING, R. and NOCTOR, M. (1983) *The Provision of Political Education in Schools: A National Survey,* Curriculum Review Unit, London.

SUPER, D.E. (1981) 'Approaches to occupational choice and career development', in WATTS, A.G., SUPER, D.E. and KIDD, J.M. (eds) *Career Development in Britain,* CRAC/Hudson, Cambridge.

SUTTLES, G.D. (1968) *The Social Order of the Slum,* University of Chicago Press.

Swann Report (1985) *Education for All: the report of the Committee of Inquiry into the Education of children from Ethnic Minority Groups,* HMSO, Cmnd. 9453, London.

TAWNEY, R.H. (1934) *The School-Leaving Age and Juvenile Unemployment,* Workers' Educational Association, London.

THOMPSON, K. (1984) 'Education for Capability: A Critique', *British Journal of Educational Studies,* **32,** 3, 203–12.

Thompson Report (1982) *Experience and Participation: Report of the Review Group on the Youth Service in England,* HMSO, London.

THRASHER, F.M. (1927) *The Gang,* University of Chicago Press.

THWAITES, A. (1983) 'Technology and the prospects for employment ifn the Northern Region of England' in WILLIAMSON, B. and QUAYLE, B. (eds.) *Technology and Change in the North East,* University of Durham: North East Local Studies, **3,** 39–47.

TOWNSEND, A.R. (1985) 'A critique of past policies of "modernisation" for the North East', in Chapman, R.A. (ed.), *Public Policy Studies,* Edinburgh: Edinburgh University Press for the University of Durham, 97–118.

TOWNSEND, P. (1979) *Poverty in the United Kingdom,* Penguin, Harmondsworth.

TUCKER, S. (1984) *Report of a Study of Education and Training on the Community Enterprise Programme,* MSC, Moorfoot, Sheffield.

TUCKER, S. (1985) *Post-YTS Initiatives: a review and recommendations for action,* Youthaid and National Youth Bureau, Leicester.

VENESS, T. (1962) *School Leavers: their Aspirations and Expectations,* Methuen, London.

WALSGROVE, D. (1984) 'Policing Yourself: Youth Unemployment, Individualism and the amplification of normality', Paper presented at British Sociol. Association Annual Conference.

WARR, P. (1982) 'A national study of non-financial employment commitment', *Journal of Occupational Psychology,* **55,** 297–312.

WARR, P. (1983a) 'Work, jobs and unemployment', *Bulletin of the British Psychological Society,* **36,** 305–11.

WARR, P. (1983b) 'Job Loss, Unemployment and Psychological Well Being', in Allen, V. and Van de Vliert, E. (eds) *Role Transition,* Plenum Press, New York.

WARR, P., BARTER, J. and ROWNBRIDGE, G. (1983) 'On the Independence of Positive and Negative Affect'; *Journal of Personality and Social Psychology,* **44,** 3, 644–51.

WARR, P., JACKSON, P. and BANKS, M. (1982) 'Duration of Unemployment and psychological well-being in young men and women'. *Current Psychological Research,* **2,** 207–14.

WATTS, A.G. (1983) *Education, Unemployment and the Future of Work,* Open University Press, Milton Keynes.

WELLS, W. (1983) 'Relative pay and employment of young people', *Employment Gazette,* **71,** 6, 230–37.

WHYTE, W.F. (1955) *Street Corner Society,* University of Chicago Press.

WILLIAMSON, B. (1982), *Class, Culture and Community: a biographical study of Social Change in Mining,* Routledge and Kegan Paul, London.

WILLIAMSON, B. and QUAYLE, B. 1983) 'Work, Technology and Culture in the North East of England', in North East Local Studies, *Technology and Change in the North East,* Durham University.

WILLIS, P. (1977) *Learning to Labour,* Saxon House, Farnborough.

WILLIS, P. (1979) 'Shop floor culture, masculinity and the wage form', in Clarke, J.,

Critcher, C. and Johnson, R. (eds) *Working-Class Culture,* Hutchinson, London.

WILLIS, P. (1984) 'Youth Unemployment: thinking the unthinkable', *Youth and Policy,* **2**, 4, 17–36.

WILLMOTT, P. (1969) *Adolescent Boys in the East End of London,* Penguin, Harmondsworth.

WILSON, D. (1978) 'Sexual Codes and Conduct – A Study of teenage girls' in SMART, C. and SMART, B. (eds) *Women, Sexuality and Social Control,* Routledge and Kegan Paul, London.

WORSWICK, G.D.N. (ed.) (1985) *Education and Economic Performance,* Gower, Aldershot.

YOUNG, M. and WILLMOTT, P. (1957) *Family and Kinship in East London,* Penguin, Harmondsworth.

Youthaid Briefing Paper (1984) *The Youth Training Scheme,* Youthaid, London.

Youth Service Review Group (1983) *Young People in the '80s: a Survey,* HMSO for Department of Education and Science, London.

Index

unemployed, 56-7, 63-8 *passim*
Work Experience, 17-18, 23, 30-31,
    88-9, 91-2, 94, 96, 105, 108,
    112-14
Worswick, G.D.N., 222
Wright Mills, C., 84

Young, M., 140, 144
young adults
    media view, 84, 181-2, 184, 210
    mental horizons, 188-9, 201-202
    new social contract, 230-31
    physical horizons, 184-8, 199-200

unemployed (comparisons), 68-72,
    80-85
    see also adulthood (transition);
    status
Young Workers Scheme, 107, 114,
    115
Youth Opportunities Programme, 4,
    46-7, 55, 59, 94, 104, 114, 142,
    206, 219
Youth Service Review Group, 201
Youth Training Scheme, 55, 78, 99,
    114-15, 142, 206, 208, 209,
    219-20